Angel on a Bridge

A Memoir

Angel on a Bridge

A Memoir

Becca Moore

TUCKER

DS

PRESS

Cover design by Scott Ryan, Becca Moore
Cover photos by Geo and Laura Villegas
Edited by Scott Ryan
Copy edited by David Bushman
Book designed by Scott Ryan

Published in the USA by Fayetteville Mafia/Tucker DS Press
Columbus, Ohio

Contact Information
Email: fayettevillemafiapress@gmail.com
Website: TuckerDSPress.com

To the angel who helped me across countless broken bridges,
who carried my burdens without ever asking for recognition,
who loved with quiet strength and unwavering grace—
Mommie, may you rest in heavenly peace.
Your love lit the way, even when the road was dark.

CONTENTS

Part 3: Becoming the Light

To those who walk through life carrying hidden scars.
I see you.
Your pain does not define you—it strengthens you.
May the battles you've endured become the fire
that drives you to bring light, hope, and change
into a world that needs your courage.
-Becca Moore

—Prologue—

"You can't be brave if you've only had
wonderful things happen to you."
~Mary Tyler Moore

I traced the red liner along the curve of my lips and filled them in with matte lipstick—bold, unapologetic, and intentional. Leaning down, I fastened the bright gold stilettos around my ankles and caught my reflection one last time. I smirked. Daddy was definitely going to have something to say.

The dress? Too tight.

The lipstick? Too red.

The glitter? Too much.

In Daddy's world, glitter was excessive—shorthand for rebellion, vanity, or relating to Jezebel. In mine, glitter meant something entirely different: proof that no one could dull my shine. My sparkle wasn't up for debate. It was defiance wrapped in confidence, a quiet rebellion that whispered, I'm not asking for permission. In fact, I'm not asking.

One of my favorite quotes—one I wish I'd written myself—comes from Deion Sanders. In an interview, he once said, "Look at me—what about me would make you think I care about your opinion of me? Your opinion of me is not the opinion I have of myself. I don't care about anyone's opinion of me. They didn't make me, so they can't break me."

That line lives rent-free in my head.

At this moment, I was standing in front of the mirror on a Monday morning, preparing to speak at the Pro Football Hall of Fame Luncheon in Canton, Ohio. A seat at that table didn't come by accident. The speakers who came before me were giants—Tony Dungy. Ray Lewis. Jim Tressel. Urban Meyer. Nate Moore, who just happens to be my husband, and now . . . me?

Who was this girl?

Nate, who coached the local football team, stepped in, smiling as he looked at me, "Nervous?"

I met his gaze. "No."

He pulled me in, forehead to forehead. "You're going to be great. You look amazing."

I laughed softly, straightened my black floor-length dress, and thanked him for being the one to introduce me. "Wouldn't miss it," he replied.

He grabbed his signature bright orange jacket—the one people would definitely ask about if he didn't wear it—and I smiled. That jacket had become part of his story. Just like stilettos had become part of mine.

We rode in silence to the venue called Tozzi's on 12th. I slid into the passenger seat of his black Ram 1500, the leather cool beneath me. Nate, history nerd and head coach, once told me that "riding shotgun" dates back to the stagecoach days. The person beside the driver wasn't just along for the ride—they were there to defend the journey. That always stuck with me.

As we arrived, we were greeted by R.J. Van Almen, the Pro Football Hall of Fame Luncheon Club's founder, President Dennis Manzella, and Scott Ryan, the co-author of my previous book and co-host of *Tiger Talk*, the YouTube show we built to cover the highs, lows, and everything in between during my husband's high school football season.

We posed for photos. I signed a helmet and football alongside the names of legends. Later, those pieces would be auctioned off to support the Hall. The moment hit me like a wave—humble, surreal, unforgettable. Someone snapped a photo of Nate watching me, pride in his eyes. When I saw it later, I smiled. Usually, it's me watching him from the background.

Inside, familiar faces dotted the room. Scott's mom waved from near the front, her pride lighting up the space. "She's having the time of her life," Scott muttered, rolling his eyes. "She's proud of you. This is a lot."

I nodded, heart full.

As lunch wrapped up, the room quieted. The president stood, gave the week's updates, and then led us in the Pledge of Allegiance. I felt my throat catch—gratitude and pride swelling in my chest. Was I really going to stand up in front of peers and tell the truth that some people would not be able to handle? Would this be another backlash?

It was a flash of a thought. Then, it was Nate's turn.

He stood, all 6'4" of him, and adjusted the mic—a ritual at this point. Laughter rippled through the room, then silence. That kind of silence. The kind that comes when everyone knows something meaningful is about to happen.

Coach Moore had the room. And I would have the moment. He began, "Thank you to the Hall of Fame Luncheon Club for inviting me to introduce you to my wife, Becca Moore. You know, back when she was Becca Garber, I first really started to think seriously about this girl, when on Fridays she would bring me homemade cookies decorated in our school colors. It was that personal touch and attention to detail that made me think maybe this is the one for me. Little did I know that both I and the Great City of Massillon would be getting much more than well-timed baked goods. I am amazed every day by Becca's commitment to her family, her commitment to her jobs as both Special Education Coordinator and Parent Involvement Coordinator, and her commitment to our football program and our players. Becca is the secret sauce. She is the little engine that could. She embodies, "When you get knocked down, get back up." She is a state championship coach who knows how to push athletes to achieve the unachievable. She supports our football program and players in ways that few see but all Tiger fans appreciate. And she does it all with beauty and grace. She is a marathoner. An ironman. An author. An educator. A coach. A mother. And dare I say, the PAUL BROWN of coaches' wives. Ladies and gentlemen . . . Becca Moore."

For a moment, the room stilled—and I heard nothing. It was as if time slowed around me. I stood in place, the lump in my throat rising, tears threatening to spill over as I fought to steady my breath. Nate hugged me gently, pressing a kiss to the top of my head. And in that quiet flash, a thought slipped in—How do I follow that? How do I live up to the way he just spoke about me?

I stepped forward, lowered the microphone to match my height, and glanced out over the crowd. Every eye was on me. I smiled softly—and just then, an image flickered in my mind.

A little girl. Hiding behind a bed frame at five years old.

What would she think if she could see this moment? Would she even believe it?

Another image came next—one I've carried for years: the guardian angel painting from my childhood bedroom wall. Two small children, crossing a broken wooden bridge, unaware of how close they are to falling. But protected. Covered. Guided.

I lifted my gaze, looked out at a nearly full room, and smiled again, not from nerves, not from pride—but from something deeper.

To understand how I got to that moment—standing in heels behind a microphone—you have to understand where I come from.

Part 1

Crossing the Bridge

—Chapter 1—
No One's Going to Save You

"If these United States can be called a body, then Kentucky can be called its heart."
~Jesse Stuart

I come from a place most people couldn't point to on a map: Clayhole, Kentucky. My family lived in near-complete isolation for over a century—no phone lines, no cars, no television sets buzzing in the background. No indoor plumbing, no electricity, not even running water. The kind of life that makes you grit your teeth and work with whatever's in front of you. But my family had what mattered: faith, grit, and each other. And even when we had little, we gave freely. My family is the kind who'd hand you their last piece of cornbread without blinking.

We come from mountain soil and stubbornness, from the kind of survival you don't learn in books. My family knows how to work—really work. How to live off the land, to pick berries and boil them down into jars of jam that tasted like sunlight. They know how to string beans and snap peas, cure meat, can vegetables, and store them up like treasure for the cold months. Even now, in their eighties and nineties, they rise with the sun, plant their gardens, and work with joy in their bones.

We've taught in one-room schoolhouses, worked deep in the belly of coal mines, shoed horses, grown tobacco, churned butter, and carved out a life with nothing but our bare hands and God's mercy. There are no Instagram reels about us—no podcasts or morning show interviews. But the kind of strength we carry? It's the kind that builds churches and carves the pews by hand.

Sometimes you'll find us tired, covered in dirt, backs bent from years of labor—but never broken. We press on, fueled by a quiet hope, a deep reverence for life's rhythm, and a belief that this isn't all there is. That someday, beyond the river, there's a sweet forever. And until that day, we plant, we pray, and we press on.

I remember once telling my cousin Margaret Ann, who was in her eighties and still working forty-plus hours a week, "Margaret, you oughta write a book on how to keep working into your eighties." She looked me dead in the eye, half-offended, half-smiling, and said, "That's easy. Get up every morning and go to work. The end." And then she threw her head back and laughed, and so did I.

We know where we come from. We don't forget. It's in the way we talk, the way we love, the way we show up with our sleeves rolled up and our hearts wide open. It's in my blood—the same blood that carried me through battles I never saw coming. The same blood that steadies me when the floor shifts beneath me.

So when people ask me why I'm the way I am—why I don't flinch, why I don't fold, why I refuse to apologize for being the way I am—my answer is simple: I am a Kentucky Combs.

My mother, Bertha Grace Combs, came from that same dirt-covered holiness. Born the baby of the family, she was the surprise no one expected and the spark no one could contain. In today's world, she probably would've been diagnosed with ADHD—restless, passionate, wildly creative. But back then, they just said she was "a handful." And she was.

With jet black hair, big brown doe eyes, and a laugh that turned heads, she never just entered a room—she took command of it. She met my birth father at a wedding, and from the moment their eyes met, she was convinced it was her fairytale beginning. He was handsome. Charismatic. A man with words that sounded like destiny and promises that felt like purpose. He wrote letters that would make any girl blush—and she did.

They believed they were going to change the world. Do the Lord's work. Build a life full of mission and meaning.

In the early 1970s, that was all she needed to say yes.

Have you ever looked at someone and thought, *They've got it all. The looks, the charm, the life?* That's what everyone thought when they met David. He was tall, with dark hair and eyes as blue and blinding as an August sky—eyes girls could get lost in and never want to find their way out. But it wasn't just his looks. David had a presence. That quiet, magnetic pull that made people lean in when he spoke. And when he did? His words sounded like poetry. Smooth, persuasive, disarming. He could make you believe in anything—especially him.

To my mother, David was everything she'd ever dreamed of. Handsome. Strong. Faithful. He loved Jesus. Worked with his hands. A man she thought was just like her daddy. He didn't just seem like the answer to her prayers—he looked like the prayers themselves, walking around in boots and a flannel shirt. It felt preordained, like God himself had tied their paths together.

They got married, settled down, and a few years later, I came along.

My earliest memories are stitched together inside a little three-bedroom ranch in West Manchester, Ohio. The kind of home where the front door opened into a modest living room with a soft hum of comfort. To the right, an archway led to a kitchen with worn brown carpet patterned in swirls I'd trace with my toes. Off the kitchen was a laundry nook with a wringer washing machine and a door that opened to the backyard— where clothes danced on the line in the wind and sunlight.

The garage smelled like sawdust and dreams. That's where David kept his tools, his projects. He was a gifted carpenter. He built toy boxes, candle holders, and even a playhouse for me in the backyard—white with black trim, so perfectly built you could almost live in it. To a little girl, it was magic. A castle. A promise that things were good and safe.

The hallway off the living room led to three small bedrooms and a single bathroom, which we all shared. It was a simple house in a quiet town—but it was enough.

West Manchester was—and still is—a tiny village in Preble County, where the population barely nudged over 400. The pace was slow, the values old-fashioned. Neighbors still knocked on doors to borrow sugar. Kids rode their bikes barefoot down the middle of the street and only came home when the porch lights flickered on. Gardens bloomed in nearly every yard, and the sound of laughter and screen doors slamming was the rhythm of life.

It looked like the picture of peace. But it was just that—a picture.

Because behind those white curtains and backyard swing sets, the fairytale was starting to unravel. And David? He wasn't the hero of it. He was the illusion.

Dreams always have endings—some bathed in light, others drenched in shadow. Ours began to slip quietly into darkness. Not all at once, but inch by inch, like a slow-moving fog that you don't notice until it's already wrapped around your neck.

To the outside world, we were perfect. A charming house. A hard-working husband. A smiling wife. But inside, something had shifted. There was an unease—subtle at first, then suffocating.

Even as a little girl, I could sense it. Children always do. I began noticing the bruises. They weren't on her face—not yet. But they showed up in places that made my stomach twist. And slowly, the brightness in my mother's eyes dulled. Her laughter faded. She moved differently—cautiously, like each step could set off an alarm. Like she was walking barefoot across broken glass, always protecting us, always protecting herself.

It was like living inside a house made of eggshells. And I learned early: step too hard, speak too loud, exist the wrong way—and everything could crack.

I remember one night, like it was sealed into my bones.

I was wearing a pink nightgown, legs folded tightly into the fabric, hiding behind the bed frame in my room. One hand on the wall, the other gripping the wood behind me. The screaming echoed from across the hallway—loud, sharp, terrifying. I didn't understand everything, but I knew enough: stay quiet, stay still, stay hidden.

Tears slid silently down my cheeks. Don't cry, I told myself. He can't find you if you don't cry.

Then the hallway light flicked on.

And I heard it—a slap. Skin meeting skin with a crack that still rings in my ears.

I looked up at the wall. There, above my bed, hung a painting—the one thread of comfort that held me together on the nights I couldn't hold myself. A storm-dark sky hovered above, casting shadows over the shattered remains of a wooden bridge. Beneath it, a torrent of black water crashed against jagged rocks, the kind of current that doesn't forgive. The bridge—splintered, missing slats, barely standing—looked one step from collapse. Two small children, no older than I was, clung to each other in fear, frozen mid-step, the girl's bare feet inches from empty air. And behind them, almost glowing through the storm, towered a guardian angel. Cloaked in a flowing white dress with an equally flowing soft blue colored shawl wrapped around her shoulders and arms. Her wings stretched the width of the scene—massive, sheltering, holy. A single star hovered above her golden auburn hair. Her face is round and soft, with rose cheeks and lips pressed together with a faint touch of pink. Her expression wasn't panic—it was peace. She wasn't afraid. She knew. I used to lie in bed and stare at her for hours, whispering prayers I didn't know how to finish. If she could get them across that broken bridge, maybe—just maybe—she could get me through this.

But the light in the hallway suddenly disappeared—blocked by a tall shadow in the doorway.

My heart froze. I pulled my knees tighter, tucked the nightgown under my feet, and buried my face between my legs. Please, God, don't let him find me. Please, not tonight.

But he did.

His hand reached behind the bed and yanked me up by my nightgown like I weighed nothing. Dangling midair, I felt his breath before I heard his words.

"So . . . you think you can hide from me?" he sneered, licking his lips.

I said nothing. I had learned by then that silence was safer.

"Get to the bathroom. And remember—this is our little secret. No one needs to know. Tiptoe—your mama's sleeping."

The bathroom was small. A tub. A toilet. A sink with a smeared mirror and a line of dim bulbs above it. One wall was covered in old floral wallpaper. I stared at the flowers, willing myself not to look anywhere else. He shut the door quietly. The lock clicked.

I was trapped.

I tried to picture the angel. I tried to focus on anything else.

Then came his voice again—quiet, but loaded.

"I told you. Put your hands on me. Get on top of me. Now."

I obeyed. I straddled him as he lay naked on the floor. My eyes locked on the yellowed lights above. Or the faded flowers on the wall. Anything but him.

And then it happened. The "lotion," he called it. It shot out like lightning, landing on my cheek and on the counter. He smeared it across my face with his thumb, blank-eyed. Hollow.

"Clean up. Go to bed."

I was four years old.

And I remember thinking—*Is this love? Is this what daughters do when mommies and daddies fight?* I wanted to believe it would get better. It had to. But the truth was, the nightmare had only just begun.

David's anger came fast and loud—over things I couldn't understand. I took refuge where I could. The neighbors' house. The backyard. Aunt Ruth and Uncle Bruce's in the summer. School became my safe place, my sanctuary. But even there, I learned to be careful—sweet, well-behaved, and always dressed to hide the bruises.

Because the bruises that once showed up on my mother's arms . . . now stained mine.

And I remembered what he always said, "No one would understand. This is our secret."

• • •

When school started, I thought things would change. Kindergarten was everything I had dreamed it would be. I got the best jobs—line leader, milk cart duty, even walking to the cafeteria all by myself. I loved pushing that cart down the hallway, my little shoes clicking against the floor. I remember staring at the milk cartons and wondering if one day, my picture would end up on the back of one, with that haunting word: Missing.

The bus rides to school were an adventure—a time where I found peace from what may have happened the night before. The rural roads twisted and curved through open farmland, and every turn felt like a ride at the fair. I especially remember one freezing morning, the kind where the frost bites through your tights. I had my heart set on wearing brown wedge sandals. I was five, and my love for heels had already taken root. My mother tried to reason with me—she said it was too cold, too slippery, too dangerous. But I didn't care. I stood firm. Wind, snow, ice—nothing was going to keep me from wearing those shoes. Besides, I thought, I'll be inside all day. How hard could it be to walk from the bus to the school doors?

I won the battle.

I remember bouncing onto the bus, beaming, and pausing proudly at the top of the stairs.

"Look at my shoes!" I squealed to the driver. "Aren't they just perfect?"

She smiled back. "Shoes are always important for a stylish girl."

I slid into my seat, grinning.

I don't remember how long I was on the bus after that. I just remember her voice—talking to me—and then, nothing. Next thing I knew, I was lying on the cold, hard ground in the middle of a field. My wedge sandals were soaked. The world was sideways. The bus had flipped—one and a half times. Most of us were knocked unconscious.

I didn't cry. I just told the EMT my arm hurt.

No one died that day, thank God. But the next day, I wished I had.

I was sitting at our little metal kids' table with my baby sister, Rachel, when I heard him. David was screaming in the kitchen.

"This could've been her!" he barked. "But no—she had to cry because her arm hurt."

He hurled the newspaper at my mother. I watched it flutter and hit her like a slap. I was five. The bus had flipped. I was terrified, bruised, and confused. But there was no room for any of that with him.

He came into the family room and threw the paper into my face.

"You see this? You see her?"

I nodded timidly.

"This girl—she's on the front page. You know why? Because she didn't cry. She didn't go to the hospital. She was brave. Not like you. You're a baby. A weak, pathetic baby."

His face twisted with rage. He yanked me from the seat by my arm, and my knee slammed into the metal table. I started to cry.

Wrong move.

He had the belt off in an instant, lashing it across my back, my legs, my arms. I cowered against the wall, sobbing, but he didn't stop. My mother ran in, screaming, trying to shield me.

"David, STOP! You'll kill her!"

And then the lamp flew—shattering above our heads. Glass rained down on us like hail. That was when he finally stormed off into the garage, leaving behind a trail of silence that somehow hurt worse than the screaming.

I don't remember if I cried after that. I don't remember when I went back to school. What I do remember is learning—quickly—that I had to act like everything was fine. Smile. Listen. Be sweet. Wear long sleeves.

When I was five, Mommie B helped me cover the scars from my washing machine accident by making a stylish arm sleeve—and my love for fancy dresses and shoes had already begun.

Say nothing.

No one ever asked if I was okay. Not a teacher, a family member, or anyone at church. No one. Even if they had, I wouldn't have known how to answer.

No one in that house was safe—not my mother, not Rachel, and certainly not me. What started in the bathroom had now become a routine. It was happening more often. Quietly. Predictably. And while other little girls were playing house, I was trying to survive in one that had become my prison.

The playhouse in the backyard—the one he built for me with white siding and black trim—became his new hiding place. His sanctuary. His secret. Mine too.

He told me it was ours, a place no one else could go.

By the summer between kindergarten and first grade, the last flickers of childhood innocence were slipping through my fingers. And that little white house in the yard? It became the place where whatever was left of me was slowly, painfully taken.

He wasn't this tall, dark, handsome man. He was a nightmare. A devil in disguise wearing human skin. The violence escalated the night he nearly choked my mother to death. He put a hook in the ceiling and strung her up with a rope. Her neck bruised and burned so badly the marks stayed on her for weeks, like a necklace made of violence. Out in public, she masked it all with long sleeves and hollow smiles so no one would ask questions. But something had shifted—maybe it was the way I flinched, maybe she finally caught glimpses of bruises on me. Maybe it was just that her body had finally hit its limit. Whatever it was, she snapped into action.

She grabbed Rachel and me, threw us into the backseat, and climbed in the passenger seat next to our neighbor Marsha, who didn't ask questions—she just drove. I clutched Rachel so tight I couldn't feel my arms. I was six, and I already knew what it meant to shield someone. We flew down the road, tires screeching into the police station parking lot. But he was behind us. Of course he was. His car swerved, slamming to a stop beside us. Marsha laid on the horn like it was a war siren, begging someone to come out. No one moved fast enough. He was already out of his car, pounding the passenger window, sobbing, manipulating, screaming, "It's a misunderstanding! Please come back! I'll die without you! Do you want me to die?" And then—glass exploded. A flash of fury. He reached in and dragged my mother through shattered glass, shoving her into his car like a stolen object, and drove off. Marsha froze. I stared at this brick building with a sign saying Police Station. But no one ever came out. Would no one ever help us? Marsha whispered, "Rebecca, I'm so sorry," and I think she meant it. But sorry didn't mean safe. She threw the car in reverse and backed away while I sat frozen, Rachel tucked in my arms, her baby breath against my neck. The wind blew in through the broken silence, and I kissed her forehead. "Don't worry," I whispered, "He'll have to kill me first." I accepted right then that I wasn't ever going to grow up. I was going to end up on a milk carton—face printed beneath the words: Missing. Just one more forgotten girl the world didn't bother to save.

Marsha drove us, and I wondered where she could be going. When the car slowed to a stop, I looked up to see the white and black playhouse and realized I was home. I laid in the bed that night and looked up at the guardian angel in all her glory, guiding the two little children across the bridge. In a whisper with tears coming down my face, I said, "When are you coming for me and Rachel?" I turned over and went to sleep.

• • •

For a few weeks, things were quiet. Less yelling. Fewer visits in the night. The playhouse stayed empty except for me. But quiet doesn't mean safe either—not when silence feels like the breath you hold before a scream. When you live in fear, days blur into each other like rain against glass. You stop living and start surviving. I learned that survival meant staying busy, staying invisible. So I cleaned. I did chores. I ran laundry through the old wringer washer we used because we couldn't afford anything else. Most of our clothes hung out on the line or were draped over chairs inside the house to dry.

The wringer washer looked harmless enough—two rollers stacked above a deep metal tub. We poured in water and let the clothes agitate, turning slowly, like a false sense of calm. I knew how to use it. I used it dozens of times. But that day, I fed a wet shirt through, and my hand went right along with it. I didn't even have time to think. My fingers disappeared between the rollers, then my palm, then my wrist. I screamed. The kind of scream that rips through your throat without permission. My mother came running, frantic and crying. In her panic, instead of hitting the release, she hit reverse. And it rolled my arm back out—inch by inch, like it was eating me alive and then spitting me out. By the time she got me free, I was inside the machine up to my elbow.

David walked in, annoyed. Not worried—annoyed. My mother was still crying, cradling my arm. "She needs a hospital—her arm might be broken," she sobbed. But he just shook his head and walked into the kitchen to make a call. I don't know who he called. I don't remember much after that, just that my arm swelled until the skin split and oozed. At the hospital, the doctor said I needed stitches, but David insisted, "No, it'll be fine." So they taped it shut, wrapped it in gauze, and sent me home.

To this day, I still carry the scar. Three inches long, tucked inside my right arm—thick, raised, and permanent. You can still see the tread marks from the rollers. Sometimes it itches. Sometimes it aches—as if it remembers. Other times, I forget it's there until someone asks, and I brush it off with a shrug, calling it a silly childhood accident. But it isn't silly. It's a reminder that some wounds never fully heal. Some pain lives under the skin. My arm was crushed that day, but I was already carrying worse injuries on the inside—ones no bandage could cover.

Somewhere in the chaos—between the bruises, the screaming, and the nights I spent curled into myself, praying to be invisible—my mother got pregnant again. Melissa came into the world loud and angry, and honestly, who could blame her? It was like she came out already carrying the weight of everything our mother had been forced to bury for the past decade. Her cries were relentless, like the pain had finally found a voice.

Melissa only seemed to sleep at our Aunt Ruth and Uncle Bruce's house. Maybe it was quieter there. Maybe it was safer. Or maybe she knew, even as a baby, that some places hold peace like a secret. I still don't know where my mother found the courage—her face looked different that day, less makeup, more resolve—but one day, she finally packed us up and we moved in with them. Aunt Ruth was my mother's sister, and they were as different as night and day.

That night, my Mother sat me down on the pull-out brown couch bed while Rachel lay there sleeping and Melissa slept in a secondhand crib beside her. Her voice cracked when she spoke. "Rebecca, your father and I . . . we're not getting back together. He's going back to Delaware with his parents. We'll stay here. We'll sell the house. We'll figure it out." I nodded, but I couldn't speak. The words felt heavy, like they were settling deep into my bones. I think I hugged her, but I honestly can't remember if I said anything at all. I was numb, as I knew this meant the end of something I shouldn't be sad about but just couldn't quite comprehend.

Later, I walked into the small bedroom my aunt and uncle had set up for me. I stood in the doorway and stared at the wall. It was blank. No angel. No children crossing a broken bridge. No glow in the dark hope. Just a plain, empty wall. The angel never came. Not for me. Not for Rachel. Not for Melissa. I laid down anyway, staring into that empty space until I finally fell asleep.

I was never going to be the same. I don't think I had the words for it back then, but I knew—somewhere deep inside—I was marked. Not exactly broken. Just . . . marked. And I didn't know which was worse.

The truth is, once you've lived in survival mode, you don't know how to live outside of it. It rewires your brain. It teaches you that silence isn't peace—it's a warning. Love isn't soft—it's conditional. That safety is an illusion. Back then, there was no #MeToo movement. No trauma-informed therapy in schools. No mandated reporting laws. There was just secrecy and shame. You didn't talk about it. You survived it. Alone. Silently. Or you didn't, and you were forgotten.

The beatings were merciless. The gaslighting was constant. The anticipation—waiting for the next blow, the next whisper in the dark, the next slammed door—that was the worst part. David didn't just hurt our bodies. He invaded our minds. He infected our joy. He made us distrust the very air we breathed.

There is a specific kind of betrayal that comes when the monster lives in your house. When the man who's supposed to protect you is the one who breaks you, piece by piece, that kind of trauma doesn't just fade. It follows you. It stains your dreams. It lingers in your voice when someone raises theirs. And even after you escape, the aftershocks don't stop.

Every statistic said I'd never make it. Girls like me? We don't make it out. But what they didn't know was this: I'd already learned to live in fight or flight. I'd learned how to listen for footsteps and read faces in shadows. I was always ready to run. Always ready to defend. Always scanning for the next exit.

I was in the driver's seat, and no one was riding shotgun.

—Chapter 2—
Marked

"Sometimes the only way to get closure is
by accepting that you'll never get it."
~John Mark Green

The clicking noise came through the intercom like static thunder, rattling across the ceiling tiles of my first-grade classroom at National Trails Elementary.

"Excuse the interruption, but could you please send Rebecca McKay to the office for dismissal—with all her things?" The secretary's voice buzzed over the speaker, distant and matter-of-fact, as if this were just another early checkout. But it wasn't. Not for me.

This was it.

I knew, somehow, without anyone explaining it, that I was leaving for good. I clutched my blue pencil box, the one with a few worn-down crayons and a broken eraser inside. My handmade school bag, stitched with little strawberries, hung off my shoulder. I walked out of that classroom and never looked back—not because I didn't want to—but because I couldn't afford to.

No teacher stopped me. No classmate asked why. I walked through those silent hallways knowing that not a single adult in that building had ever truly seen me. Not the bruises, not the sadness behind my eyes, not the way I sometimes winced when someone brushed against my arm. I'd become a professional at pretending. I knew how to smile through pain. I knew how to laugh at just the right moment so no one would dig deeper. I was six years old and already fluent in the language of hiding.

No one ever asked about the scar that marked my arm. I learned early that people don't ask questions they're not ready to hear the answers to.

When I got to the office, my Aunt Ruth was waiting, her hand steady and warm when I slipped mine into it. My mother stood beside her, trying to smile. She had that look again—like she was holding her breath inside her own skin. Like if she exhaled, the whole house of cards might collapse. I didn't know how this would end, but I knew we were at the beginning of something else.

Something quieter.

It wasn't the perfect setup—none of this was ideal—but I was going to live with my Aunt Ruth and Uncle Bruce. For now, it meant being separated from my mother and sisters. Rachel and Melissa were still too little to be in school, and they'd stay with our mom while she finished her teaching license and tried to start her life over. That was the plan. Or at least the hope.

Children's Services had been involved for months. We had been under their microscope like bugs on a slide. They had rules. Lots of them. You couldn't just move a child across county lines, even for safety. They came to inspect the house—measuring rooms, opening pantry cabinets, even pacing off the backyard. I didn't understand it all at the time, but I knew enough to be nervous. What if they said no?

My aunt and uncle were solid people. Aunt Ruth was a respected second-grade teacher at Tri-County North. Uncle Bruce was a land surveyor with a quiet spirit and even quieter voice with the kindest blue eyes that could pierce your soul. They didn't have children of their own, which meant—ready or not—I was about to become the center of their world. I was used to fading into the background. This would be new.

The lady from Children's Services scribbled into her folder, barely looking up.

"I guess this will suffice for now," she muttered.

Suffice?

I blinked. Suffice? I had a whole room to myself. Apple trees in the backyard. Strawberry plants. A place where no one yelled at night. Where the floors didn't creak with footsteps that made my stomach twist. Where the bathroom didn't feel like a prison.

I didn't know what the word "suffice" meant exactly, but I knew this: it felt like everything I'd ever wanted.

I think back to that moment. The measuring tape. The checklist. The way they treated my potential safety—like it came down to square footage and shelf space. Today, the system is drowning. Too many kids. Too few homes. There are bunk beds crammed into corners and closets turned into bedrooms. Anyone with a roof can become a foster parent. But back then? They measured Uncle Bruce's house to the inch. And even then, they called it "sufficient." It makes me ache when I think of what "insufficient" must've looked like.

A few days later, I stood in the doorway of a new classroom—West Milton Elementary—first grade, second attempt. My teacher's name was Mrs. Maccumber. She had short black hair and deep brown eyes that sparkled, like the sun had been hiding behind them just waiting to shine. Her smile lit up the whole room. It didn't just stretch across her face—it stretched across the distance between us.

"Welcome to my classroom," she said warmly. "I'm so happy you're here."

She didn't ask me questions. She didn't need me to explain. I think my aunt and uncle had given her the kind of quiet warning you can't put into words—handle with care. And she did. Every single day. Same smile. Same gentle voice. Same morning hug. I wasn't a hugger, not then. I flinched the first time. My body didn't know what safety felt like. But she didn't stop hugging me. And slowly, I stopped pulling away.

She paired me with kind kids. Gave me space to read. Let me help erase the board at the end of the day and hand out papers like I was someone she could count on. She never treated me like I was fragile. She treated me like I mattered.

It was strange—being seen. Not because someone was checking for bruises or measuring my pain, but just . . . because I was there.

For the first time in my life, when the bell rang, I wasn't afraid. I was going home to a place that felt like a safe haven.

The days that followed were bright in ways I hadn't known to hope for. Everyone in class was kind. Sweet. They didn't know what I had lived through, and it didn't seem to matter. I started laughing more—real, belly laughs that didn't come with fear attached.

And then one day, something unexpected happened.

I was sitting at my desk with my head down, quietly tracing the lines on my spelling test, when I heard a whisper.

"Psst. Hey, Rebecca, did you study for the test?"

I looked up and I saw a little girl—her name lost to time now—leaning toward me without ever turning her head. She was looking straight ahead, eyes locked on the chalkboard.

"Are you talking to me?" I asked, confused.

"Don't look at me," she said quickly. "She'll know."

Mrs. Maccumber was walking slowly up and down the aisles, calling out each word, using it in a sentence, then repeating it. I looked back at the girl.

"Yeah, I studied . . . Didn't you?"

"I'll tell you later," she whispered. "Can you help me?"

I stared down at my paper—the kind with thin blue lines that tore if you erased too hard—and I knew what she was asking. I waited for Mrs. Maccumber to pass, then tilted my paper just enough for her to see. I pretended to be erasing, the pencil squeaking against the page. The girl copied the answers, word by word, while I kept one eye on the teacher and one on the paper. It was like a quiet game of cat and mouse.

When we finished the test, we walked up together to turn them in. As we reached the front of the room, she grabbed my hand and gave it a little squeeze.

"Let's play together at recess," she said with a grin.

My heart did something it hadn't done in a long time—it leapt. Someone wanted me. I wasn't just the new girl. I wasn't just the quiet girl who hugged the wall. I was going to have a best friend.

For the first time in a long while, I felt like a kid.

I was so excited at recess that I ran outside like the air itself had turned to gold. She grabbed my hand and we skipped to the far corner of the playground—away from the swings, away from the aides, away from anyone who could overhear. She stopped suddenly and turned to me, her voice barely above a whisper.

"Don't tell anyone, okay? You promise?"

Her eyes locked on mine, and for a second, I couldn't breathe. There was something hollow behind them, something I recognized but couldn't name at the time. I just nodded quickly, eager to prove I could be trusted.

"Cross my heart, hope to die, stick a needle in my eye . . ." I trailed off. I didn't know if there was more to that chant, but it didn't matter.

My heart was racing.

She leaned in and slowly pulled down her bottom lip. I gasped. The inside was torn, raw, like meat.

"What happened?" I whispered.

Her eyes dropped to the gravel beneath our feet. "My mom got mad. Kicked me with her boot. There was something sharp on it . . . it cut my mouth."

I stood there frozen. I wanted to reach out, say something, anything, but the words locked up inside me like a room I didn't want to go back into. I didn't tell her I understood. I didn't say, "Me too." I just looked at her and nodded. My silence was all I could offer without breaking open.

I knew we were bound at that moment. We were marked. Not broken—just carrying scars that the world couldn't see.

The next few days at school were the happiest I'd ever known. We were inseparable—whispering at lunch, braiding each other's hair at recess, pretending we were secret agents on the playground. She made the lonely parts of me feel less lonely.

But then, it all shattered.

One afternoon, Mrs. Maccumber called me to her desk. Her face was serious, her voice quieter than usual, but it still held that tone adults use when they've already made up their minds.

"Rebecca, I have a serious question, and I need you to be honest with me."

I froze. My stomach dropped like it did when David used to yell. That same panic. That same flash of shame.

"Your spelling test . . . You and another student had the exact same answers. The same words are correct. Same mistake in the same place. Rebecca? Did you cheat?"

I looked away. My face flushed. The room felt loud, even though no one was talking.

"I didn't mean to . . . I just . . ."

She cut in gently, "Go sit down. Think about what you want to say. I'll call you back up."

I trudged back to my seat. My friend was staring at her paper, her face pale. A few moments later, she was called up too. I watched her walk slowly to the desk, then back again. And then it was my turn.

"I let her cheat off me," I admitted, barely above a whisper. "She needed help. Her mom . . . her mouth . . ."

I trailed off. I couldn't say the rest. If I opened that door, everything I'd buried might come flooding out.

Mrs. Maccumber said nothing. She just nodded and motioned for me to sit down again.

A few days later, they came for my first friend. My recess giggle-buddy. The girl who shared her story because she thought I was safe.

And just like that—she was gone.

No one told me anything. No one said her name out loud again. Kids whispered behind their hands when I passed in the hallway. I became that girl. The one who made their friends disappear. Like I was cursed.

After that, no one came to sit with me at lunch. No birthday party invitations. No sleepovers. Just whispers and side eyes, like I was too different to touch, I was cursed. I wore my frilly dresses and little heels anyway. I prayed before I ate lunch and bowed my head with my hands folded while kids around me snickered. I learned how to pretend their laughter didn't cut.

First grade faded into second. Then third. Then fourth. Still alone. No friends.

And then came Mr. Williams.

He was my fourth-grade teacher—stern, gruff, and tired-looking. One day, he called a parent-teacher conference, and I had to come along.

"There's no denying her intelligence," he said as he glanced at my aunt and uncle. "Rebecca is sharp. Academically, very strong."

My aunt beamed, proud. My uncle sat stone-faced, hands folded in his lap.

"But," Mr. Williams continued, his tone hardening, "I think she's a spoiled brat. And honestly, I doubt she'll amount to much. She doesn't have friends. She acts like she's better than the other kids."

The words hit me like a slap across the face. And not just any slap—a memory. My mother getting struck. That sharp, hot sting of humiliation. I felt it all over again, only this time I couldn't cry. I sat there in silence, trying not to shatter.

I looked at my aunt. Her face had fallen. She had no words. My uncle didn't move, didn't flinch, just stared ahead.

The ride home was quiet. No one brought it up again.

But I heard his words in my head for years. "Spoiled brat. Won't amount to much." They crawled in and nested. They whispered to me in middle school and screamed at me in high school. They would knock on my door later in college.

Why did he say it? Was it the dresses? The books? The way I didn't try to belong because I already knew I didn't?

I laid in bed that night and stared at the ceiling. No angel painting now, no bridge. Just white silence.

But maybe my uncle was the angel. Quiet. Steady. Always showing up. Maybe not all men were dangerous. Maybe one of them was sent to guide me.

I wasn't sure yet.

And Mr. Williams didn't help.

Life carried on after that conference. I kept being me—the girl no one talked to. My mother had remarried by then, settled into a teaching job, and started a new life. I visited sometimes. I saw my sisters on weekends. Played awkwardly with my new step-siblings.

But no one ever said, "Come live with us."

At their wedding, they mentioned it like a passing thought, but I was never really invited into the fold. And honestly? I didn't mind. I didn't want to leave.

Because for the first time in my life, I was safe. I had my own bed, my own space, and a home that didn't make me flinch when the garage door opened.

And sometimes, safe is enough.

• • •

Christmas rolled around, and truthfully, I never really loved Christmas. Not the way kids are supposed to. The lights, the songs, the presents— none of it held magic for me. But traveling to Tennessee to see my grandparents? That part I loved.

They lived down a long gravel lane in a modest three-bedroom ranch surrounded by woods and a creek that ran along the back of the property. Two large gardens bordered the side and back of the house, and in the summertime, it felt like a childhood dream—barefoot days filled with fishing, swimming, and swinging from branches into the creek. A place where you could breathe, where the trees kept secrets and the water washed away whatever hurt you were holding.

Christmas in Tennessee with Grandma and Grandpa Combs was a little chaotic and a lot of magic. Grandma cooked like it was a sport, dirtying every pot, pan, and plate in the kitchen. The older cousins stuck with dish duty would grumble, "Does she really need this many bowls to make biscuits?" They'd roll their eyes and whisper under their breath while scrubbing casserole dishes, but somehow, it was all part of the tradition.

We went to church, Southern-Baptist-style, where the pews shook and the walls felt alive. People would rise out of their seats and walk straight into the choir mid-song, their voices rising like a storm of praise. I didn't even know the words, but I joined anyway, just to stand among them—to be part of something that felt big, and joyful, and safe.

They weren't rich. Their house was small. But now I know they were angels—helping to guide me over the broken bridge while the troubled waters raged below.

The best part was that my Aunt Ruth and mother were sisters, so for just a few days, I got to be with my sisters again. Rachel and Melissa would arrive with my mom, and we'd run around barefoot in pajamas, string popcorn for the tree, and decorate aluminum foil ornaments with our cousins. My mom's brother, Uncle Phil, and his wife, Aunt Julie, would bring their kids too, and sometimes there were others—children my grandparents had quietly "adopted" into the fold. No one asked questions. Everyone belonged.

Every year, Grandpa would lead us out into the woods behind the house to find a tree for Christmas. We'd argue and vote until we all agreed. Then, like a team of tiny lumberjacks, we'd drag it back—often down the railroad tracks that ran next to the house. It was imperfect, messy, and magical.

But behind the laughter and the popcorn strands, something else was happening.

One night, I wandered down the hallway and saw that the back bedroom door was slightly cracked open. Inside, the adults had pushed the bed against the wall and were sitting in a loose circle—on buckets, on the floor, wherever they could find space. It didn't feel like a family meeting. It felt like something bigger—like decisions were being made. Serious ones.

"I just think it's time for a change for all of them," someone said, voice clear and steady. "This is the best way to give them a chance. A new beginning."

The words hung in the air like smoke. A new beginning? My stomach tightened. Was I in trouble? Was I leaving again? What had I done this time? Was I too much? Not enough?

Before I could think of another question, someone saw me standing in the hallway. The door closed quietly. And that was that.

The next clear memory I have is standing inside the courthouse in Troy, Ohio.

That conversation in Tennessee—those hushed, emotional, grown-up voices—had led to this. A moment of impossible sacrifice. And a strange, fragile kind of joy.

The judge's chambers were warm, the air smelled of old paper and polished wood. He sat behind a towering desk that looked like it was carved out of a tree that had lived for a hundred lives. His eyes were kind. His smile didn't feel forced.

I sat across from him in my new dress and shiny patent leather shoes, the ones with the tiny heel that made me feel older than I was. To my right, my mother sat in a chair so big it seemed to swallow her whole. She looked like a shadow of herself—fragile and tight—but she wore her best smile. She sat up tall, her back straight, like she was holding it all together with a thread.

To my left sat Aunt Ruth. Calm. Steady. Her hands folded in her lap. Behind her stood Uncle Bruce, quiet as always, his face unreadable, but his presence solid and grounding. He didn't say much. He never did. But he was always there—like gravity.

The judge looked at me.

"Rebecca," he said softly, "sometimes life asks us to be very brave."

I don't remember the exact words after that. I just remember a feeling. A heavy, beautiful stillness in the room. The shifting of something enormous.

I was being adopted.

By my Aunt Ruth and Uncle Bruce.

My mother's tears welled but didn't fall. She nodded through it. I think she knew this was the only way to give me a real shot—a life without chaos. Without fear.

She let me go so I could be free.

And somehow, in that moment, love looked a lot like loss. And sacrifice looked a lot like salvation.

I walked out of the courthouse with my new Mommie and Daddy. The sun was shining, and the wind brushed my face like a soft kiss— gentle and light, almost like an angel's wing. For a moment, I imagined one had passed by me. I don't know for sure, but I picture my mother, whom from this point on I would refer to as Mommie B, walking to her car, tears silently streaming down her face.

That moment reminded me of a Bible verse Grandma Combs always said, "Greater love hath no man than this, that a man lay down his life for his friend." —John 15:13.

The ultimate sacrifice: giving up your child, not because you want to—but because you know they deserve more than you can give. Losing a child, even when they're still alive, must leave a scar on the heart that never stops aching.

But for me, in that moment, it felt like my hell on earth had cracked open—just wide enough to let some heaven in.

Things started to look up. I was headed into fifth grade with a fire in my chest and a stubborn whisper in the back of my mind: Prove Mr. Williams wrong. I had a new name, a fresh start, and something I hadn't felt in a long time—hope. I'd even made a couple of friends. I'd spent the night at a girl's house from the bus, and for once, I hadn't felt like an outsider watching life from the sidelines.

It was early fall, and something inside me felt wide awake. I was finally allowed to join the school band, and after school that day, we were going to try out different instruments. I had taken piano lessons for four years and was ready to try something new. I had my heart set on the flute—delicate, precise, beautiful. I imagined myself mastering it, twirling through parades one day, playing the piccolo. I was going to march myself right down that fifth-grade hallway and leave every whispered word behind me.

I yelled to Mommie that I was riding my bike over to our neighbor, Lettie's, house to tell her about the big night ahead. Lettie was an older neighbor I stayed with in the mornings until the bus came, since my parents left early for work. She always spoiled me—and I always had big plans to share. I'd tell her about the places I'd go, the dreams I had, how I was never going to settle down. She'd just laugh and hand me one of her fresh chocolate chip cookies.

Daddy was working in the backyard. I didn't even tell him I was leaving—I just hopped on my bike, turned left out of our driveway onto Rangeline Road, a two-lane country road that could be busy at times, and then made a left onto Emerick Road. I was already imagining Lettie's cookies and the way her eyes lit up when I told her my stories.

The wind played in my long brown pigtails as I smiled, sticking my arm out to make the familiar left turn onto Emerick. I'd done it a hundred times before.

Then everything went black.

"Mrs. Garber! Mr. Garber! Hello!" The neighbor girl was pounding on the door, breathless and panicked.

My mom rose slowly from the couch, grading papers. No one ever knocked on our front door.

"Mrs. Garber!" the girl cried again, louder now.

"Well, hello?" my mother replied gently, still in her soft teacher voice.

"She's been hit! It's Rebecca. It's bad." The girl collapsed in the doorway, sobbing.

My mother dropped her red pen and bolted out the door. "Bruce! Bruce, come quick—it's Rebecca. Something bad has happened!" she screamed, running barefoot down the driveway.

Nothing could have prepared them for the sight just two houses down. My bike was twisted and broken, the wheel still spinning beside the body of a little girl in pigtails and a dress, lying motionless in the road.

I don't remember much. I remember one car passing me on the left, and I put out my hand to signal my turn. I was too excited to look again. I was going to get a new instrument. I was going to be the best at it, get first chair—whatever that meant—and prove Mr. Williams wrong. I was going to show Lettie and tell her everything.

I didn't see the second car.

The driver was an eighteen-year-old German Baptist boy. He hit me going fifty-five miles an hour. My brand-new blue Schwinn went under the car and crumpled. I flew through the air. My forehead hit the windshield, denting the roof six inches. I skidded forty feet on the back of my head.

There was blood. So much blood.

Neighbors said it looked like a horror movie—the villain had caught the girl, and now she lay gasping for air, unable to speak, knowing somewhere in her mind that this might be the end.

The paramedics arrived and quickly realized I wouldn't survive an ambulance ride. "We're too far out. The local hospital isn't equipped," the captain radioed. "She won't make it unless we use CareFlight."

An EMT ran to Lettie's house.

"Ma'am, we need to land a helicopter in your front yard. I can't promise it won't tear something up—they'll be coming in hot."

"Do it," she said. "Now."

I was CareFlighted to Dayton Children's Hospital. Mommie would later say she thought, *Funny, she always wanted to ride in a helicopter*, as she watched it disappear into the sky.

The doctor was waiting when my parents arrived.

"I'm not going to lie. It's bad. Her brain is bruised to the core. One centimeter more and she'd be dead. She might be a vegetable. She may never wake up. But there are no broken bones."

He paused. "I tried not to shave her head before stitching her. Just in case . . . just in case she doesn't make it. I didn't want that to be how people remembered her."

So everyone waited. And prayed for a miracle.

I was in the ICU. I don't remember any of it. They told me later my head was so swollen it didn't look real. Alien-like. Daddy said my eyelids looked like tiny dimes. A few days later, I started coming around. They moved me out of the ICU to recover, but I didn't know who I was. I didn't remember names. I couldn't read. I didn't even know the colors on the walls.

I was broken again.

No angel had come this time. Just darkness—and me, trapped in it— trying to claw my way toward the light. What was left to live for if all I could see was shadows?

They moved me into a room with another little girl. Mommie sat beside me, trying to keep her voice steady. "The kids at school made you cards. Maybe we can sit up and read a few?"

She looked so pale, so exhausted. Later, she told me that I had woken up while she stepped away and asked the nurses where she was. They told me she had left.

She hadn't. She never left. The idea that I might have thought she abandoned me broke her heart.

The nurse came to help sit me up.

No one had prepared me for what I would see. Directly in front of me was a sink with a mirror over it.

As I was lifted upright, I caught my reflection.

I screamed. Loud and uncontrollably. A sound that didn't feel human.

I couldn't speak, couldn't form words. I just pointed at the mirror. My face wasn't mine. It was bruised, raw, burned. My eyes looked like they were trapped inside someone else's skin. I looked like a monster.

Another nurse came running in. I felt a pinch in my arm.

Then darkness again.

Recovery was slow. Painful. My memory returned in fragments. Mommie labeled everything in the house. One night, I looked at my plate and asked, "What are these?"—pointing at green beans.

She cried.

Bit by bit, my face healed. My knees, my skin. I relearned how to walk without limping. I relearned how to read. I tried to relearn how to be whole.

One night, about a month after the accident, I woke up screaming. Mommie came running in. I was drenched in sweat, crying hard.

"Why do I only remember the bad things?" I sobbed. "Why would this happen? Why do I forget the things I want to remember and remember the things I wish I didn't?"

She pulled me close and whispered, "I don't know, sweetie. I'm just glad you're here. That's enough."

I looked at the wall in my bedroom.

Blank. No angel.

That night, I made a decision. I would bury the past so deep it could never climb back out. I had lost pieces of myself, and no one knew if I'd ever get them back. So I promised myself I wouldn't go looking. I would lock the door, throw away the key.

Forget the past. Live from now. You have a second chance. Close the chapter. It doesn't exist.

You're not marked anymore.

But the truth is—

You can never really forget.

A smell.

A song.

A memory.

A careless word.

A hard season.

They can all yank it back to the surface, right when you think you've finally outrun it.

Sometimes it sounds like Mr. Williams' voice again:

"She won't amount to much."

But now, I whisper back: Just you wait.

—Chapter 3—
Fighter's Blood

"Our very survival depends on our
ability to stay awake, to adjust to new
ideas, to remain vigilant and to face
the challenge of change."
~Martin Luther King Jr.

Life was different now. When you have a near-death experience, it changes you. Maybe you feel it right away, or maybe it creeps in quietly, revealing itself in the way you start to see the world. Either way, you're not the same.

I had to work harder in school than I ever had. Things that used to come easily—reading, remembering, even simple math—felt like trying to walk through deep water with weights tied to my ankles. My brain just didn't work the same anymore, and that frustrated me. It wasn't just that I had to relearn things; it was the constant fear that maybe I wouldn't. That maybe the version of me before the accident was gone forever.

Mommie was patient—so patient. She gently corrected me when I used the wrong words. She studied with me every night, sometimes holding flashcards in one hand and stroking my hair with the other, like she could will my brain to heal with her touch. But even with all her effort, I still felt behind. I still felt broken.

And while the outside of me began to heal—bruises fading, skin smoothing, hair growing back over scars—the inside stayed tender and raw. I couldn't quite explain it, but there was this constant ache. I wasn't just the girl who got hit by a car—I was the girl people whispered about. The one they stared at just a second too long. The one who made them uncomfortable. I could see it in the way other kids looked away, or worse, didn't look at all.

I spent most afternoons outside with my dog, who didn't care how slow my brain was or how many scars I had. He just laid beside me and listened. Sometimes that silence was better than any conversation I could've had.

My parents could tell I needed something more. They didn't say it out loud, but I think they saw it too—that the pieces of me weren't quite fitting back together. So they decided I needed counseling. But not just anyone. Someone who was kind, trustworthy, and could help pull me from the shadows I kept slipping into.

They turned to Pastor Lawson.

He was the kind of man who made you feel like everything would be okay, even when nothing felt okay. He had a warm voice and a laugh that made your shoulders drop. He'd married my parents and pastored a small church in Trotwood, Ohio. Born and raised in Tennessee—which he always called "God's country"—he loved telling stories about home, and I loved listening to them. It gave me a place to dream about when I didn't want to be where I was.

His wife, Fayth, was an elementary teacher and played the organ at church. Together, they just . . . fit. Like a pair of old shoes that had walked through a lot of life and still held strong. Pastor Lawson started coming to our house once a week to meet with me. At first, I wasn't sure how much I wanted to talk, but he didn't push. He'd just sit there with me, sometimes telling me a story, sometimes asking a quiet question, sometimes just letting the silence do the work.

I started to believe maybe, just maybe, I was going to be okay. I thought that with enough prayer and Pastor Lawson's visits, this new sixth-grade year could be different. I thought I would walk into that school building with a new name, a second chance, and maybe—finally—kids would see me for who I really was.

The first day of school proved that everything I had hoped was wrong.

I sat on my milk jug seat on the porch, legs swinging, nervous and excited, hoping this year would be different. I told myself someone—anyone—would want to sit next to me on the bus. I'd smile, they'd smile back, and just like that, I'd have a friend.

But the whispers hit before I even found a seat.

"There's pigtails."

"She's probably gonna pray at lunch."

"She's so weird."

I sank into the green faux-leather seat and stared straight ahead, my face hot. The bus rumbled forward, and the space beside me stayed empty.

So here I was, sixth grade—no friends, no welcome. Just the girl who got hit by a car and lived. Nothing special about that. I wasn't admired. I was avoided. At lunch, kids physically scooted their trays away like I was contagious. I couldn't escape the isolation, so eventually, I stopped trying. They thought something was wrong with me. But the more they stared, the more I convinced myself there wasn't.

What did they know anyway?

I stopped caring. Or at least I told myself I did. If someone said hi, I'd just look them dead in the eye and keep walking. Indifference became my armor.

There was a group of kids who made sure I knew exactly where I stood. The "popular" ones. Jenny, with her perfect blonde hair and icy blue eyes. Marcy, her shadow. And Jeff—the first boy I ever thought was cute—who laughed right along with them. They lived to mock me. I can't say I ever did anything to earn their attention, other than existing in a way that was different. I wore dresses because my family believed girls shouldn't wear pants. That was enough.

So I made a decision. If people were going to talk about me, I was going to give them something to talk about. I didn't know it then, but that defiance—that quiet, inward rebellion—was the beginning of a fight I'd carry for years. The beginning of my complicated relationship with clothes, shoes, and the way people measured worth by how you looked.

Looking back, I know that something in me shifted that year. Maybe it was the head trauma. Maybe it was early PTSD. Or maybe it was just the human response to feeling so deeply unwanted.

Toward the end of sixth grade, I couldn't take it anymore. I went to Daddy. He was always good at listening, and I knew I needed him to hear me.

"I don't think I can keep going back to this school," I said, trying to hold it together. "I want to go somewhere else. I don't have any friends.

I don't fit in."

I didn't know exactly what I wanted—but I knew it wasn't this. I could feel myself going numb, turning into someone who didn't feel anything at all. And that scared me more than being lonely.

Daddy didn't say much, but I saw it hit him. I saw him really hear me.

By the end of the year, my parents had applied for me to attend Dayton Christian School. I interviewed. I was accepted. And just like that, I was closing this chapter.

Kids were mean. That much I knew. But maybe—just maybe—there was a place for me out there. A place where I wasn't the girl who got hit by a car, or the girl in dresses. A place where I could be seen.

And maybe, if I were lucky, I'd finally have one real friend.

On the first day of school, my life would forever change.

I had an hour-long bus ride from our house to downtown Dayton to go to school. It felt like a drag most days, but that morning I was wide-eyed with excitement. I knew everything was going to be different.

We made several stops along the way. At one of them, a girl stepped onto the bus. She wore a dress and sparkly slip-on shoes—just like me. She had brown hair and brown eyes, so similar to mine that I sat up straight.

"Hi," I said, smiling widely.

"Hi," she replied, a little quiet, a little shy.

"I'm Rebecca. What's your name?"

"I'm Hannah. Hannah Miller," she said, looking right at me.

And that was it. From that moment on, I knew—we were going to be best friends. We'd grow to be nearly inseparable through middle school and high school. We looked so much alike that even our parents would get us mixed up during sporting events. We'd flip through old photos and laugh, realizing their camera rolls were filled with each other's daughters.

Dayton Christian School was a world away from what I'd known. Private school was different—structured around faith, built on kindness, and more patience. It was exactly what I needed. For once, I wasn't just tolerated. I was welcomed. I was seen.

Seventh grade meant I could join sports. I chose cross country; something about running just felt right. Naturally, I talked Hannah into joining too. We'd go on to do cheerleading and track together. The truth was, we were always looking for more time together—since we lived so far apart, practice and meets became our shared world.

Hannah and I started running together in seventh grade, and over the years, our journey has grown from cross-country and track to marathons, triathlons, Ironmans, and ultraraces.

Running quickly became more than just something I did. It became a part of me.

In junior high, I was the fastest runner on our team, and Hannah—well, Hannah just wanted to finish before they took down the clock. I'd always run back after I crossed the line and find her. I'd cheer her on, run alongside her, push her forward. No matter how tired I was, it felt good to help her finish. Our motto was "2 Legit 2 Quit"—corny, but it was ours.

Helping Hannah and others like her started to feel just as good as running fast. Sometimes even better. Watching the look in their eyes when they crossed that finish line—tired, proud, victorious—it filled me up. It made me believe in something bigger than winning.

In high school, we ran for Coach Jay Johnson. He'd give out tiny teddy bears when we beat our personal record at a race. I earned a lot of teddy bears. Every one felt like a little piece of healing, a little patch over the broken spots inside me.

Running started to mend me in ways I didn't expect. It was quiet and hard and personal—but when you pushed yourself past the point of giving up, something shifted inside. It was the only time I felt truly unstoppable. The only place where pain felt like power.

I was still meeting with Pastor Lawson, and now another counselor too—he focused more on family dynamics. By the time I was heading into my senior year, I finally felt grounded. I had friends. I had goals. I felt like I had a grip on my story again.

Then, almost overnight, everything started to unravel.

Maybe it was the loss of my Grandpa Combs, who had moved in with us after Grandma Combs passed. Maybe it was the quiet panic that came with senior year—college, dating, adulthood looming. I don't know exactly what triggered it, but something cracked.

I had set a goal: to finish in the top fifteen at state for cross country. I had trained hard all summer and felt ready.

Then came the first meet of the season—Triangle Park, late August.

I don't remember much about the race. One moment, I was running, and the next, I was wandering out of the woods. My legs were shaky. My vision was blurry. I saw my Daddy's face and walked toward him.

"I don't know what happened," I said softly, confused. "I just don't feel good."

He didn't say much. Just pulled me in close, his arm around me. We walked to the car in silence.

Something was wrong.

Things went downhill from there.

I started throwing up every time I ran. Races that once gave me energy now left me shaky, dry heaving behind the team tent. I felt sad all the time, and I couldn't figure out why. I still had friends. I still ran. But something had shifted inside me, and it wouldn't shift back.

One night, I couldn't sleep. My brain wouldn't stop racing. I was exhausted, both in body and spirit. I felt like I was going to lose my mind. I just needed rest—real, deep sleep. I crept downstairs in the dark, opened a bottle of sleeping pills, not even thinking, and took a handful. I wasn't trying to die. I just wanted the chaos to stop, just for a few hours. I went back to bed and pulled the covers over my head. But something felt off almost immediately.

I got up, walked into my parents' room, and quietly said, "I think I did something wrong."

That was it. I collapsed, hitting my head on the wall as I went down.

Mommie's voice, panicked and pleading, as they rushed me to the car, I heard, "God, please don't let me lose her. Wake her up. Dear Jesus, help me—help me."

She was praying over me like a whisper underwater. Daddy didn't speak. He just drove—eyes ahead, focused, unmoving.

At the hospital, they dragged me from the car. I was limp, unresponsive. A nurse cracked an ammonia inhalant under my nose, trying to snap me awake. I barely flinched.

"Ma'am, get back—right now!" the nurse barked at her, wheeling me through the ER. She froze in her tracks.

"Call the doctor. We're going to have to do a gastric suction immediately!"

Everything became muffled, distant. It felt like I was watching it happen from somewhere else—hovering above, invisible. This is it, I thought. This is how it ends. I'm dying because something is broken inside me, just like they've always said.

Getting your stomach pumped is something I wouldn't wish on anyone. It was sudden. Violent. I felt the tube scrape down the back of my throat as they forced it in, suctioning the contents of my stomach as quickly as they could. My throat felt like sandpaper for days. My voice came out raspy and raw.

To this day, I struggle with taking pills. I still taste the bitter, chalky aftertaste—the kind that clings to your tongue and won't let go. And I do everything in my power not to throw up. Whenever I have to take a pill, I immediately go back to that moment. That hospital. That tube. It triggers something deep. A kind of darkness that still feels too dangerous to walk through.

It turns out I had taken a handful of Mommie's prescription pills. My body violently rejected them.

I kept telling the doctors—and my parents—I wasn't trying to kill myself. I just hadn't been sleeping. And when I did, I'd have these vivid, awful dreams. I couldn't even remember what they were. Just that I'd wake up in tears, confused, heavy, like I didn't belong anywhere. I hadn't told anyone. Not even Hannah. I wore the mask too well. Smiles. Laughter. Cross-country meets. No one saw it coming.

I laid in the hospital bed with my eyes closed, listening to the nurse talk in hushed tones near the door.

"If I were you, I'd seek serious help. This is nothing to take lightly. She could've died."

Concern filled her voice. My parents said nothing.

I rolled over and stared at the blank, white wall. No angel hung there. No Jesus portrait like the one at church.

Just a blank white wall.

A few weeks later, and after a lot of tears, I was on a plane with Daddy, headed to a mental health clinic in Texas.

Mommie couldn't come with us. She couldn't take me there and leave me behind. I'd overheard her one night, whispering to Daddy through tears, "It'll feel like I'm losing her." So he took me instead. I didn't argue. I was empty. Angry. Scared. Mostly numb.

When we got to the clinic, we walked into a room labeled Intake. I didn't say a word. I didn't want to be there. There was nothing wrong with me. I wasn't crazy. I wasn't broken. I just needed sleep. I needed to run. I needed my senior cross country season—not this.

I looked at Daddy. He looked back at me, concerned and sad, but silent. The doctor behind the desk kept talking, flipping through my chart.

"Well, Rebecca," he said matter-of-factly, "Here's how this will go. You'll say your goodbyes here. He'll walk out that door. And there will be no contact for the first four to six weeks. Understood?"

I just nodded. What else was I supposed to do?

Daddy came over and put his arm around me. I tried to smile.

"Well, Bumpkins," he said—the old nickname he'd given me when I was little because I bumped into everything—"Get better, and you'll be home soon." He gave me a quick squeeze.

I didn't hug him back. I didn't speak. I just stared. And as he walked to the double doors, I opened my mouth and let out the sharpest, hardest thing I could say.

"I hate you for bringing me here."

He froze for just a moment, then turned away without ever changing his expression. The double doors clamped shut behind him.

And once again, I was someone else's problem.

The story of my life.

So began my hospital stay. I was placed on 24-hour suicide watch, which meant nothing I did was private. If I went to the bathroom, someone followed me. If I showered, someone stood nearby. If I went to sleep, someone sat beside my bed and watched me breathe. My own clothes and shoes were taken away. Every part of my life was monitored, managed, and stripped down.

There was no space to breathe, let alone heal.

I was surrounded by other teens, boys and girls. Some of their stories were terrifying. Some heartbreaking. Some kids were court-ordered to be there. Others, like me, were brought by parents holding out for a miracle.

I cycled through several roommates. Some came and went like shadows. Others left an imprint. Everyone was broken in their own way.

My diagnosis came back: sports-induced bulimia and severe depression.

The wing I lived in housed teens from thirteen to seventeen, dealing with everything from eating disorders to anxiety, depression, drug addiction, and more. Girls on one side, boys on the other. We only crossed paths during school hours and group therapy.

Everything ran on a schedule. You got up at 7:30. Ate breakfast. Did some kind of guided meditation or breathing exercise. Then it was off to school. After that came lunch, one-on-one sessions, group therapy, art or music therapy, dinner, and—if earned—free time.

The therapist figured out pretty quickly that running was a core part of me. So they made a deal: if I took my protein shakes and didn't purge, I could go to the pool three times a week and run in the water.

I agreed. It was the only piece of me I had left.

Almost four weeks into the routine, I received a bouquet of flowers with a small card attached. The card read:

"I am praying for you. Love you — Dad."

I hadn't had any contact with family or friends since arriving, so I brought it up to my therapist. They agreed it might be a good time to call and thank Daddy. I was so excited—just hearing his voice was going to be the best part of my day.

"Daddy," I said, smiling through the phone, "Thank you so much for the flowers. They're exquisite." I knew he loved it when I used big words, the kind that made him proud.

There was silence on the other end.

Then I heard him mumble something to Mommie. A pause.

"I didn't send you flowers," he said, softly. "There must be a mistake."

My heart started pounding. My breathing became shallow and fast. This couldn't be happening.

The nurse must have noticed because she gently took the phone from my hand. She stepped out to talk to someone, and moments later, I was sent back to my room—back to stare at the flowers.

A therapist came to get me. She led me into a smaller, quieter room, and then she broke the news as gently as she could.

It was my birth father who had sent the flowers.

My world shattered.

I started screaming. I bolted for my room. The nurses chased after me, but I was already grabbing the cheap plastic vase. I hurled it at the wall. Water exploded, petals flew, glass cracked.

How did he know where I was? How could he find me?

How dare he say he was praying for me? That he loved me?

"Liar!" I screamed at the wall.

The nurses were talking, trying to calm me down, but I couldn't hear them. All I could hear was the rush of my own blood pounding in my ears. I was trying to speak, to scream something that made sense, but nothing came out—only broken sobs and raw sound.

Before I could come down from it, two nurses had me in the "cool down room"—what I called the bubble room. I had always said I'd never end up there.

But now I was.

It was padded and ice-cold, designed for kids who needed to break down safely. I kicked and hit the walls until I was drained and collapsed in a heap. I couldn't feel anything anymore. I just melted into the floor like water. Curled up in a fetal position, shaking from the cold.

Eventually, a young male nurse came in. He crouched beside me and whispered, "Are you ready to go back to your room? Do you feel calm now?"

I nodded.

And I shuffled back down the hallway in silence, back to a blank wall and a bed that wasn't mine. I was placed back on 24-hour suicide watch.

That night, as I laid staring at the sterile white wall, I remember thinking, *This must be the end.*

By week five in the hospital, something shifted.

Therapy became more intense. They introduced the empty chair exercise—something I wasn't ready for but did anyway. You sat facing an empty chair and imagined the person who hurt you most sitting in it. Then you told them everything.

Everything you'd never said. Everything you were afraid to admit. Everything they deserved to hear.

Most kids screamed at the chair. Cursed at it. Spit years of pain into the silence. Eventually, the chair would get thrown across the room.

And just like that, the bubble room would come calling again.

No one wanted to end up there. Because once you were dragged out and back to your room, the truth would hit you like a freight train: Maybe I am broken. Maybe I really am crazy.

And that's a truth that's harder to face than any padded wall.

After weeks of putting it off and refusing to do the empty chair exercise, I finally realized I wasn't going to get out of group therapy unless I faced it. Around week seven, I decided to volunteer. I thought if I volunteered, maybe I'd have more control over my emotions. I hated every minute of it. And still to this day, I'm not ready to reveal more than that.

It made me unbearably emotional, and I completely fell apart. So much so, I fell right out of my chair and curled into a sobbing ball on the floor. I didn't even have the energy to throw the chair—I had surrendered. I was a girl going nowhere.

That night, they put me back on suicide watch.

I was drained walking into group therapy the next day. Hope was slipping away fast. I felt like I was doomed to be the "girl interrupted"— in and out of clinics for the rest of my life.

Then, a guest speaker came in. I don't remember his name, but I'll never forget what he said.

We sat in a circle around the room. His voice was soft, comforting, but serious.

"Look around at each face you see here. Look closely. Statistically, only one in ten of you will make it out there—into the real world."

I counted the kids in my group—one, two, three . . . nine, ten.

Only one of us was going to make it?

In my head, the voices started swirling: You're a statistic. It's just the cards you've been dealt. Here's your proof.

No. I screamed inside.

I looked around the room again, and something inside me stirred.

I am going to be the one who makes it.

Something told me, "Say it again."

Without thinking, I stood up and shouted, "I will be the one! I'm getting out of here, and I will make it out there!"

Most of the kids froze. Some snickered.

The speaker smiled and said, "You can. You can be the one who changes everything—for yourself and for others."

It wasn't my parents, my best friend Hannah, my counselor, or Pastor

Lawson who got me to believe this, not that they hadn't tried—it was a stranger. Someone whose name I don't even remember. But his words—those words changed everything.

People may forget your name, but they will never forget what you've done.

A few weeks later, I was on a plane headed back to Dayton, Ohio, to finish my senior year. I had a layover in Atlanta, Georgia, where my Great Uncle Charles was waiting for me to have lunch during my three-hour layover, so I wouldn't have to be alone.

He was as Southern as they come—a school teacher, principal from Breathitt County, Kentucky, now a retired superintendent of the Warren Robins Air Force Base School District.

"You know, Rebecca," his Southern drawl always made me listen closely, "God has a plan for you. I know you're going to be something to reckon with."

I smiled. "You think so?"

"Oh, I know," he said with those sweet, sparkling eyes. "You've got fighter's blood. You are a Combs. We survive. And we love."

He was right.

I thought this wasn't my undoing.

This was my new beginning.

And as the plane touched down in Dayton and I saw my parents waiting anxiously at the gate, I believed it. For the first time, I began to realize the angel was there all the time, right in front of me.

—Chapter 4—
Fighting for My Voice

"You just have to find that thing that's special about you that distinguishes you from all the others, and through true talent, hard work, and passion, anything can happen."

~Dr. Dre

I was a changed girl. Something inside me had shifted—permanently. I couldn't wait to finish my senior year and step into the next chapter. I was ready to share my story, to change the world, maybe even save a life. I wasn't waiting for a storm to pass anymore—I had been the storm, tossed and thrown, and now I knew: I was the storm. And nothing was going to stop me.

I needed a platform. Somewhere to pour out what had been poured into me. Hannah, my best friend, had gone on a summer-long mission trip the year before called Operation Barnabas. Seven weeks of traveling, serving, and sharing the Gospel—her stories lit something inside of me. I couldn't think of a better place to begin. The program was created specifically for high school juniors and seniors, and I was all in. I couldn't wait to apply.

Operation Barnabas got its name from the biblical Barnabas—his name meaning "son of encouragement." That was the heart of the program: to go wherever a church needed encouragement and serve in any way possible. It taught teens how to share their faith boldly and to fall deeply in love with Jesus Christ. When I thought about it, I could almost see myself standing in my childhood bedroom, reaching my tiny hand toward that angel on the wall. As if she were still there, looking down on me, whispering, *I brought you across that bridge for this very moment. Now go.*

Only ninety students would be accepted that summer. We'd train for a week and then be sent out in small teams. Street ministry, vacation Bible schools, service projects, sharing our stories through drama or puppet shows, feeding the hungry, helping the homeless—whatever was needed. This wasn't just a trip. This was it. My chance to take everything I had lived through and let it mean something. Surely I wasn't the only one who had survived something and made it to the other side. Maybe someone needed to hear that they could survive, too.

Operation Barnabas had four simple, powerful goals: to develop a heart for God, a heart for the unsaved, a heart to encourage other believers, and to consider full-time ministry. That last part tugged at me. I couldn't shake the feeling that my life was meant to help others heal. Our team would travel through Florida and the Carolinas and finish the trip at the massive youth convention at Liberty University. Even better? Our training week would be hosted at my Uncle Phil's church in Norton, Ohio. That just felt like confirmation.

All that was left to do was wait for the envelope.

It arrived sometime in March. A standard white 8½ x 11 envelope stamped "Operation Barnabas" in the corner—but to me, it felt like a key to something bigger. I screamed the moment I saw it. I had been chosen. One of ninety. I was going to be the *one* of ten who made it. And not just make it—I was going to make a difference. I was going to help someone else find their light, just like I had found mine.

My parents stood nearby, watching through tear-filled eyes. Mommie hugged me tight and whispered, "This is just what you need. God is good."

She was right. But first, I had to finish track season.

Track season, my senior year was different. I came in changed—physically, mentally, emotionally. But I was ready. What I wasn't ready for was a new coach who had one focus: his daughter. She was wicked fast, and I'll give her that. But from day one, it was clear—this season wasn't about the team, it was about her. I was about to learn something I never forgot: some coaches don't coach to make a difference. They coach to win, and they coach for their own child.

Still, our 4x800 team was unstoppable that season. A true force. We swept the invitational meets with ease. I loved that race. The 800 is gritty—two laps of pure sprinting until your lungs want to give out. It's not for the faint of heart. You have to want it. Every second. Every step. I wasn't as strong as I'd been in years past—how could I be, after what I'd done to my body in the fall? But I was working my way back. I was trusting the process. And I knew we were good enough to make it to state.

I always ran the first leg—my job was simple: get us in position to place, or win. With the coach's daughter as our anchor leg, we almost always did. We cruised through districts. Easy.

Then came regionals.

That morning, the coach pulled me aside. His voice was flat, almost bored. "Listen, if you don't have us in the top three when you hand off, I'm going to have the girls back off. My daughter's got a shot to win the mile and the 800, and I'm not wasting her legs on this race."

I blinked. Was he serious? He was.

Pressure like I'd never felt before slammed into my chest. This was supposed to be a team event. Not a solo mission. I walked to the line, holding the baton in my hand, and realized it was shaking. I was shaking. I never got nervous. But suddenly I couldn't hear anything except my own thoughts screaming at me.

You can't do this.

You're not strong enough.

Just another statistic.

Just a dreamer.

You're going to choke.

"On your mark," the official called.

Just give up now. Don't embarrass yourself.

"Set."

The gun fired.

I took off.

That race was a blur—wind, breath, spikes pounding, lungs burning. I gave it everything I had. Every single ounce. When I handed off the baton, we were in fourth. Not third. Not the top three. But I had nothing left in the tank. I collapsed on the side of the track, gasping, heart pounding through my ears. Maybe it wasn't my best time, but it was everything I had in me.

Then I looked up and saw him—the coach—standing on the edge of the track. He made the signal. The one I'll never forget.

Back off.

And just like that, it was over.

My high school track career ended not with a personal best or a shot at state, but with a wave of a hand and a team pulled back.

All because one leg wasn't fast enough.

All because I wasn't enough, and I felt a crack open in my soul.

• • •

A week after high school graduation, I headed to Norton, Ohio, to begin training for Operation Barnabas. The sting of disappointment from track season had started to fade. I was moving forward—eyes on the next chapter. I was thrilled, impassioned, ready to change lives and bring hope to others like me. This was it.

I don't remember the main leader's name—maybe Cheryl? She seemed nice enough. Welcoming. She explained that the week would be full of icebreakers and evaluation activities, all designed to help place us on the right team—where we'd be most effective in ministry. I couldn't wait. I was ready.

As the days wore on and training intensified, they announced we would break into small groups to share our personal testimonies. These stories would help them coach us on how best to share our faith in churches, on the streets, wherever we are called. I was buzzing with anticipation. This was what I'd come for—to tell my story, to show that you can go through hell and still carry light.

Our group gathered in a small Sunday school room. A plain white table sat in the center, surrounded by tiny wooden chairs. One by one, teens shared their faith journeys. How they'd found Jesus. What He meant to them. I listened closely, soaking it all in.

Then it was my turn.

I smiled. I closed my eyes. Took a deep breath.

"In Isaiah 40:31, it says, 'But those who wait on the Lord shall renew their strength. They shall mount up with wings like eagles. They shall run and not be weary. They shall walk and not faint.'"

Nods. Smiles. My heart felt light.

I continued, "When I was little, I was born into a family full of turmoil. My father was abusive—physically, emotionally . . . sexually. I had this painting of an angel—"

Suddenly, a voice cut in sharply. The leader stood up, flustered. "I think that's enough sharing for today. Let's take a break. Everyone is dismissed."

The room froze. Wide eyes locked on me. No one moved at first.

"GO," she snapped again. "See you at dinner."

And just like that, it was over.

I laid down in my sleeping bag, staring up at the ceiling, trying to make sense of what had just happened. Tears pricked the corners of my eyes, but I blinked them back. I wasn't going to cry. Surely they didn't stop the group because of me. I wasn't lying. I wasn't exaggerating. It was the truth.

An hour later, one of the staff members came to get me. "Someone needs to speak with you," she said gently.

I followed her into a side room. The head leader sat waiting. She gave me a thin smile and motioned for me to sit.

"Rebecca, come have a seat."

I sat, instantly on guard. The room was too quiet.

She folded her hands and spoke in a tone that was strangely flat. "Listen, I understand you think these things happened to you . . ."

Right then, something snapped. A cold weight settled over me. Like a dark curtain falling.

She kept talking. ". . . but we don't discuss things like that here. Not if it draws attention away from the purpose of our ministry. We're here to help others."

I wasn't even listening anymore.

She thinks I'm lying.

She thinks I made it up.

Did I exaggerate?

Do people not talk about this stuff?

I couldn't stop the tears this time. They came hard and fast.

Then she said the words I'll never forget:

"Maybe this just isn't the right fit for you."

I snapped. "Call my Uncle Phil. Call him right now. He'll tell you it's true. He'll tell you I'm not lying."

She studied me for a moment. "Okay," she said. "Go wash your face.

I'll talk to him and find you later."

I walked straight to the last bathroom stall. Locked the door. Sat on the closed toilet seat and pulled my knees to my chest.

And I cried.

Alone. In silence. With the fluorescent lights buzzing above me like a lie I'd been told too many times.

Was something wrong with me?

Was I some kind of scarlet letter?

My Uncle Phil was the pastor of Norton Grace Brethren Church at the time. He had taken a small congregation and built it into a thriving community hub, loved and respected by many. He always started conversations with a joke—claiming he was the good-looking one— which broke the tension and made people laugh. When he showed up to meet with the leaders about me, I could tell his presence carried weight.

After that, Uncle Phil sat down with me alone.

"Rebecca," he said gently but firmly, "I might not explain this perfectly, but some people just aren't ready to face the truth—that as Christians, we too sometimes go through terrible things, even from other so-called Christians." His voice held both passion and kindness.

The Operation Barnabas group—me in the third row, three from the left, seated next to a boy. I often wonder where everyone ended up.

I listened quietly. I knew he had lived a lot longer and seen far more than I ever had.

"I'm not trying to diminish your story or what you've been through. People sometimes think these things get exaggerated. But we know the truth—you're not exaggerating. I told them, 'Let me help you find a way to minister in a way they feel comfortable with,' because I believe you need this experience."

After that long conversation with Uncle Phil and the adult leadership, the verdict came: I was just a girl, adopted, who loved Jesus and wanted to help others. No more, no less.

A wave of sadness and darkness seeped deeper into my soul.

I realized then that I'd have to pretend—from now on and maybe forever—that I was just that girl: adopted, loved Jesus, and could maybe help. Nothing more, nothing less.

I stayed and was placed on a team. We traveled through Florida, running vacation Bible schools, doing physical labor at churches, and joining in whole-group singing. But I was never allowed to be alone with anyone, never trusted to work one-on-one with kids or teens. I was always under the watchful eye of someone older, someone in control of what I was saying and doing.

When we arrived at the grand finale youth convention at Liberty University, my heart raced. Over two thousand teens would be there, and we'd get to perform and share a few words. I was especially excited to see Hannah after not seeing her all summer.

But the morning of the performance, the senior leader—the same woman from our training who had made me feel so small—came to get me.

She looked me up and down with those cold, judgmental eyes.

"I've decided you will sit with me through tonight's performance," she said flatly.

I gasped, shocked. "What? Why? What did I do?"

She smirked like it was obvious. "You're just too showy. You draw too much attention to yourself. We are not about that. I think I told you that before."

Darkness crashed over me like a tidal wave.

True to her word, she escorted me to a seat high above the stage, far away from the crowd.

During the performance, I got down on my hands and knees, tears streaming down my face.

Afterward, she looked at me with a small, almost satisfied smile. "I hope you understand. I see you prayed. Looks like you're learning."

I smiled through the burn of tears and quickly walked away. That wasn't what I was doing. I was trying not to lose it on her and tell her what an awful person I thought she really was.

I wouldn't give her the satisfaction of seeing me break.

That night, on my knees, I prayed with everything I had.

"God, help me control this anger. I want to punch her, hurt her the way I'm hurting right now. Please get me through this. Help me walk away with my head held high. No matter the situation."

I thought I had found my passion, helping others, showing them there is light.

Turns out, according to others, it wasn't mine to have.

—Chapter 5—
Educating the Educated

"Sometimes we can only find our true
direction when we let the wind of
change carry us."

~ Mimi Novic

Choosing a college turned out to be way harder than I expected after being gone all summer. My family had a long history with Bryan College in Dayton, Tennessee, but I was determined not to follow their path. I didn't want to be boxed in by family tradition. My best friend Hannah was heading to Grace College in Indiana, and honestly, that felt too close to home—no real fresh start there. I thought about Liberty University, but after the intense experience of Operation Barnabas ending there, I just couldn't picture myself going back.

Then I found Toccoa Falls College, a small Christian liberal arts school tucked away in the foothills of northeast Georgia. Something about it spoke to me. Their mission to create a Christian community where truth and godly character meet, preparing graduates for service—that was exactly what I needed. I wanted more than just classes and tests; I wanted purpose.

The campus sat on over a thousand acres of rolling hills beneath the Blue Ridge Mountains, a place where I could climb rocks, raft wild rivers, hike endless trails, run free—and most importantly, heal my soul. And then there was the waterfall. The historic 186-foot Toccoa Falls is taller than Niagara Falls and the tallest free-falling waterfall east of the Mississippi. I could already feel the mist on my face, the water's soothing power washing over the pain I'd carried for so long. It was more than beauty—it was medicine.

By the end of August, I was ready to move in. I already knew I wanted to study journalism. Teaching was out—too many teachers in my family, too much expectation. I didn't care about "summers off." I wanted to write stories that mattered, stories that could inspire and change lives. Since I couldn't tell my own story, maybe I could tell someone else's. I was ready to go against the grain, blaze my own trail.

Toccoa Falls had both dorms and houses where students lived, and I was placed in one of the houses with my roommate, Shawn, a girl from Lenox, Massachusetts. We hit it off instantly—laughing, joking, and carrying on like we'd known each other forever. I had found my place. This was exactly the fresh start I needed. Shawn, Erika, Courtney, and I, along with a few others, became inseparable. Whether we were rollerblading to class or just walking across campus, we were always together—talking about everything from cute guys to the classes we thought were pointless, and dreaming about what we wanted to be when we grew up.

But TFC came with rules—and dress codes—that they took very seriously. I was the kind of girl who pushed limits, especially when the rules felt ridiculous, which was often. One of the more absurd rules was that every Sunday, to get into the cafeteria for lunch, you had to be wearing a dress or a skirt. I love dresses—always have—and I love a good pair of stilettos. I'm five feet, two inches tall, so a flashy pair of heels made sure you noticed me. So naturally, I showed up on Sundays ready to turn heads.

One Sunday, the lady at the cafeteria counter eyed me up and down and said, "Fancy shoes." I smiled and said, "Thank you." Then she dropped the bomb. "Miss Fancy Shoes, your skirt's too short. You can't come in unless you change it." I rolled my eyes, but then she added, "I'm going to need you to get on your knees. If your dress touches the floor, then it's long enough. If not, change it or no lunch for you."

Are you kidding me? I was screaming inside. What did my knees have to do with anything? But I got down on my knees. "See? It doesn't touch the floor. Change it or no food." My friends went in without me. I changed and ate alone.

This became a Sunday ritual. Kneeling for the skirt test, no jeans in the library, no sweatpants anywhere. I got fed up and started speaking up about the dress code and how unfairly we were treated. Word got to the Dean of Students, and I was called in.

"Rebecca," she said, her voice urgent, "I hear you have concerns about the rules."

I sat, trying not to explode, pinching myself to keep calm.

She looked me in the eye. "We're a school of integrity, preparing you for ministry and servanthood. There's no room to question those in authority who guide you to success and blessing." It sounded sweet but felt like a slap.

I snapped back, "Really? Where in the Bible does it say you can't show your knees to eat? Or that I must comply without question? I grew up in church, I'm minoring in Bible, and my parents are pretty conservative. Daddy's German Baptist, Mom's Southern Baptist. I couldn't wear pants until middle school, and even then, I fought for it."

She shook her head slowly. "Then maybe you should consider another

Cheerleading at Toccoa Falls College left me with lasting friendships. I still laugh about getting in trouble for my skirt not being long enough, even though none of ours reached the knee. I'm the second girl from the right, next to our coach.

school. I don't think this is a good fit. Think hard. I'd hate to make the decision for you. You're dismissed."

I left fuming. Seriously? Over knees? I decided I'd fight to stay just to prove I could survive anywhere. I signed up for intramural sports and tried out to be a cheerleader for basketball. I'd cheered freshman through junior year of high school, but was cut in my senior year. This time, I made the team with Erika, Courtney, and the girls I hung out with. I was pumped. Intramurals and cheerleading became my lifeline, reminding me that home, good sports, and exercise were essential for my mental health.

At the end of my freshman year, I went home for the summer. This was the only summer I would spend working back home. I decided landscaping would be the way to make the most money. Hard work, long hours—it would keep me busy. I had no desire for free time or distractions. I just wanted to work.

Then, mid-summer, a letter arrived from Toccoa Falls College. My heart dropped the moment I saw the official-looking envelope. I opened it, and the words hit me like a punch:

> Dear Rebecca,
>
> You have been brought to the attention of the admissions office. Due to your first year at Toccoa Falls College, we are suspending you for a semester and up to a year. Suspension means you are not allowed to participate in classes or any college-related activities during this time. The suspension will be noted on your academic record and transcript as "Administrative Withdrawal."

The rest of the letter detailed the conditions for possible readmission and states that failure to meet these conditions may result in denial of your return to the college. They even had the nerve to sign the letter, "We wish you the best."

I couldn't believe it. My college career was over before it even started. After just one year, I was "not good enough." Just like everyone had predicted. All the old voices in my head screamed back to life: You'll never amount to anything. You're just another statistic. Too showy. A total weirdo. That girl's crazy.

I called Hannah. She was my constant reminder to never back down. "Yeah, you can apply to come to Grace College with me," she said, excited.

"I don't want to go there, Hannah. I like it down South. It's where I want to be—away from reminders," my voice cracked as I fought back tears.

"Okay, but there has to be an appeals process. Someone to talk to, or a letter to write," she encouraged.

She was right. There had to be a way. I didn't think I'd get through the appeals, so I decided to write a letter directly to the president of the college.

Dr. Paul Alford had been TFC's president since 1979. He was one of the kindest, most approachable people I'd ever met. Every year, he'd invite all the new freshmen to his house for a meet-and-greet, offering encouragement and a warm smile. His house was full of pictures, stories, and finger foods set out in every room—a true reflection of the man and his accomplishments.

I don't remember every word I wrote, but I poured my heart and soul into that letter. I promised to become a better person, to represent the school and its mission with pride.

Then, in the middle of August, a letter arrived. My suspension was lifted. I could come back.

And I did. I kept my promise. I tried out for the very first girls' soccer team, made it, and played left wing. I continued cheering for basketball and focused on my writing, pursuing my degree in Journalism. My sophomore year became my best year yet.

And then it was time to branch out. Shawn invited me to live with her in Massachusetts for the summer, working at a bed and breakfast. I said yes without hesitation.

Lenox, Massachusetts, was breathtaking—rolling hills, blooming gardens, and charming bed and breakfasts on every corner. It felt like the perfect escape, and I had the privilege of working at some of the most beautiful B&Bs in town. The work was steady, the scenery peaceful, and for the first time in a while, I was surrounded by people who didn't know my past. I was just Becca—hardworking, witty, passionate. And maybe, just maybe, I was ready to start dating seriously.

I wasn't attending college to get my "Mrs. Degree," as many of the girls at TFC called it. I hated that phrase. I didn't want a ring just to say I had one. But I did want to be known and loved for who I was, not for what had happened to me. In order to fully step into the future, I realized there was one thing left undone. And it was just a little over five hours away.

David.

My birth father.

· · ·

I hugged Shawn goodbye, boarded a Greyhound bus mid-summer, and headed for Delaware. I can't quite remember how I got in touch with someone from his side of the family—maybe it was a letter or a phone call—but I had told them I was coming. I was going to stay with his parents, my biological grandparents. I would see David, his brother, his sister Cindy, and apparently, a half-brother I had only recently learned about—David's son from his second marriage. He was currently on his third wife, and she would be there too.

I wasn't nervous. I was resolved. If I wanted to move forward, I had to stop dragging his shadow with me. There had always been tension between David and the rest of his family. Cindy even tried to talk me out of the visit. "You don't need to see him," she had warned. But I wasn't there for them. I was there for me. I was there for closure.

When I arrived, I stood outside the house—a two-story white home with black shutters. At least, I think it was white and black. Funny how memory fogs up when emotions run high. My first reaction was bitter: This? This nice house? This is the man who left my mom and sisters with nothing? Who left chaos behind? And this is where he gets to live?

I knocked on the door. His wife answered with beaming excitement. "Come in, come in! We're so happy you came," she gushed. Her joy spilled out too easily. I felt numb.

"He's just finishing some things in the backyard," she chirped. "Come on, let me show you around."

We walked through a hallway lined with framed photos. About halfway down, I froze. There it was—a photo of me with my sisters. Taken thirteen years ago. Same with the photo she pointed to in the room where my half-brother stayed. The same dusty memories hung like they were sacred. It all felt too carefully placed, too perfectly staged, even.

And then I heard it.

A throat cleared.

I turned toward the doorway, and there he was—taller than I remembered, standing in the very room where my feet had just stepped away from a photograph that I didn't give permission to hang.

I don't know what he said. His voice didn't register. I just stood there, frozen in the one place I had never expected this to happen—a bedroom. A space where I had cried myself to sleep night after night as a little girl.

My knees trembled. I closed my eyes. The angel from my childhood room flashed into my mind.

And then I said it. Through tears that spilled without warning:

"I don't think I can forgive you."

That was it.

I turned and ran out of the house. I can't tell you how I got back to his parents' place. I just remember waking up the next morning, boarding a bus back to Lenox, and promising myself I was done.

That door was now closed. Sealed. The key was thrown into the deepest ocean. The next time I would want to speak his name would be the day he died—so I could stand over his grave and spit on it.

And I meant it.

I went back to school with fire in my bones.

• • •

I finished my degree in Journalism at Toccoa Falls College. That moment—walking across the stage, hearing my name, holding my diploma—wasn't just for me. It was for every girl who had ever been told she wouldn't make it. My parents were there. My entire family. Pastor Lawson, too—my steady compass and source of truth throughout the storms.

I had played three years of soccer, cheered, performed in church musicals, and thrived in classes that illuminated who I could be. I loved every minute of it. College became more than a season of learning. It was the place where I rebuilt myself—piece by piece.

After college graduation, I landed a job in Sumter, South Carolina, as a copy editor for the local daily paper. It wasn't glamorous—I had to work my way up to writer—but I was determined. I wanted to cover sports. Sports have always made me happy. There were underdog stories, last-minute victories, and teammates becoming family. That was the kind of world I wanted to live in. That's what I wanted to write about.

But about six months in, the reality hit hard. This was a man's world. And I wasn't invited to the table. The glass ceiling wasn't just above me— it was right in my face.

At the time, I had a boyfriend who lived near Toccoa, so with help from my parents, I packed up my things and moved back to Georgia. I took a job at Walmart. I was lost. Directionless. I had a college degree and no idea what I was doing with my life. After Walmart, I became an assistant manager at Wendy's. It was a paycheck, nothing more. The work didn't ask much of me, and honestly, I didn't ask much of myself either. I went through the motions. I traveled some. Laughed a lot. But deep down, I knew I was wasting my God-given talent.

I called my mom.

"So . . . I think I need to do something with my life," I said, half-laughing.

"You think or you know?" she shot back, classic Mommie-style—cutting through my nonsense with love and no sugarcoat.

"I don't know . . . I was thinking, maybe I could sub or something. I mean, I have a degree," I said, barely above a whisper, because teaching was the last thing I wanted to do. Everyone in my family taught. I didn't want to be a carbon copy.

"Well," she chirped, clearly trying to rein in her excitement, "You could try a Christian school—maybe they'd let you do a long-term sub position using your journalism degree."

It didn't take long to find a school. A small Christian school just outside Atlanta offered me a second-grade teaching position. The principal connected me with a woman from the church who had a little apartment in her basement. It all fell into place. I taught for a year—and surprise—I didn't hate it. In fact, it started to feel like I had a purpose. I finally admitted to myself that maybe teaching wasn't such a bad idea after all.

With my parents' unending patience and support, I applied to Kennesaw State University to pursue my teaching degree. I got in.

KSU was everything I didn't know I needed.

I snagged a position at the student newspaper writing and editing, found a house to live in, and picked up a lifeguarding job at the YMCA to make ends meet. Summers, falls, winters, springs—I stayed busy, and I loved it.

KSU was vibrant. The student life was rich and diverse. The newsroom was filled with passionate, quirky, smart humans who challenged me in all the right ways. I wrote nonstop—sports stories, human interest pieces, student government spotlights. I fell in love. Fell out of love.

Laughed loud. Cried hard. Learned who I was and who I didn't want to be. This was finally my college experience, and I soaked up every minute.

Then came student teaching.

Before the final semester, we had a preparatory phase—spending time with professors at partner schools, designing lesson plans, and developing classroom centers. That's where things unraveled.

Our professor was new, freshly minted with a doctorate—and she made sure we knew it. Everything was by the book. No room for flexibility. And busy work? She was the queen of it.

One day, I couldn't take it anymore.

I raised my hand and said what half the room was thinking.

"I mean no disrespect, but writing out these detailed pretend lesson plans—where we guess what a child might say and then write how we'll respond—it's just insane. We don't know what kids are going to say. This is busy work. My mom's a teacher. My grandpa taught in a one-room schoolhouse. My uncle is a superintendent. No one is doing anything this ridiculous."

Her face flushed with fury.

"Well, I never—" she started.

"And having a doctorate is just a piece of paper. I could get one," I blurted out before I could stop myself.

"Get out. You're dismissed," she snapped.

Just like that, I was suspended from the teaching program.

I called Daddy, sobbing. I couldn't say the words out loud—I couldn't tell him I'd been kicked out. Not after everything he had done for me. Not after choosing me to be his daughter. I just told him to come. Please come. And without hesitation, he did. He drove all the way from Ohio to Kennesaw overnight.

The next morning, I couldn't get out of bed. I lay there, feeling like a complete failure. Again. That girl with the cool stilettos and big dreams who couldn't seem to stay out of her own way.

Daddy didn't say much. He went to the store, bought groceries, and baked me a cherry pie. Later that night, I heard him talking to Mommie on the phone:

"She looks pretty bad. She's thin. Doesn't look well. I couldn't even get her to eat pie. I don't know how this one is going to end."

That broke something in me.

I got up. I fought back. Again.

I stood in front of a faculty committee and made my case. The head of the program had already decided I wasn't a good fit. But the committee listened. They saw something in me. Somehow—grace, maybe even a miracle—they voted to let me stay.

Afterward, Daddy hugged me.

"Keep your head down. Stay strong. Just finish."

And I did. I now had a degree in Journalism and Early Childhood Education. So is this where life begins? I didn't even know what life even meant yet. But I was about to find out. I'd spent years, and no one could seem to handle me. I told myself I was ready for the world, but deep down, I wasn't sure what that even meant. Something was still missing, but where was I gonna find it?

Part 2

Accepting the Angel

—Chapter 6—
The Boy Who
Changes Everything

"No one believes in love at first sight
until that special person comes along
and steals your heart."

~Unknown

After graduation, I needed something different—something bold, something healing, something far away. So, I took a trip to Bangkok.

What started as a two-week trip to teach English in Thailand turned into a love story I never saw coming. I fell hard. For the people. For the language. For the blinding sun and the buzzing city streets. For the night markets that lit up like fairytales. For the temples that felt sacred even to someone still sorting through what sacred even meant. I fell for the chaos, the food, the color, the freedom. And I knew if I couldn't find a teaching job back in the States, I was coming back here for good.

So I did.

By June, I had bought a one-way ticket to Bangkok. I packed my bags, shipped a couple of trunks full of "necessities" that I probably didn't need, kissed my parents goodbye, and flew across the world to chase something that felt like purpose. I landed a job teaching English at the University of Bangkok and moved into a three-story apartment in the heart of the city. My interpreter was a college student, and somehow the two of us made the perfect roommates. The days were long, the sun was hot, and for the first time in a long time, I felt like I was exactly where I was supposed to be.

Thailand greeted me with ninety-degree weather and warmth in more ways than one. Even during the "cold" months, the temperature never dropped below seventy. There was constant sunshine. Constant movement. Constant wonder.

I set out to visit as many temples as I could—golden, glowing spaces that left me breathless. Once a month, I taught English to a group of Buddhist monks. That experience alone could be a whole chapter. They were kind, curious, and incredibly wise. I felt honored just to be in the room.

Every morning, fresh fruit and Coke were delivered to my door. Street food became my go-to, and my taste buds were living their best life. I rode tuk-tuks around the city like I was in a video game, half-laughing, half-convinced I wasn't going to survive the ride. I snorkeled down the coast of Phuket and wandered markets where smells and spices danced through the air like something magical. If you ever need to believe again, go walk through a Thai night market.

Eventually, I bought a motorcycle because I figured if I was going to live in the wild, I might as well go full throttle. Riding a motorcycle in Bangkok is not for the faint of heart. There are no rules—only chaos, horns, and adrenaline. Traffic is a never-ending maze of buses, tuk-tuks, taxis, and daring motorcycles like mine. One time, I got on a bus where the driver had toothpicks jammed in his eyelids to keep them open. The bus was jam-packed, rusted out, and vibrating with uncertainty. I got off at the next stop and swore off public transportation forever.

That motorcycle became my wings. I could race to the front of the pack at every red light and feel the wind slap my face like a welcome back to life. It was madness, but it was mine. Did I wear tennis shoes? Nope. High heels on the bike were my signature look.

I had found my rhythm. I was teaching. I was living. I was healing. Eighteen hours ahead of everyone back home, I was living a version of myself that felt finally free.

Sure, it was hard being far from my parents and everyone who had helped shape me, but for once, I wasn't defined by where I came from. I wasn't the girl with a complicated story, or the girl who spoke up too much, wore too high of heels, or wore skirts that didn't touch the floor. I was just me. And in Thailand, that was more than enough.

Life had finally settled into a rhythm in Bangkok when Hannah decided to visit me for ten days. I took her everywhere on the back of my motorcycle—no helmet, no hesitation—and not once did she question my wild driving. We laughed nonstop. One of our last adventures was a trip to a private island, the kind you could only reach by boat once a day. The sun was setting in hues of pink and gold as we walked barefoot along the beach. She looked at me—and I knew that look.

"Okay, out with it," I sighed, my eyes fixed on the horizon as waves lapped at our feet.

She didn't even pause. "I think all of this is amazing and beautiful," she started, "but . . . are you going to live here forever?"

I let the silence breathe. I looked down at the ocean soaking into our footprints. I turned to her. "I love it here. I feel peace. I'm dating someone—I like him, I like his family. I love my job. Yeah, I think this is good for me."

She didn't miss a beat. "Well, I miss you. I think you should come home. You could live near Kenneth and me. We could run together. I'm sure you'd find a teaching job."

Hannah came to visit me in Bangkok, Thailand, and we had a blast sightseeing—first with me biking and towing her along, then upgrading from pedal power to a motorbike for a whole new kind of adventure.

"You're married now. I'd be the third wheel. No, thank you," I said, rolling my eyes.

"Seriously," she said. "Married life is great. Come home, find a man, we'll have kids together. Our kids can be best friends."

I laughed and shook my head. "I am never having kids! No man could handle all this," I said, shaking my hips and sprinting toward the water.

But when I hugged her goodbye at the airport, something about the way she looked at me lingered. It was the kind of look that stays with you, even when you try to forget it. The kind of look that makes you question what's waiting around the corner.

That look. That conversation. Plus the fact that I kept getting strep throat over and over—and there was no way I was having my tonsils taken out in Thailand—finally pulled me back home. My plan was simple: fly home for the summer, have surgery, heal, and go back to Thailand in the fall. I stored my trunks with a local family in Bangkok, said my goodbyes, and flew home. I booked my tonsillectomy, expecting a painful but standard 10–14 day recovery.

It was anything but.

The surgery went fine at first. I was four days in, sore and tired of popsicles and the smell of my own bad breath. I was standing over the kitchen sink at my parents' house, trying to take my liquid pain medicine. Mommie was in her green La-Z-Boy, Daddy on the couch. I took the medicine and immediately felt it come back up. I coughed out the words "Something's wrong," just as bright red blood began gushing from my mouth—and then my nose.

I heard Mommie scream, "Bruce, call 9-1-1!"

And then I passed out.

While I was crumpled on the kitchen floor, Daddy called for the ambulance. Mommie called Mommie B and told her to meet us at the hospital. The EMTs arrived to find me lying on my side, just like the dispatcher instructed. They started suctioning, but the battery died. Panic flared. They hoisted me onto the gurney. One of the paramedics straddled me on the stretcher, jamming gauze down my throat in an effort to stop the hemorrhaging. We were at least twenty minutes from the hospital, even speeding.

Mommie B was waiting when we arrived. The paramedic was still on top of me, shouting. Mommie B would later tell me I looked dead— white as a sheet, completely limp, not a trace of life in my face. They rushed me straight to the OR.

Daddy didn't come to the hospital right away. He stayed home to clean up all the blood. He never said it out loud, but I think he didn't want my mom to come back and see it if I didn't make it.

While all that chaos was unfolding, I was somewhere else entirely.

I remember being in the ambulance. I looked over and saw a figure bathed in blinding light—so bright I couldn't tell if they were male or female. The outline of wings behind them shimmered. Sitting next to this angelic being was my Grandpa Combs. He had been gone for years.

He smiled and nodded. His lips were moving, but I couldn't hear him.

I tried to speak. I couldn't breathe. I was gagging. I started to panic. And then I saw him mouth the words again—"Not today. It's not your time."

Tears spilled down my face. Not today? But I wanted to be with him. I loved him. I didn't want to go back.

Then—darkness.

When I opened my eyes, I was in the hospital. My parents and Mommie B were beside me. They were relieved. They told me I'd hemorrhaged and needed emergency surgery, but I would be okay.

But I wasn't thinking about stitches or blood loss. I couldn't stop thinking about the vision. What did it mean? Why wasn't it my time? Why was I still here? My life had been a series of close calls and unanswered questions. How many times could someone cheat death before the universe said enough?

I felt like a failure with two degrees, no job, and nothing but a story that made people uncomfortable.

I went home the next day to recover and try—once again—to figure out what in the world I was going to do with my life.

• • •

Hannah convinced me to look for a job. After scouring the internet and sending out what felt like a hundred resumes, I finally landed a long-term subbing job at City Day Community School in Dayton, Ohio, in late September. It was a K–8 charter school, tucked into the middle of downtown Dayton, where you did not want to find yourself after dark.

This would be my first real teaching job in the States. I had only taught older students before, so first grade was going to be a whole new world.

My classroom was on the first floor, right across from Ms. Jones. She greeted the kids every morning with a smile that made it feel like sunshine had cracked through the hallway windows. Every morning, she'd flash me a grin and said, "Have a great day, girl," like she meant it.

The school had all the essentials—music, computer class, art, and physical education. I had met all the special teachers except for the elusive PE teacher. The principal, Mrs. Goff, was giving me a tour one afternoon when this man came down the stairwell. Actually, filling the stairwell doorframe might be more accurate. Top to bottom. Side to side.

"Oh! You haven't met Mr. Moore," she said, pausing. "Mr. Moore, this is Ms. Garber. She's our new long-term sub in first grade."

He stood there silently for a beat, then stuttered out a polite but brief hello.

I smiled and replied, but he didn't say another word.

Okay, I thought. *Big guy. Seems shy.*

I turned and headed back down the hall, the click of my silver heels echoing off the floor. I caught a glimpse of my reflection in the glass and smirked at myself. I'd been a lot of things, but being nervous wasn't usually one of them.

A few days later, it was time for my class to head to PE. I hadn't seen Mr. Moore since that first awkward introduction, and I had almost forgotten about him until I led my students up the stairs to the gym. And there he was—across the room—striding over to greet the class.

Even from a distance, he looked tall. As in, I'm 5'2"-and-wearing-heels-and-still-a-foot-shorter-than-you tall.

He walked up, all calm and professional. "Ms. Garber, is your class ready?"

I shrugged and smiled. "I guess. Some of them seem a little scared of you," I said, laughing.

He didn't miss a beat. Just looked at the class and told them to head in and find their spots. And just like that, they scurried in like obedient little mice. He would later laugh and say teaching the little ones was like herding cats.

I turned and headed back down the stairs. But something weird was happening. My stomach did a little flip. Not a nervous flip. More like . . . fireflies on a summer night. Or . . . butterflies.

Out loud, I whispered to myself, "Well . . . this is different."

That night, I could barely wait to get home. I had moved into a little townhouse just one street over from Hannah. The second I walked in the door, I called her.

"Hannah, you are not going to believe this," I said, practically out of breath. "Something crazy happened today."

"What? What is it?" she asked, instantly on alert.

"I met this teacher. His name is Mr. Moore—I think his first name is Nate—and . . . something's just different," I said, trying to wrap my head around what I couldn't quite explain.

"Different how?" she asked, intrigued.

"I don't know. Like I was drawn to him. There were butterflies, Hannah. But I don't even know why or how."

"Did he ask you out?"

I laughed. "No! He could barely even talk to me."

"Well then," she said, matter-of-factly, "you have to talk to him."

Over the next few weeks, I did my best to spark conversations with Mr. Moore, but it was clear—he was a man of few words. Polite. Reserved. And impossible to read.

One morning, as I was standing at my classroom door, Ms. Jones leaned against her frame across the hall, arms crossed, one eyebrow raised like she was reading me top to bottom. Her head tilted toward the mailboxes and then back at me.

"What?" I asked, suspicious.

"Hmm-mmm," she hummed. "Mr. Moore never checked his mailbox. Not once since he got this job last year. And now—suddenly—he's down this hallway once or twice a day? Mmm-hmm. I see what's going on here."

Sarcasm practically dripped from her grin. I laughed and rolled my eyes, mouthing a dramatic whatever.

And as if on cue, Mr. Moore strolled by. "Good morning, Ms. Garber," he said calmly, then paused. "I have a football game Friday . . . you should come."

I blinked. Smiled. "Okay—just send me the details, and I will."

Friday night came, and I bundled up and showed up to the game. I spotted him immediately on the sideline—towering over the players, holding a whiteboard, pacing with purpose. At halftime, I saw him standing in midfield, staring at the scoreboard. The second the clock ticked to halftime, he hit the button on his watch and bolted toward the locker room.

Khaki pants, Nike sneakers, short-sleeved green polo with the school logo. I smiled. That man is tall and fine.

After the game, he called and asked me to meet him at a local spot—Tanks, a little hole-in-the-wall place in Dayton. I didn't like eating that late, so he bought me a Coke. When a couple of my friends, who met us there, and I left that night, they all turned to me at once.

"I think Mr. Moore has a thing for you," they chimed in unison.

We laughed the whole way home.

The next week, he invited me to another game. But by Friday, I wasn't feeling great. I had a fever pushing 102, and it was snowing—the bitter, wet kind of snow Ohio loves to dump on you when you least need it. Still, I dragged myself there. It was the school's big rivalry game and the last one before the playoffs.

I made it through the entire freezing night, barely. Afterward, I texted him, told him I had to go straight home—I wasn't feeling well. I didn't hear from him again until Monday at school. We were friendly, still talking at work, but not really spending time outside of school—aside from my three Friday night football appearances.

Around Thanksgiving, I asked him to help me study for the test I needed to pass for my Ohio teaching license. He said yes.

The day after Thanksgiving, I found myself at his house, sitting with textbooks and flashcards scattered between us. He glanced up at me, eyes half-lidded with boredom.

"We need a study break."

I looked at him, grateful for the excuse. "Okay . . . what do you want to do?"

Without saying a word, he pulled out his guitar and started strumming.

Wait. What?

He can coach . . . he can teach . . . he can play an instrument?

That was it.

That was the moment.

It was over for me.

This man was it. My person. There would never be another.

Without thinking, I leaned in, gently pulled his face to mine, and kissed him like I had never kissed anyone before.

From that moment on, we were inseparable.

In mid-December, we were getting ready to spend time with his parents. I was fixing my makeup in the mirror, and he sat on the edge of the tub watching me. I caught him staring, gave him my best crooked smile.

"What?" I asked, teasing.

Without blinking, without hesitation, he said, "I love you."

I froze. Stared. That wasn't a test-the-waters kind of confession. It was honest. Steady. Real.

I already knew I loved him too—but no way was I going to say it first.

I walked over, touched his face, and whispered, "I love you too."

There was no big label. No need for one. No defining moment that turned us into boyfriend and girlfriend. Just a quiet knowing. It was enough.

On January 8, 2005, we were in my townhouse, dancing in the living room. Music played softly, echoing off the walls. I could hear Van Morrison's voice drifting into the room:

"I can hear her heartbeat for a thousand miles

And the heavens open every time she smiles . . ."

I looked up at Nate. His lips moved with the lyrics as he gently kissed my forehead.

"And when I come to her, that's where I belong

Yet I'm running to her like a river's song . . ."

He dropped to one knee.

Nathaniel Adam Emerson Moore asked me to marry him after two months of dating.

And I said yes.

Five months later, on June 18, 2005, I walked down the aisle to the sounds of "Crazy Love" played softly on the piano. Pastor Lawson—who had married my parents years before—stood at the altar to marry us.

The same Pastor who had counseled me through darkness, who reminded me that healing would come, not from finding someone, but from finding myself.

I found myself in Thailand.

I found love in a hallway in Dayton.

It was love at first sight.

It was crazy love.

A love that would be submerged in fire and tested quickly.

—Chapter 7—
Advocate

"There is no trust more sacred than the
one the world holds with children.
There is no duty more important
than ensuring that their rights
are respected, that their welfare
is protected, that their lives are
free from fear and want, and that
they can grow up in peace."
~Kofi Annan

We were young and in love, full of dreams and blind hope—the kind of hope that comes easy when the world hasn't broken your heart yet. Nate was coaching at Chaminade Julienne, and I had just enrolled full-time in grad school to become a school counselor. We bought a small house in Kettering, not far from Hannah, and began building a life we thought would unfold like a fairytale.

But life doesn't care about your plans. It rewrites them without warning.

The fall of 2006 was a blur of textbooks, late nights, football practices, and holding it all together because I was pregnant. First came the happiness, then came the sickness. And it never stopped. Day after day, I would vomit until I couldn't stand. In the morning, I crawled into the school building. During the day, I'd teach with a trash can next to my desk. Then at the end of the day, Nate carried me out to the car. I would pray every night that my body wouldn't betray this little life growing inside me.

The doctors told us I might not be able to carry to full term. I was so dehydrated, they hooked me up to IV nutrition. Nate had to inject me with needles in my legs every morning—legs that became bruised and yellowed from the constant sticks. One morning, he looked at me, tears in his eyes, and said, "I'm so sorry, baby. This hurts me more than you know."

But I didn't cry. Not yet. Because when you're in survival mode, you don't feel—you endure.

At five months, they found something. Our baby's intestines were growing outside his body. They suspected more abnormalities. Down syndrome. Risks. Needles. Miscarriage. My mind spiraled into darkness. I had never even wanted children—I had been too afraid. And now here I was, being asked to carry a life that might not survive. It felt like punishment. Like my worst fears were finding me anyway.

I'll never forget how Nate held my face in his hands and said, "It doesn't matter. He's ours. And I will love him no matter what."

With Nate's words, something shifted. Not in my body—but in my soul.

We didn't agree to any risky tests. We waited. And somewhere between specialists and tears, the baby began to heal. "A little miracle," the doctor said. Skin was growing where there shouldn't have been any. Hope, where there had only been fear.

Then came October 23rd.

Game week. Rivalry week. Chaminade Julienne's biggest moment. I woke up to pain, panic, and water breaking too early. I slipped on a dress and heels—because if I was going to fall apart, I was at least going to look like I had it together—and we rushed to the hospital.

Eli Nathaniel Moore came into the world six and a half weeks early. He didn't really cry. I didn't get to hold him. They whisked him away and left me in a sterile room full of doctors I didn't recognize and fear I could barely name.

Three hours later, I was wheeled to the NICU (Neonatal Intensive Care Unit). And that's when the pediatrician looked at me like I was already guilty. "Did you drink or do drugs while you were pregnant?" she asked coldly. I nearly came out of my skin. She hadn't read the file. She hadn't seen the fight. She just saw a baby with signs. I fired her on the spot. I realized: I wasn't just a mom anymore. I was an advocate.

Eli had surgery. He gained weight. And slowly, our lives started to settle—not into ease, but into resilience.

I returned to work two weeks later. We couldn't afford for me not to. Daddy came every day to care for Eli while I taught. Nate was coaching, chasing playoffs, chasing purpose. And I—well, I was becoming something I never thought I'd be strong enough to be.

A mother.

A coach's wife.

A warrior. And almost immediately, this would be put to the test.

Some stories never leave you. Some moments redefine you.

For me, it started with a jacket and a refusal to do a sit-up. It ended with my career torn apart—and my soul set ablaze, and a mindset that would become unwavering.

Nate was quiet when he came home that day. The kind of quiet that makes the world pause. "I have a problem," he said, "and I don't know if I want your help."

I was offended—of course, I wanted to help. That's what love does. That's what we do. But then he told me.

A girl in his PE class had refused to take off her jacket and wouldn't lie back for the physical fitness test. When he gently asked her why she couldn't take her jacket off or lie on the ground, she broke. Not emotionally, but physically. Her voice trembled as she told him her mother had beaten her in the shower until blood circled the drain.

He did the right thing—he reported it, because as a teacher, you are a mandated reporter. But when he told the principal, she became angry. "Do not call CPS," she barked. "They think they're God. You don't know what happens when kids go into the system." She told him to stay out of it.

This is when I began to think and reflect that silence is not safety. And neutrality is not justice.

That night, I held Eli close. I knew what it meant to hide bruises under Sunday dresses. I knew what it was to be a child silenced by fear. By 4 a.m. I had made my decision. If no one else would confirm her story, I would.

Nate asked other teachers if they could check her back to confirm her story, and they were too afraid to get involved. They just couldn't risk getting fired. So, I brought her into a small, quiet room. She looked tired—too tired for someone her age. I gently asked what happened, and her eyes filled with tears. "Sometimes my mom gets angry," she whispered. "I honestly don't remember what I did this time." And then she described it—the beating, the cord hitting her back repeatedly, the blood running down her legs and out the drain.

She raised her shirt to show me.

I will never forget what I saw. Her back was a tapestry of torment—open wounds, scabs, lash marks that never should've been on a child's skin. It looked like the paintings of Jesus after the scourging. I gasped. Then I cried. I held her as she pulled her shirt back down. "We'll get through this," I said. But my voice cracked, because I wasn't sure how.

Nate made the confirming call to CPS, and within an hour, she and her sister were removed from the school and taken into protective services.

That should've been the end of it.

But it wasn't.

The principal came into my classroom like a storm. "Do you know what you've done?" she spat. "You're going to regret this." By the end of the day, I was escorted out. Fired. Not allowed to collect my things. Not even a goodbye to the kids I'd poured myself into.

I lost my job. I lost my title. But I did not lose myself. The principal actually called security and had me escorted out.

And then came the subpoenas. I had to testify against the mother. The principal was charged. Cameras followed us in and out of the courtroom. It was ugly, public, and painful. And just when I thought it couldn't get worse, Nate and I were summoned before the Ohio Department of Education. Separated. Grilled for hours. Accused of being liars, racists, and insubordinate.

I was the one on trial now—not the woman who ignored a child's cries.

No lawyer. No advocate. Just my truth, and Nate's unwavering eyes from across the room, silently saying, "You can do this."

And I did.

Eventually, justice came. The mother pleaded guilty. The principal lost her license and failed in her appeal to the Ohio Supreme Court. I returned to the classroom—for the kids. Not for the system. Not for the adults who failed them.

I left that job at the end of the year because I knew I was going to choose a kid over policies and politics.

The next year, I worked remotely as a counselor. I enrolled in an administrative master's program because I was done being powerless. Done being quiet. Done being the teacher who gets fired for telling the truth.

Nate got a new job teaching special education and coaching with his mentor at Hamilton City Schools for the next few years. This led to my being hired as a kindergarten teacher at Hamilton. I was so thankful to be back in a brick-and-mortar school and on the same schedule as Nate.

That moment in the room—with a child's scars laid bare—was my turning point.

I decide then and there that I will always be the one who looks. The one who listens. The one who acts.

I know what it is to hide pain. I know what it means to suffer in silence. I know the price of doing the right thing.

And I would do it again. A thousand times.

I will never sit quietly while a child cries in the dark.

Coach Moore and my first event together—sharing a Thanksgiving meal I cooked for my City Day first-grade class, filled with gratitude, love, and community.

—Chapter 8—
Becoming the Head
Coach's Wife

"We interrupt this marriage for football
season and pre- and postseason, and well,
the rest of your life . . ."

~Unknown

Nate had been grinding for years, building his coaching resume one stop at a time, and it finally paid off—he landed his first head coaching job in Minster, Ohio. The only problem was that we were still living in Kettering, and the housing market was in shambles. Selling a house during a recession felt impossible. But the job couldn't wait. Nate was already living out of the coach's office in Minster, pouring everything he had into this new opportunity. We had to make a decision, so we did what we always did—we adapted.

We put our house in Kettering up for rent, and Eli and I moved in with Nate's parents in Mason. It wasn't ideal, but it gave us a weekend landing spot in Minster as a family. I was still teaching kindergarten at Hamilton City Schools and working to finish my principal internship. Baby number two was due in February, and the pregnancy was already weighing heavily on me, both physically and emotionally. Everything felt like it was being held together by threads, but I was determined not to let any of them snap.

Minster was straight out of a postcard. A small village tucked in rural

Auglaize County, where people didn't lock their doors and left keys in their cars. The kind of place where Friday nights meant the whole town showed up for football, and the local taverns were known as much for their charm as their specialties—Willy's Drive-Thru, the Wooden Shoe Inn, Bud's Pizza. There was a rhythm to life there that was slower, but somehow fuller.

I found a yellow two-story house with a wraparound porch right across from the Catholic church. The landlord lived in the back half with her own entrance, and we barely saw her. On Sunday mornings, I'd sip tea on the porch and watch the town filter in and out of church mass. And on Friday nights, we'd bundle Eli up and walk the three blocks to the field.

That first year stretched me in ways I didn't know possible. I was juggling motherhood, finishing my second master's, teaching kindergarten, dealing with a complicated pregnancy, and learning to accept life without my husband during the week. The miles between us weren't just physical; they tested our communication, our endurance, and our ability to keep choosing each other amid the chaos. This life— being the wife of a head coach—was not for the faint of heart. It wasn't for the type of girl who needed constant attention or reassurance. But I'm not that girl. I loved him, and I believed in what he was building.

The beauty of Minster wasn't just in the tree-lined streets or the porch lights glowing warm through the fog. It was in how the community wrapped its arms around us. People showed up with casseroles and open hearts, thrilled that Nate had come to lead their team. That team had only won one game their junior year—six total in their high school careers—and yet there was hope.

I'd come to learn something about Nate in those early days: he wasn't just a coach. He was a rebuilder.

Nate had decided, entirely on his own, that he was going to visit every single player in their home before the season started. Since I was only in Minster on the weekends and he had all the time in the world, I suppose it made sense. I mean, how hard could it be to plan football practices when you've never actually run a program? (Insert sarcastic eye roll here.)

So, Nate pulled out his best suit and tie and started making house calls. Keep in mind—this is Minster. Rural Ohio. Farm country. One of his first visits was to a player who lived on a cow farm.

He knocked on the door, the mom answered, smiled sweetly, and said gently, "Oh, you'll want to talk to my husband. He's out in the barn. Just go around and yell." So Nate, in his freshly pressed suit, walked through the mud to the barn. And there was the dad, arms deep in a cow helping it give birth. Nate just stood there, frozen. The dad looked up from his work and, completely unfazed, asked, "You wanna help?" Nate shook his head, wide-eyed, and replied, "No, I'm good. I can wait inside." That night on our Skype call, he told me the story, and I laughed so hard I nearly fell off the bed. "Well," I said between giggles, "This is definitely not a city school." He gave me a look and muttered his classic one-word response when I'm pushing my luck: "Clearly."

That summer, Eli and I would walk down to watch practice. The field was tucked behind the school, just a short walk from our little yellow house. Eli would roll down the grassy hill while I sat watching the team. A few of the dads would show up too—not the loud, obnoxious type, but quiet, steady observers. They didn't critique Nate's plays or gossip. They just talked, laughed, and watched.

Over time, those dads became known as the "Grassy Knoll Dads." They even had hats and shirts made with GKD stitched across the front. To this day, those men are some of our biggest supporters, showing up at games long after their sons graduated. I could never find words big enough to capture the gratitude I hold for their quiet loyalty.

Then came the first game. You could feel the electricity in the air as the Minster Wildcats took the field. I watched as Head Coach Nate Moore—my Nate—ran out in front of the team. For a moment, it was like seeing him for the very first time. I felt those old butterflies take flight, and just as they did, baby Ella kicked in rhythm with the marching band. My heart was so full. I couldn't wait to see his first win and kiss him at the fifty-yard line. It felt like a movie moment just waiting to happen.

Except it didn't happen.

We lost a nail-biter to Fort Loramie, 14-12. And yet, no one seemed upset. Everyone kept saying how much better the team looked. I was confused. We lost—wasn't the point to win? I didn't move to the middle of cornfield country to lose football games. This wasn't what I imagined.

Week 2 was another loss, this time to Lehman Catholic, 34-13. Then Delphos St. John's, 35-7. Then Marion Local steamrolled us 41-6 in Week 4. We were 0-4, and I was starting to wonder if maybe Nate had jumped into this head coach position too soon. Maybe I wasn't being supportive enough. Maybe this wasn't going to work out.

But Nate never complained. Not once. He just kept showing up early, staying late, grinding every day. I kept driving back and forth between Mason and Minster—pregnant, exhausted, and disheartened. I started to wonder quietly, "Is this what I signed up for?"

And then came Week 5.

New Bremen. Just two miles down the road. The air felt different. Nate's team walked out of the locker room through a tunnel made of cheering parents, arms linked in celebration. "We want Moore! We want Moore!" They chanted. And then—there he was. That elusive smile spread across his face as he ran under their outstretched arms. I wiped away tears. In that moment, I knew. This is what my husband was made for. To rebuild. To inspire. To give people something to believe in again.

We won. 27-20. Nate's first win as a head coach.

The Minster Wildcats went on to win the next four games, one after another. They closed out the regular season with a 5-5 record—just enough to make the playoffs. For that group of seniors who had only known losing, it was magic.

Week one of the playoffs, they dismantled Catholic Central 44-21. Confidence was building. Then came the news: we'd be facing Marion Local again. The same powerhouse team that had crushed us in Week 4. A team that had owned Minster for years.

But something felt different this time. Nate had laid a foundation—and win or lose—people were starting to believe.

I was six months pregnant, exhausted but surviving, and completely amped for the rematch against Marion Local. Nate was in the zone, the town was buzzing, and it felt like all of Minster was holding its breath. But my body had other plans.

On Tuesday night, I called Nate. "I hate to tell you this," I said, trying to keep my voice steady, "but something's wrong. I can't keep anything down, and I feel . . . off." I didn't want to say the word scared, even though I was. I knew how much this game meant to him, how much he had poured into this team. He couldn't miss a single practice that week, not with the biggest game of the season looming. Still, he didn't hesitate. "What do you need?" he asked, his voice calm and steady, like it always is in a storm. I smiled through the nausea and said, "For you to win."

By Wednesday morning, the doctor admitted me to the hospital. There were serious complications with the pregnancy, and no chance I'd be released before Friday night's game. I was devastated. I didn't want anyone from my family in the hospital with me—I wanted them at the game. That's where the magic was going to happen.

So, I made them bring me an orange wig. No joke. I wasn't allowed to wear Minster gear (thanks to the hospital dress code), but that didn't mean I couldn't get into game mode. I had the nurses hook my hospital computer to the radio broadcast and warned them: no interruptions unless it was a full-blown emergency.

One of the nurses laughed and shook her head. "You know you're in a hospital, right? Not at the game." I looked at her with the wig proudly on my head and deadpanned, "You know I'm in game mode, right?" She walked out, probably rolling her eyes, but I didn't care. My team was about to take the field. And my coach—my husband—was about to take a swing at the giant.

Everyone said Marion Local would dominate. Coach Tim Goodwin had a dynasty, and the smart money said this game wouldn't even be close. But Nate Moore? He loves being the underdog. He lives for it. And that night, in a down-to-the-wire thriller, Minster pulled off the unthinkable. Final score: 30–26. When the scoreboard hit 0:00, I was sitting in a hospital bed in Kettering, Ohio, rocking an orange wig, hugging my baby bump, crying happy tears—and puking into a plastic bin. It was probably the most beautiful mess of a win I've ever witnessed to that point in Nate's career.

Minster lost in round three of the playoffs, a 27–14 heartbreaker against Lehman Catholic, played on the cold turf at Piqua. But for a guy who started the season 0–4? A regional runner-up trophy didn't look too bad sitting on Nate's desk.

That Christmas, we got flooded with cards from Minster families—many of them with pictures from that game. I still have some tucked away in a box in the basement. They remind me that support doesn't always mean being on the sidelines. Sometimes, it looks like a hospital room, a busted radio feed, and a whole lot of love from a distance.

A few weeks later, we ran into Coach Goodwin and his wife. He grinned and said, "Let me introduce you to the man who ruined my December." I died laughing. I love Tim Goodwin. I really do. At some point—I don't remember if it was that night or a later conversation—he told Nate, "You won't be coaching in Minster long. You're too big."

At the time, I didn't understand what he meant. Too big? Why would we leave? I was still so naïve.

That February, I finished my second master's degree in administration—early, thank you very much—and on February 17, 2011, we welcomed our daughter Ella into the world.

Now it was time for me to job hunt in rural Ohio while on maternity leave, so we could stop living across counties and finally be a real family in the same zip code.

The chapter of Nate's coaching dreams had just begun. And I was determined to make sure mine weren't left behind.

While looking for a job, nursing a baby, and recovering in the spring of 2011. I began having pains in my back and lower side. On doing a check-up with my doctor, he called Nate and me into his office. When you leave an exam room and head to a doctor's office where it is "comfortable" to speak, it is never good. The doctor looked solemnly at Nate and me, and I felt Nate gently take my hand as I sank into the single chair's leather seats. Looking at me, he smiled and said, "I have been your doctor since you were a teenager. We have kick-started your cycle, treated major endometriosis, and lived through hyperemesis gravidarum (HG), and now we are looking at what could develop into pre-cancer cells." There was silence in the room. I knew Nate wanted more children, but at that moment, I knew it wasn't in the cards for us, and my gut and heart literally started weeping before the tears reached my eyes.

Smiling and looking at us both with genuine empathy, he said, "I am recommending that you get a full hysterectomy as soon as three months postpartum. This way you won't have to worry about anything, in my opinion." I knew Nate was thinking as he sat there and squeezed my hand. He didn't look at me, but at the doctor, and without taking a breath or pausing, he responded, "Having my wife here to raise our son and daughter is more important than having more children, or risking her health. So we will do whatever we need to do."

At the end of May, I still had no prospects for a job. I had moved back to Mason, living with Nate's parents during the week so I could finish up my teaching job at Hamilton City Schools. Nate's mom graciously watched Ella during the day. I was prepped and ready for surgery at the end of May. I looked at Nate one last time as they were getting ready to wheel me into surgery that would take away my ability to give Nate any more children. He leaned over and kissed my forehead and said, "You are more important, no tears." I closed my eyes and I don't remember anything else until I woke up in my hospital room a few hours later. That was the end of the conversation. We had Eli and Ella. A boy and a girl. He was a head coach, our life was complete, we just had to live it, and I had to find a job.

In rural Ohio, there are not a lot of teaching jobs, administration jobs, or counseling jobs. I had certification in all these areas, and still, there was nothing available for my qualifications. I was not feeling supportive as a wife. I didn't know how we could live another year apart, but I knew I couldn't be jobless. One for my own sanity, plus we both had major student loans. I was feeling desperate when something caught my attention. St. Marys Middle School in St. Marys, Ohio, was looking for a guidance counselor. It was about ten miles away from Minster, and I thought, *This would be perfect!*

I landed an interview, but I couldn't drive because I was only two weeks out of surgery. I was interviewed by the principal, Mary, and her assistant, Cory. I immediately fell in love with Mary. She was a passionate, witty, funny, driven, and no-nonsense kind of woman. I wanted to work for her more than I have ever wanted to work for anyone else. When I got in the car, Nate was like, "Well, how did it go?" I just started crying, "I was in pain the whole time, but I think I would love this job and be really good at it." Nate just squeezed my hand and drove me home. On the way home, I lay my head against the window and closed my eyes as I let out a breath. As the sun hit my face, I prayed, "Dear God, I cannot take another year apart from this family. Please, please help me get this job. Nate needs me, even though he doesn't say it; Eli needs me; Ella needs me. We need each other to live this life. I'll give it more than 100 percent." The next day, Mary called and said they would like me to have a plan and present the following morning on how I would run groups, track students, work one-on-one, create behavior plans, and anything else I could think of to impress them. I could hear the challenge in her voice and picture the smile on her face when she said, "Good luck!"

I hung up the phone, and Nate said, "Well?" I rolled my eyes, "I have to put together a presentation in less than twenty-four hours that will make me stand out more than the other candidates." He just looked and grinned and replied, "Well, if anyone can do it, you can."

Within twenty-four hours of presenting, I had the job offer. Mary told me later that they gave me little time because they wanted to see what I would come up with under pressure. Would I crack or perform? St. Marys Middle School counseling job to this day is my favorite job.

Don't get upset if you are reading this and think I don't love my job now. I absolutely do. But St. Marys City School, Principal Mary, and the kids there would forever change my life. My passion to advocate harder for kids came from my experience there.

• • •

Going into the summer before Nate's second season, my sister Rachel was starting to go through some major life issues, which began to affect her young son Ashford. After long discussions with extended family, we decided it would be good for Ashford to be in a small place like Minster. So our family of four became a family of five once we obtained legal guardianship. All summer long, Ashford and Eli were constant fixtures with the Grassy Knoll Dads during practices. The town of Minster embraced Ashford, and our family, going from four to five, seemed seamless.

As we settled into life in Minster, I began to try to settle into being a middle school guidance counselor at St. Marys City Schools. Within my first couple of weeks, I could feel that the teachers didn't know how to handle me. They just saw me as a diva in dresses with high heels, who didn't understand life in a small town. I was pretty used to being misunderstood by this point in my life, so I tended to ignore people's scoffs or glares. Eli was starting kindergarten, Ashford was in second grade, and Ella was staying home with Mommie, who loved being Grandma Garber.

I continued to show up to school in my stilettos and dresses and worked on building my relationship with the kids who had been labeled the "troubled kids." I'm not sure why, but I found myself very drawn to helping these kids and coming up with ways that would motivate them. For example, for attendance and making a good grade, I created "Moore Money." I ordered money with my face on it, and they earned it for achieving goals. When they had 100 Moore bucks, I would take them to eat at Buffalo Wild Wings. I had a blast doing this and formed a close bond with a student named Alyssa. She was a very outspoken girl who was an IEP (Individual Education Plan) student. She was on probation, but there was something about her that just drew me to her. I had her join a group that I formed with other students who were labeled as troublemakers. We stayed after school, where I brought snacks to share with them while they had time to complete homework. We had a really great time together and learned along the way.

St. Marys opened my eyes to how important the relationship between an educator and a student can be. I learned so many heartbreaking things about students and their lives. There was drug addiction, alcoholism, and child abuse. It was all a daily part of so many children's lives, and they were just trying to make it through high school and graduate. I made a silent commitment that I would always look for the student that others thought wouldn't graduate or make it, and I would be there, giving it my all to make sure they did. Besides, I live for a challenge and love to prove everyone wrong. No one should just be a statistic.

. . .

Nate proved to be the head coach that Minster hoped he would be. In the 2011 season, he was named Ohio Division VI Coach of the Year. He was the head coach in the MAC All-Star Game and Assistant Coach in the Ohio-North South Game. In 2012, he was named Miami Valley Football Coaches Association Division VI Coach of the Year with a record of 9-3. He lost to Coach Tim Goodwin of Marion Local in the 2nd round of the playoffs. I guess it was Tim's turn to ruin Nate's December.

Already upset about the season ending before we wanted it to, I had a meeting with my principal and superintendent at St. Marys schools, where I was told that if the district didn't pass the levy in the spring, my job would be one of the first to be cut. I was distraught and felt the pressure mounting. Nate was so happy in Minster. He could stay in that job forever. We lived on the corner of the school and the football fields. Ashford and Eli walked through the yard to the school. They played baseball in the spring and had made great friends. We never worried about where they were or who they were with. It was the perfect place to raise our family. But we were in a crisis. We had student loans and bills to pay, and just couldn't afford for me not to have a job, which was rare and far between. I knew the chances of finding a job were going to be very difficult. I had two bachelor degrees and two master's. In the education world, once you have over five years of experience and a master's, you are considered expensive for a district.

Nate and I sat on the couch one night, when the kids were tucked into bed. We knew Ella wouldn't stay in bed long. She always tended to wander into our room at some point in the night. The doctor had said she would grow out of this. I'm pretty sure Nate thought she never would. Nate looked at me with his serious, determined brown eyes, and without a sigh or gasp, he said, "You want me to look for another job?" I scrunched my lips to my nose, trying to fight back the tears. "Can we afford for me not to work?" I silently mumbled. "I know you are happy here and are building something amazing." He nodded, like he was contemplating his words, and thinking about next steps. He took out his computer and started pulling up sites that posted head coaching positions. He looked at me and said, "What are your conditions?" I was so confused, I didn't know what he meant by conditions. He must have sensed it because he went on, "Do you need to be close to someone, or something?" I sighed, "Well childcare is expensive, and I want to work. So I would like to be close to our parents, so maybe we could have a balance. I don't want to leave Ella with just anyone."

I leaned back and closed my eyes, and the flashbacks of my childhood came flooding in. I had learned to lock this part of my brain, but in tense situations that I can't control it automatically unlocks. And I start thinking about leaving my baby with a stranger, and thoughts take over me. I wasn't going to be able to leave my kids with a sitter. I felt the tears seep out of my eyes. Nate pulled me close, kissed my forehead, and whispered, "In this together, for better or worse." I opened my eyes as the flashbacks vanished and that compartment in my brain became locked again. When I went to bed that night, I was plagued with dreams of dark rooms, hot breaths, and touches that didn't feel good. I woke up in a sweat early in the morning, with Nate fast asleep beside me. I whispered to myself, "He doesn't need to be reminded how weak I can be. I am strong, and we will get through this." I laid awake until it was time to get ready for work and went about my day.

• • •

A few weeks later, Nate landed an interview at La Salle High School, which is an all-boys catholic school located in the suburbs of Cincinnati, Ohio. The process was going to be long since La Salle, although not a powerhouse in the GCL (Greater Catholic League), was considered a premier job. Nate felt like if we were going back to Cincinnati, this would be a great move for him and a place we could continue and retire from our careers. There would be multiple school districts that I would be able to apply to if Nate got this job. We could also live near his parents in Cincinnati. I would be closer to Hannah! This was a win/win situation.

The interview process dragged on. Where Nate was patient, I was a mess. It wasn't looking good at St. Marys as they had begun to make cuts after the first levy did not pass. The home economics teachers had been told they would be let go and their program would be closed. I knew if the levy didn't pass in the spring, that I would be next. It wasn't looking promising. Finally, Nate got a call back for a second interview. This meant he had made the top three.

My phone rang, and it was Nate calling. "Babe, the interview went great, I feel pretty good." I could almost hear him smiling through the phone. I took a breath and felt relief. How could you not hire this guy? He oozed confidence and had a plan. I laughed, "Thank God, when do you think you will hear?" He responded without hesitation, "I would say a few days."

A few days came and went. I started losing sleep. I couldn't shut my brain off. What were we going to do? I would have to work two jobs if I were let go. I would be away from my family more with no control over my schedule. But I would do whatever it took to help Nate continue as a head coach. I knew even then that his way of coaching would impact kids into adulthood. It was my duty to support him and his dream, and no one could convince me otherwise. Nate decided to send an email to someone who was part of the process after a week of silence. They responded that they were still in the process of making a decision and hadn't been able to meet, and to please be patient.

About two and a half weeks and many sleepless nights went by before Nate got the call. He was offered the job. He accepted. So one of us now had a job, and again, it was up to me to be the one to find a new job in Cincinnati. I could not resign from my current position, in case I wasn't let go. The pressure of finding a job was on. But in all honesty, the pressure of becoming a head coach's wife in a high-profile job would prove to be a bigger undertaking than I had ever imagined.

—Chapter 9—
Baptized in a Sea of Red

"All the art of living lies in a fine
mingling of letting go and holding on."
~Havelock Ellis

When Nate called the Minster football team in and told them he had accepted the head coaching job at La Salle, it all felt oddly seamless. There weren't any angry outbursts, no bitter Facebook posts or snide tweets. Just some solemn nods, firm handshakes, and a steady stream of "Thank you, Coach." The Grassy Knoll Dads stood tall, told him they'd be watching—and they meant it. That kind of loyalty? That doesn't fade.

But while his transition looked smooth from the outside, mine felt like dragging a house through the mud.

The stress hit me in waves—finding a job, packing up our lives, enrolling Eli and Ashford in new schools, figuring out housing—and Nate? He was doing what he does. Drawing up plays, meeting the new players, putting together a staff. He was building something again. From scratch. And I was trying to hold it all together with a glue stick, grit, and gold heels.

Gone were the days when you could walk into a school office, shake a principal's hand, drop off your résumé, and charm your way into an interview. No, this was the era of online applications and algorithms. I spent hours on job sites, tweaking cover letters, navigating portals that crashed halfway through submission. I'd make it to the top three candidates, only to hear crickets—or worse, "We've decided to go in another direction."

It didn't even help that Nate's dad worked in the Cincinnati Public School system. Name-dropping wasn't helping me at all. I was tired. I was tired of trying and tired of feeling like I was chasing a moving train. I kept picturing living apart from Nate—again. But that is what I would do because I believed in my husband's calling. I knew he was doing what he was born to do. Being the coach's wife isn't all ribbons and roses. It's messy. It's lonely. It's a series of hard choices you make without cheers from the stands.

And just when I was bracing myself for another long-distance year, a sliver of hope cracked open. Right before the school year ended, I landed a job at McAuley High School as the assistant principal. It was an all-girls Catholic high school—just down the road from La Salle. I was ecstatic. This was it. I'd always wanted to be a principal, and now there was a path. I also thought, *All girls? How hard could that be?*

Oh, bless my heart. I miss that sweet, naive version of me.

When I broke the news to my students at St. Marys, they weren't happy. Alyssa looked me square in the eye and said, "You promised you'd get me to graduation. I'm not gonna make it without you." My heart split. I bent down and told her, "If you make it to graduation, I'll show up with a hundred bucks, and we'll go out to eat—just the two of us, one more time." She smirked and said, "Okay, but I'm not promising to stay out of trouble." I laughed. Because that's who she was—bold, sharp-edged, and full of fight. I wonder who that reminded me of?

Cincinnati brought bigger stakes and a bigger stage. And once again, I was trying to keep up—not just with Nate's career, but with my own expectations of motherhood, leadership, marriage, and identity.

It's one thing to move towns. It's another to move mountains.

St. Marys ended up passing their levy after all, and one night, Nate asked me if I regretted leaving. I paused longer than I expected. The truth? I loved Minster. I loved the people, the rhythm of that sweet small-town life, and my job—it was hands down the best one I'd ever had. But deep down, I knew something Nate would never have admitted: he was meant for something bigger. His journey wasn't meant to end in Minster.

That place was almost too perfect, and Nate thrives in a challenge. I knew then that supporting him wouldn't always mean standing beside him. Sometimes, it meant pushing him forward—and being willing to pull myself back.

I had to toughen up. I had to hold space for his growth, even if it meant pausing my own. Not stopping forever—just long enough to let his light catch fire.

After a ton of searching, we finally found a house to rent that I absolutely fell in love with—less than a mile from Nate's parents in Mason. Ashford was going to stay with us for one more year while we slowly prepared him to transition back to living with his mother, my sister Rachel. Mason City Schools were enormous, but organized in a way that made a big place feel small. Families stayed clustered together, and that was a blessing. The best part for our kids? They'd be close to Pop—Nate's grandpa—and just down the street from their grandparents. Mommie was still committed to driving in twice a week to help with Ella, who was only two at the time. We were going to make it work.

Do you remember when your media life began? When did your actual life become a highlight reel for strangers? Because for me, it didn't creep in slowly—it smacked me straight in the face. Social media, news crews, radio stations, all of them, lined the halls of La Salle High School the day Nate was introduced as the new head coach. I had Ella on my hip, and Eli and Ashford trailing behind me like little ducklings. Ella wasn't having it—she buried her face into her crocheted bunny, as cameras flashed and people called out congratulations. Hats were handed to the boys like souvenirs. The lights were blinding. I stepped back and took it all in, my heart racing, trying not to drop Ella or break into a full panic attack.

That was me, but not Nate. He was front and center. Confident. Steady. Smiling like he was right where he belonged.

It started to come into focus. Everything was about to change. This wasn't Friday night lights in a small village anymore. This was a stage. And every move we made would be watched, talked about, posted, and judged. From that moment forward, I had to be more than a coach's wife. I had to be a rock. I had to rise to match him. There was no room for insecurity, no time for self-doubt. I had to channel everything I had survived, everything I had fought for, and become someone Nate—and this program—could count on.

He caught my eye across the room and winked. That was all I needed.

Just as the clarity was settling in, someone shouted, "We need a family picture for social media!" In a blur, we were whisked in front of a WLSN La Salle Network backdrop. Ella on my hip, dressed in her red Lancer t-shirt, black tutu, red tights, and her ever-present bunny in her mouth. Ashford and Eli in matching tees and red hats embroidered with "#LRD"—short for "Lancers Roll Deep." Nate stood tall, sharp in a black suit with a red and black striped tie, a matching hat perched on his head. I wore a red dress, my favorite earrings, and yes—heels. Stilettos, actually. I didn't know it yet, but they'd become my trademark.

When the photo hit social media, I laughed out loud. Ella, sweet as ever, wasn't even looking at the camera—she was gazing at Nate, bunny in mouth, like she already knew her daddy was doing something big. That picture still makes me tear up. Sometimes kids see things more clearly than adults ever can.

About a week later, Nate was prepping for his first parent meeting. He was setting up in the cafeteria, fiddling with wires and slides, when he looked at me and said, "Are you ready for this?"

I laughed, "What do you mean? Of course. We're already in it."

He just smiled, kissed my forehead, and whispered, "Just making sure."

Then they started coming. Parents, aunts, siblings, grandparents, friends—filing in one by one until the cafeteria was standing room only—some pressed against the doors. I remember looking around and thinking, *They're here for him. And they all want something.* Expectations hung in the air like tension before a kickoff. Some greeted each other with hugs, some whispered in corners, but all eyes eventually found Nate.

I turned back toward the entrance and saw this towering kid walk in—baby-faced, but tall enough to pass for a college player. He had a huge smile and wore even bigger shoes. I remember thinking, *Good Lord, these kids are built differently.*

This wasn't just a new coaching job. This was a new life.

In true Nate style, he flipped the coaching switch on without warning. His voice cut through the cafeteria with force and clarity, commanding the room:

"Eyes. I want everyone looking at me so you don't miss anything I say. Make no mistake—there are going to be changes. You can fall in line and build something or choose another path."

I nearly choked trying to keep a laugh from slipping out. I brought my hand to my mouth and looked around, wide-eyed. Nate had never felt intimidating back in Minster—he was steady, approachable, even soft-spoken off the field. But tonight? Tonight, he was different. This was head-coach-in-the-big-city Nate. He wasn't asking for respect—he was demanding it.

And the room felt it.

Some of the boys looked stunned, like deer in headlights. You could see it settling in—they were realizing that seniority didn't matter anymore. Star power didn't matter. Neither did what position your dad played, who your uncle was, what number you wore—none of it mattered. The best athlete was going to play, and Nate Moore was not going to discuss playing time with parents. Period. The message was loud and clear: if you wanted a spot, you'd have to earn it.

The air was thick. Questions were few. Mostly, there were glances—sideways looks, quiet realizations. The football life they'd known? It was gone.

August was a blur. Nate caused a stir before camp even started when he made the bold call to interview every single coach on staff. Not out of disrespect—but because he needed to know: who was all-in, and who was holding on to the past. If they weren't aligned with his vision, they wouldn't be on the sideline. Simple as that.

People whispered. People pushed back. But Nate didn't flinch. That's one of the things I admire most about him—when it's time to lead, he leads.

The first big test of the season came fast. We were opening against Oak Hills on the University of Cincinnati's football field for the Crosstown Showdown, sponsored by Skyline Chili. It was bigger than anything we'd ever experienced at the high school level—TV cameras, spotlights, media everywhere. I felt my heart pounding as we walked in.

I looked up—and there they were. Our people. Hannah. Our family. Even the Grassy Knoll Dads drove in from Minster. They were all decked out in black and orange, like they never left us. The hugs were tight and familiar. Their presence was everything.

Then it all became real. Kickoff with the cheers of the crowd roaring as La Salle drove their offense down the field, over and over again.

La Salle dominated. It was beautiful. A 42–14 win. Clean, focused, fast, aggressive. The team looked sharp, confident, and totally bought in.

Nate was awarded the game ball for his first win as La Salle's head coach. When I found him after the game, his smile was so big it almost didn't fit on his face.

"So," he asked, wrapping his arm around me, "What do you think?"

I looked at him and laughed, "I think you're going to win here—and maybe be the first one to really do it."

He nodded, grinning, and said with that low, steady voice I know so well, "One week at a time."

But week two came with its own chaos.

Nate called me the morning of the game, and I could hear something in his voice that I rarely heard: panic.

"What's wrong?" I asked, bracing myself.

He lowered his voice. "I can't be sure yet, but I think someone tampered with the headsets. They're not working. I can't communicate with the box."

I sat in stunned silence. "Wait—what?"

"Yeah," he said. "I don't think we got all the keys from the old staff. I don't want to jump to conclusions, but it's bad."

I couldn't believe what I was hearing. Someone might've sabotaged the communication system before a game? At this level? Would someone really go that far—risking a team's performance—just to take a shot at a new coach? Was this what our life was going to be now? Smiles in public, sabotage in private?

But Nate didn't sit in the mess for long. He got in touch with a rep from the headset company, and within hours, they had someone flying in from Florida with new equipment. Unreal.

That night, under the lights, Nate and the Lancers took the field again—and delivered another blowout: 56–14 over East Central. The headsets worked. The team worked. And Nate? He worked through every single obstacle like he always does—with determination, focus, and a steady refusal to be shaken.

Two weeks in. Two wins. And I had a front-row seat to what would soon become one of the most unforgettable seasons of our lives.

Week three brought another commanding win. La Salle dismantled Princeton 55–7, and the stands were electric. The buzz about Coach Moore was growing louder. "He's going to change the GCL map," someone whispered near me. "We're going to be state champs, no doubt," another voice added. The boys were playing like they had something to prove. And the truth was—they did.

Late that night, after the win, my phone rang. A student I had just started mentoring over the summer—Rachel—was killed in a car crash, along with another student from a nearby school. My knees buckled. I'd lost a student early in my teaching career, and it shattered me. This time was no different. You don't ever get used to losing a child. There's no training that prepares you for it. It cuts right through your soul.

Rachel and I had a connection—we used to joke that we were kindred spirits. She said she always felt like she was standing on the outside of the circle, just watching everyone else be part of the crowd. I told her that it was okay. I had been there too. She was growing, adjusting, trying. She struggled with getting to school on time, lived with her sweet grandmother, and always seemed like she was carrying a weight that didn't belong to a girl her age. Her grandma would continue visiting me long after the funeral, and every time, I'd fight tears.

Rachel's service was held at the school. They roped off the casket in the gym because her injuries had been so severe. It was unlike anything I had ever seen. For over two hours, the line of mourners never stopped—student after student from every part of the city, many of them needing to be physically held up just to walk through. Our girls wept and leaned into each other for strength. The weight of grief blanketed the gym, thick and unmoving.

The next morning, we gathered again in the auditorium for the official funeral. The music started, and the words from "After the Storm" by Mumford & Sons spilled into the space:

"And there will come a time, you'll see, with no more tears.

And love will not break your heart, but dismiss your fears . . ."

I closed my eyes and let the music carry me.

Time slowed. No one sobbed loudly—the sadness was too deep for that. It was as if we were all frozen in place, unable to move under the weight of what was lost. The priest spoke, but nothing could reach that part of me where the grief had taken root.

As the casket rolled down the aisle, I couldn't look away. I thought of the line from the song again: "Because death is just so full, and man so small."

That was it. We were so small. And she was so young.

I bowed my head and whispered: God, please use me. Help me reach the right kids for the right reasons. Help them over their hills. Help them live full, bright lives. Because this pain—this loss—is too much to bear.

In the quiet that followed the funeral, Nate began telling me about a student he had taken an interest in. "Becca, this kid's failing every class," he said. "No backpack. No supplies. Just shows up in his uniform and goes through the motions. I think he's got potential, but he's just been overlooked. No one's checked in to see if he's okay. I'm going to keep him in my office during practice until he brings his grades up."

I nodded. "Sounds like a plan."

I didn't even ask the kid's name—I was too weighed down. I was still adjusting to the pressure cooker of my new job, trying to stay afloat after Rachel's loss, and doing my best to navigate an unfamiliar world: an all-girls Catholic school.

• • •

I was called into the McAuley president's office. She started with, "Some of the girls and a few parents have concerns about your attire. It's making them uncomfortable. Especially when you're addressing the dress code with students."

I blinked. I looked down. I was wearing a tailored dress from White House Black Market. It fell below my knees. It wasn't revealing. My nude stilettos matched the embroidered floral detail. Yes, the dress fit me well—I was in shape, I worked out, I dressed professionally. This wasn't inappropriate.

She continued, "You need to think about whether this place is for you, because if you want to continue working here, you're going to need to get a new wardrobe."

I felt the burn rise behind my eyes—but I held it back.

"Are you offering to pay for my new wardrobe?" I asked, locking eyes with her. "Because I'm not sure what I'm being reprimanded for—dressing professionally, or dressing confidently."

She didn't answer. She tapped her pen.

I kept going. "Are you singling me out because I don't dress like the other assistant principal who's twice my age and wears a button-down blouse and slacks every day? Are we holding the students to the handbook or bending it to avoid making waves with parents?"

I stood up. "I'll leave for the day. But I won't change who I am to make people more comfortable. That's not what leadership looks like."

I walked out, shoulders straight—but inside, I was unraveling.

I went straight to Nate. "What have we gotten ourselves into?"

I was exhausted. Miserable. Disoriented by this new world of tuition, privilege, and the illusion of rules that only applied when convenient. I couldn't understand how a student could challenge authority, break dress code, and still win—because their family wrote a check.

Public education wasn't perfect. But it was fair.

This? This was going to be a long, hard year.

And it was only just beginning.

Week four brought Nate's first loss at La Salle—31 to 24 against Bishop Dwenger, a team out of Fort Wayne, Indiana.

It stung. But we figured it was just one game.

Then we lost again. And again. And again.

Six straight losses.

The cheers faded. The excitement dimmed. The buzz in the stands turned into whispers. By the time we hit the back end of the season, the conversation had shifted from he's going to turn this around to he was too young for this job.

I'd hear things like:

"This program's too big for him."

"He's in over his head."

"They should just cut their losses and move on."

"Why did that first guy back out? Think he'd take it now?"

That last one hit hard.

We found out later the truth—Nate wasn't even the first choice for the job. Another coach had been offered it and turned it down. Nate had been the second call.

Second choice.

Second best.

But you know what? Even knowing that, he still showed up. Every day.

Because that's what real leaders do.

Still, the reality was undeniable: 3–7 wasn't going to cut it in the GCL. Not in a place like La Salle. Not with the hype that surrounded his arrival. This wasn't small-town football anymore. This was the big stage—and it was merciless.

To top it off, my job was coming to an end. I was pulled into a meeting and told the school was hiring a new president, and they were looking for "new leadership." Translation: one year of me was enough.

They wanted someone who would blend in. I never did that well.

So there we were—two careers hanging in the balance. No wins on the field. And a family to support.

But this wasn't the end.

Not for us.

For the first time since Nate had accepted a head coaching job, I stopped trying to plan five steps ahead. I looked around at the mess, at the fear, at the critics, and I made a decision:

One year at a time.

That's how we'd survive.

I'd been through worse. I knew how to weather storms—heck, I'd lived through a hurricane of a childhood, funerals, firings, and everything in between.

No season, no rumor, no job loss was going to break me now. I was made for this.

We were made for this.

We weren't just chasing success—we were building something deeper. And if that meant spending the summer looking for another job, if it meant picking up the pieces again, if it meant Nate pouring himself into one single kid who needed someone to believe in him, then so be it.

—Chapter 10—
To Every Thing
There Is a Season

> "When the winds of change blow,
> remember . . . sometimes what appears
> dead is simply preparing for a new
> season."
>
> ~Jane Lee Logan

Summer is supposed to be a stress-free season-having fun in the heat, going to the water park, and riding the rides at Kings Island. You're not seeking work because you're worried about how you'll make ends meet or whether you'll ever be able to retire. On top of that, if you don't reside close to the school where your spouse is the head coach, you may endure what is known as a widow football coach's wife. Nate would leave early in the morning, often before the kids were up, and would rarely return before they went to bed. I'd go to the gym at 4:45 a.m. and arrive just in time for him to get in his vehicle and pull out to pick up this student on his way into work. This kid was stealing my alone time, and I wasn't happy about it.

Soon after, I began expressing my displeasure to Nate. It was most likely the stress of job interviews. Nate, in my humble opinion, was never under pressure because he excelled at his profession. There were a lot of people looking for employment in school counseling, administration, or teaching, and I needed to have a connection with someone to land a job. I was always the one looking for work. I practiced doing interviews. I worked on my resume and created experience books, but it was never quite enough. I am quite confident in my abilities. I am a competitive person who strives to be the best at whatever I do. So going through interview after interview and rejection after rejection is taxing, especially when your husband is focused on developing a program and assisting a teen you know nothing about.

After an interview, I went straight to watch practice at La Salle. A young man by the name of Thayer Munford was seated with Nate and the other coaches in Nate's office. Thayer was the young man whom Nate left early in the morning to pick up, and had worked with him on academics the year before. He recognized his untapped potential. Because he needed a lot of assistance with his schoolwork, Nate had been there for him throughout the winter. Nate and Thayer did not have a snow day; rather, he was driving through the snow and slush in order to bring Thayer to a Panera or Chipotle so that they could connect to the internet and get caught up on work.

When I stared at his feet, I couldn't help but be shocked; he was sporting the largest pair of shoes I had ever seen. When I saw his feet, I said, "OMG, what size shoe do you wear?" As soon as he heard this, his bright grin spread over the room, and he said, "I think like a 16 or 17." With a giddy expression on my face, I said, "What!?" adding, "I didn't even know they made shoes that big!" I couldn't help but snap a photo! I hastily propped up my size six heels next to his and took a photo. I was about to leave when Nate grabbed my elbow and pulled me to the side. "You can't post that picture," he said, glaring at me. Astonished: "What? Why?" I made more of an inquiry. To put it bluntly: "Because I don't want people thinking he is getting special treatment, and that is that." They walked out of the office, and I just shrugged. Nate was notoriously secretive about his work for others, and his relationship with Thayer was no different. Our family soon embraced Thayer as one of our own. Ashford enjoyed being in his company and would become his little shadow on the sidelines. Eli and Thayer, along with some of the other players, would get into epic Nerf gun fights all summer long when they came over to our house for team bonding meals. The team was really starting to click, and our family was settling into life as a head coach's family in a more high-profile job.

After several interviews, late in the summer, I was hired as the Director of Special Education at St. James School, where I would collaborate closely with Cincinnati Public Schools. A hilarious comment was made to me a few weeks before school started while I was walking down the hall with a teacher and the principal. "You know what I remember about your interview," she stated flatly. "It was something about your yellow nails and sky-high heels. I'm curious if you intend to wear those every day." Without hesitation, I grinned and responded, "Of course!" while winking at her.

Home life was going to look a little different going into the fall. After a year-long procedure and the sorrow of making a decision, as well as having a guardian ad litem, Ashford was granted permission to return home with his mother by the courts. This was a difficult decision for me because Ella and Eli had gotten so attached to him. Plus, I wasn't sure whether Rachel was truly prepared. In the end, it was the correct thing to do because she is his mother, and she was working hard to establish a better life for herself and her three children. We became a family of four again, and I was sure our family was complete.

August came in like a roaring lion, and it was straight to work and reshaping the special education department at my new job. I absolutely loved the teachers I was working with, and I was even able to hire the aides who would be working in the classroom. These co-workers would become my biggest supporters and help me fall back in love with my job.

On our first day of school together, a parent arrived in her van, and she appeared frazzled when she got out. "Please, I need your assistance," she pleaded as she glanced at me. "I got him in the van, but I couldn't dress him." The teachers and aides glanced at me as if to say, Ms. Heels, what are you going to do? I've always admired pupils who present a challenge and those whom others find difficult to work with. This mother was so kind, and you could tell she simply wanted what was best for her son and was prepared to go to any length, so I had to be willing to go to any length as well. I went into the van next to a fourteen-year-old boy who was completely nude and annoyed that I was in there with him. Every eye was on us.

"Well, Matthew, I suppose your mother told me that's your name. Ms. Becca is here, and we're going to put something on and head inside to have some fun." He gave me a sidelong glance, muttered something, and squished himself entirely against the back of the van. We battled together in the back of the van for about 30 minutes before I was able to put on some shorts and stroll into the school, him barefoot and me in my stilettos. I smiled at the aide and mother, who were still waiting. "We're going to be the best of friends! This is going to be a fantastic year," I said with a smirk to Matthew's mother. Chris, one of my aides, simply smiled and shook his head. "Yeah, it'll be interesting." I noticed tears in the mother's eyes as she smiled and thanked me.

Nate, meanwhile, was settling into his second year as head coach and intervention specialist, just across the city. During the summer, the team underwent a transformation. Nate thought they needed to go camping far away from civilization. He planned for the team to be in a remote camp outside of Cincinnati, so they wouldn't have access to phones. The only people at the facility were the players, coaches, and the people who maintained the facilities. One night into their three-night stay, I dropped by, and it looked and felt like something out of the movie *Remember the Titans*. These players were fully committed to Coach Moore's vision for the team. They came back from camp with goal cards and units, and Nate frequently referred to them as "one of the tightest teams in America." The concept of "team above self" also originated here.

The first game of the season was set to be a big one. La Salle would face the powerhouse D1 school, Colerain High School. Colerain and La Salle are located less than four miles from each other. However, there hadn't been a varsity football game played between the two schools since 2004, when La Salle lost 35-7. Colerain went 15-0 that year, winning the state title undisputedly, 50-10, against the Canton McKinley Bulldogs.

The game was set under the lights at 8:30 p.m. at Miami University Yager Stadium as part of the annual Skyline Chili Crosstown Showdown. I showed up with my white shirt proudly marked with an LS and my new stiletto football heels on. Ella struggled to keep up in her little white sundress and pink sandals. She made us stop and smell every red flower around the stadium because she said it meant we would win. The stadium was filling up with fans and students from both schools. I wondered how there could be a game bigger than this that we would ever be a part of. This game was going to set the tone for the season. "Deep breaths, Becca, just breathe," I said quietly under my breath as the kickoff approached.

It took until after midnight for La Salle, led by rushing quarterback Nick Watson and the unstoppable running back Jeremy Larkin, to beat Division 1 powerhouse Colerain 40-21. The GCL school, which some whispered just couldn't compete with others, was now breathing new life into the league. For us, that meant more time without Nate. If you want to win, you have to continue to put in the work, which means long hours not only on the field, but off.

Nate began leaving by 6:15 a.m. I would be coming back from the gym, and it was a quick kiss and goodbye. I would get Eli up and get him ready for either Nate's mom or my mom to show up. I would always kiss and hug Ella before I left. Nate would pick up Thayer most mornings to make sure he got breakfast, had his school work done, and was prepared for the day. I had a lot of conflicting feelings about this because I felt like it was taking up more time in the morning, and Nate had no time for his kids. Nate would look at me and say, "Don't you always tell me someone invested in you and believed in you? This kid may have a chance to break the cycle like you did. Don't you want to give him all the opportunities to do so?" I would hang my head and say, "Yeah, you're right." So the cycle continued in the early mornings, and then most nights the kids would already be in bed when Nate got home. He couldn't watch films or get anything done at home since the kids were so young. They wanted his attention, and he needed to run a program. Being a head coach's wife and being willing to take a back seat to the job takes a lot of humility, understanding, and, most importantly, independence.

So for me, getting up early in the morning and spending time at the gym was important to my sanity. I had to have some goals and dreams to work towards. So, I started setting goals that would test my mental capability. I had already qualified for the Boston Marathon, and now I had my eyes set on a half Ironman and then a full Ironman. If you don't know, a marathon is 26.2 miles, and a half Ironman is a 70.3-mile competition consisting of swimming 1.2 miles, biking 56 miles, and running 13.1 miles under time restraints for each section. A full Ironman is a 140.6-mile competition consisting of swimming 2.4 miles, biking 112 miles, and running 26.2 miles under a time constraint for each section. I figured if I am going to live this life, I had to be so mentally tough that nothing could hurt or be more painful and agonizing than competing and training for an Ironman. I would have to be able to balance up to 20 hours of working out per week while being a coach's wife, mom, and running a household. I mean, really, how hard could it be?

The season rolled on, and the excitement really started to build. La Salle won five in a row and was now ready to face another GCL team, Archbishop Moeller. The game was played at home, and it wasn't even a nail-biter; La Salle won without a hitch, 34-9. The team's confidence was through the roof. Who could beat them?

The following Friday, they faced St. Xavier, and the tension could be felt around the stadium. The "King of the Road" trophy was on the line. Everyone was on the edge of their seats the whole game. La Salle was down 14-0 at the half, and the crowd was not happy. Whispers started in the line for the concession stands. "Oh, they can't beat really good teams; they aren't as good as they thought; here we go; we will lose from here on out." I'm not sure what Nate said at halftime, but they came out looking stronger. Our star players, Jeremy Larkin and Jarell White, teamed up in the backfield and drove the team to tie the game 21-21 with 4:01 left to play.

Do you know what it's like to watch a clock tick down? It is like everything is in slow motion around you, and you can hear nothing except the ticking of the clock. With 44 seconds left and the ball on the two-yard line, the La Salle defense, led by Jordan Thompson at noseguard, had a crucial third-down stop. But St.X's head coach, Steve Secht, is no newbie and knows how to win in tight games. He ran the clock down to 01 and called a timeout. It felt like the air went out of the stadium as they set up for a field goal. As if it were a movie, everyone slowly took their place in line. The ref's whistle blew, and the snap was off. In my peripheral vision, the clock hit zero as the ball floated perfectly through the air directly in the middle of the uprights, and La Salle was dealt their first loss of the season, 24-21.

Not a word was really said after the game. The ride home was silent. What was there to say? We learned that we were beatable. We learned that nothing was a given, and winning can also be a distraction. This moment was either going to make or break this team. I knew this was going to be a defining moment in Nate's career. He came home and said, "You are going to want to hear this." I stopped and looked at him, thinking, *Oh no*. He said, "The team has made a decision. They have decided there will be no more interviews. They are going to go out and play and move on to the next week. They want to be focused and allow no distractions, or the hype of this season to get in." It was at this moment that I knew something that Nate wouldn't ever admit. He was the captain, the general, and the leader, but his leadership style empowered and led by example to create the tightest team in America. Again, he would deny it, but I knew then he was going to be one of the greatest coaches in Ohio. This season, this moment would be his defining moment.

The next game La Salle played St. Charles and won 42-0. Nate decided from then on that he wanted Eli on the sidelines. I was like, "He is in first grade; this couldn't be a good idea." I hadn't let him go anywhere near practice or the game since the day in Minster, when I was riding up to practice where he had gone with Nate, and I saw him walking on top of football equipment seven feet in the air, unsupervised! Before I could even say, "Eli, get down," he fell off. He tried to play it cool, but it turned out he broke his arm. This meant that in his kindergarten picture, he would be smiling a couple of weeks later with a bright orange cast. I was not smiling. But Nate was sure Eli had learned his lesson, because I had never allowed him to go back to practice or be on the sideline since that fall. I never understood why Nate was so anxious to have him with him on the sidelines when Eli wasn't even the slightest bit interested in football.

The next Friday night, in the middle of the game, La Salle was leading by two touchdowns against Winton Woods, and I saw the trainer frantically waving to me. I had just seen Eli running around the sideline and standing by Thayer, and now I didn't see him. I groaned and headed down to the sideline. "Listen, the kids had me check on Eli because he fell while playing around on the sidelines, and I think he is going to need stitches." I looked at him and said, "You've got to be kidding me." He shrugged, and I knew he wasn't. So Eli and I left for Children's Hospital in Mason, and sure enough, he needed stitches. The doctor looked at me and said, "Well, Mrs. Moore, it seems like you are going to be a regular here." I literally wanted to hide. It was the third time in a little over a year that Eli needed to get stitches. I was either going to get a call from children's services or be known as the bad mom.

When we first moved to Mason, for Nate to take the La Salle job, Eli and Ashford were jumping on the bunk beds with the ceiling fan on. All of a sudden, I heard Ashford running down the stairs screaming, "Aunt Becca, Aunt Becca!" Eli was not far behind, with his hand on his head. "Mommie, I think I did something." As he took his hand off his head, he started screaming as he realized blood was all over him and felt it pour down his face. The fan basically scalped him, and he needed a ridiculous amount of stitches. Nate was at practice, so I didn't even call him before I loaded up the kids and got to the emergency room. I was immediately ushered in once the nurse took one look at Eli and yelled, "We got a bleeder!" These are the moments you face alone as a coach's wife. I had to learn to handle emergencies on my own, without panicking or falling apart, because Nate's job always came first. I understood that, and I wanted to win, so I was willing to sacrifice my emotions to win. But Eli was starting to test my patience with his recklessness.

Back on the field, La Salle beat Winton Woods 29-6. The following week, La Salle played Elder in The Pit, where we scored the most points ever to date: 56-35. The Pit cleared out by halftime, and all that was left were a few parents on Elder's side. This was a shock to their system and something they hadn't experienced before. It was quite satisfying to see people filing out in disbelief.

The regular season ended with La Salle going 9-1, and that one loss lit a flame that was growing as each week passed. The boys were focused, and you could see it in their eyes as they took the field on Friday, November 14, against Harrison. La Salle took the lead and never looked back. They won their first playoff game *ever* in the history of the school, 56-24. On the ride home, I looked at Nate and said, "Can you believe it? The first playoff game ever in the history of the school? How is that even possible?" He sat there quietly for a while, as if contemplating his response. Then he said very matter-of-factly, "It's just one game; the only meaning it holds is that we go on to the next week." I knew not to say anything else because he would just find me annoying, and Nate just really doesn't like to talk about football outside of when he is working. So I savored the win and the fact that Nate would be in their record books as the first coach to win a playoff game, and that made me smile as we drove home in the dark of the night.

Next up was the regional championship game against Mount Healthy. They were coached by Arvie Crouch, whom Nate had coached with at Hamilton High School early on in his career. Both were assistants, and both aspired to be head coaches. It was an amazing moment to see two guys take the field with their teams who had been mentored by Coach Jim Place. Now they stood on opposite sides and battled to win and head into the state semi-finals. At the half, La Salle led 24-0 and only allowed Mount Healthy to score a touchdown in the third quarter. When the clock hit zero, La Salle hoisted up their first regional trophy with a 38-6 win. It was their first-ever regional championship win. Nate's only comment on the paper was, "It gives the Lancers a great deal of pride to represent the area." He was always a man of few words. On to the next.

The next week was Thanksgiving, so the schedule was a little crazy since there was no school on Wednesday through Friday. It was miserably cold that week. We had to arrange everything around when we would eat our Thanksgiving dinner. I was busy planning how we were going to get bundled up for Friday. I bought running tights that I thought could keep Eli warm on the sidelines, because I was sure, even with heaters blowing on the field, it was going to be cold. Eli thought they were stupid and didn't want to wear them under his windbreaker-type pants because he thought they were girls running tights. Nate agreed. I was insistent and said I didn't care. He was wearing them because if he got sick, he was the one who was going to miss the next game when we won. I would just get him a babysitter because I wasn't missing the game. He rolled his eyes and put them on, complaining the whole time.

The wind chill was in the teens. We were all huddled together in the stands while Nate, Eli, and the team were on the sidelines waiting for kickoff at the University of Dayton field. I sat there thinking how iconic it would be for Nate to win this game and move on to the state championship. We faced Olentangy, and as they warmed up, they looked pretty confident. Their record was 13-0. They had videographers on the sidelines, filming their moves. One of their players waved at our players as they went through their warm-up rituals, and for the first time, I got nervous. This was going to be a hard fight. Olentangy players were yelling into the camera, "They are not ready, they are not ready."

Olentangy kicked off, and the ball landed in the arms of running back Jeremy Larkin. He returned it for a 98-yard touchdown. It looked like he was just floating on the field; no one could touch him or catch him. Olentangy didn't seem to get discouraged, but our defense, led by Jordan Thompson, wouldn't let them come back and score a touchdown. At the end of the first quarter, they had two field goals, and the score was 7-6.

Halfway through the second quarter, we have more of a lead, and I'm more relaxed. I looked for Eli on the sidelines. Eli was always around Thayer and the other big guys. He loved running under their legs. He was pretty much a nuisance on the sidelines. As I scanned the sidelines, Mommie grabbed me and screamed, "Eli's pants are on fire!" I screamed, "What?" I was horrified and stood up as I looked down and saw Eli's pants were on fire. Was this really happening? He stood too close to the player's heaters and literally caught himself aflame. I was raising Dennis the Menace. Players hit his legs with their varsity jackets to put the flames out. I ran down the stands as the doctors took him to the locker room. A guard stopped me and told me I couldn't go further. I looked up and said, "Listen, I am the head coach's wife, and my son is on fire, and I need to get in there right now!" I didn't even stop; I pushed right by as one of the trainers walked out, shaking his head. "Becca, he's okay. He could have had third-degree burns, but he had some kind of tights underneath his pants," he said very matter-of-factly. I literally started laughing. Both Eli and Nate had given me such a hard time about him wearing the "girls running tights," and they saved him from a trip to the burn unit and scars on his legs for life. "He will sit with me for the rest of the game," I told the trainer to let Nate know, as I took Eli to the stands. We all laughed as we welcomed Eli under the blanket in the stands.

Nate continued to coach the game, clueless to what had happened because there was no way in the world I was interrupting this game. In the end, La Salle won and was headed to its first-ever state championship game with a 48-13 win over Olentangy. I went back and watched the video on YouTube that Olentangy had posted, made by Storied Rivals Sports Media. In his pregame talk, Olentangy head coach Mark Solis said to his team, "Honestly, I think you have a chance to get these guys on the ropes. They haven't been on the ropes. They haven't played a team like us. They don't know." After the game, the same coach told the *Columbus Dispatch*, "Their defensive front, goodness gracious, we knew they would be a storm we'd have to weather, and we didn't, and Larkin, he's got a burst we haven't seen all year." It was interesting to see how the tables turned. I felt a sense of pride as I read a quote from their senior defensive lineman, Dalton Endres, who said, "We put forth the best effort we could and came up short against a great, well-coached team." Nate doesn't care what others say, but I find it a source of pride as a coach's wife that others, including athletes, recognized that coaching played a huge part in players' success.

Going into the state championship week, looking at the weather, I wasn't too sure if I wanted Eli on the sidelines. When I recounted the Eli story, Nate laughed it off and said that I obviously knew how best to dress him. That got an eye roll and a playful shove from me. Nate was insistent that Eli be on the sidelines, and Ella and I would ride the bus to Columbus with the team to attend the state championship game.

We had a police escort out of Cincinnati, and the sendoff had screaming fans and parents lining the parking lot and street. It was a cold and rainy night at Ohio State Stadium. To be honest, I was a little disappointed that we were playing at OSU. The state football games had always been about the road to Massillon, where the state games had been held over the past twenty-some years. However, I wasn't going to complain; this was a moment. How many coaches' wives get to be on a charter bus with a police escort over the course of their husband's coaching career? I thought maybe I would never experience a moment like this again. If we could win, La Salle would have their first-ever state football championship, and Nate would go down in school history as the first ever to win it. I wanted that for him and our family. For the sacrifices we made every day, including snow days when he would brave the streets to go get Thayer so we could make sure he was on top of his academics. There were no days off for Coach Nate Moore, and I knew that was why we were here.

After a team dinner, we got to head into a little holding area. The TVs were showing the current game that was being played on the field. What a pleasure it was for us, as it was our former team, the Minster Wildcats. They were down by nine points with 4:18 remaining in the game. I felt my heart rate go up as I wanted them to win so badly. Some of their players were guys that Nate had coached. Of course, I couldn't help but smile, knowing the Grassy Knoll Dads were out there in their gear. I texted one of the guys I knew was there, Brian, "Brian, how are we looking? Can we pull this off?" The bubbles popped up almost immediately. "Becca, I think we can. Hold tight." I waited as Ella was becoming impatient with being tied to a room, so we were walking the hallways. I heard cheering from the distance and received a text within seconds from Brian: "The score is 42-40 with Minster down, and there is 1:56 left to play. We have to do an onside kick. Pray we recover it." I held my breath while watching Ella run down the hall. Again, I hear the crowd roar, but I had no clue what was going on. Brian texted: "Wildcats recover!" All I could do was think, *Oh my goodness, they are going to win, and then La Salle plays!* What an amazing story it would be if Minster won a state championship and we did too!

Eli Wolf was one of our younger players at Minster and was Brian's nephew. Brian texted me that the Minster quarterback had scrambled on first down and been tackled for a loss of yards. I was becoming frantic for a game I couldn't even see. The quarterback found Eli across the middle, broke free of a tackle to outrun the defense, and scored. It gave Minster the lead 46-42 with just 34 seconds left in the game. I was in tears as I chased Ella down the hall and listened to the crowd roar. The Minster defense held. Minster won its second state championship in school history since 1989. In my mind, Nate helped inspire that win, even though a different coach led them to that championship. But I've learned there has to be a foundation, and I felt Nate turned their program around and laid the foundation for the next coach, who deservingly won the state championship. Brian texted, "We did it! You're next!"

—Chapter 11—
Champions to
Touchdown Town

"Your strength doesn't come from
winning. It comes from struggles and
hardship. Everything that you go
through prepares you for the
next level."

~Germany Kent

An usher (of course, at Ohio State, they are respectfully called Red Coats) led Ella and me up to a private box in the stadium. It was rainy and cold, and Ella had no interest in the game. Someone had donated a box for us to sit in, so I was thankful to turn on some cartoons for her and keep her entertained. La Salle had come in as the underdogs in this game. Nordonia was expected to win. They had the experience and talent to back it up on the field. But I knew something they didn't know. Nate loves being the underdog. It drives him, and that drive spills over to any team he coaches. I have watched him make something out of very little many times. I knew a show was coming.

I looked to my left out the window of the box and saw Nate leading the team down the away team tunnel. Nate's hair was already wet from the rain coming down. He had on black tennis shoes, black pants, and a gray sport shirt with red striped short sleeves. He walked with purpose and looked straight ahead, not giving the cameraman the satisfaction of a good picture. Behind him, standing tall with their classic white uniforms and white helmets that had a red stripe down the middle and LS on the side, his team followed two by two. There were no smiles. Most had black paint under their eyes. The focus was there, and I have no idea what was said pregame, but you could tell they were not to be denied.

Nordonia had future Ohio State and NFL player Denzel Ward on their team, and no team had stopped him all season. The stadium seemed empty, and later, we would learn that there were over 9,570 people in attendance. It did feel like more when I stepped out of the box into the stands to hear the roar of the crowd on kickoff. La Salle won the coin toss, and in true Nate style, he wanted to set the tone, so he chose to receive the ball.

On the kickoff, Kevin Ferguson returned the ball 43 yards, which set up the offense on the Nordonia 47-yard line. First down, Jermey Larkin rushed for 1 yard; second down, Jarell White lost 5 yards; third down, we were third and fourteen. Great, I thought, *I am going to be stressed out with this defense the whole game.* I looked back, and Ella was content watching cartoons on the television in the box and was paying no attention to me or the game. Jarell took the handoff, and we got the first down! We were in the red zone! I felt the excitement burning. We bobbled on first down, and the quarterback, Nick Watson, rushed for 4 yards. On second and goal, Jeremy Larkin punched it in for a touchdown, and the extra point was good. La Salle was up 7-0 with 9:19 left in the first quarter.

Nordonia's offense was up next. All eyes were on their quarterback, David Murray, and one of his favorite targets, Denzel Ward. La Salle's defense came out with a vengeance and kept up with the Nordonia no-huddle, shotgun offense. We forced a punt on fourth-and-eight. "Okay," I said out loud to myself, "They have no response. This is good; we've got this." Our offense took the field, and Nordonia was a little more ready this time for the challenge. Larkin and White got some rushing yards, but not quite enough. Dru Chrisman punted on a fourth-and-two.

La Salle's defense took the field with 5:51 left in the first quarter. Nordonia found a rhythm, and Denzel Ward caught a pass over the middle for 40 yards. "Oh, no, here we go," I said out loud again. "We are about to see why Ward will be playing in this stadium this time next year." I hear a little voice say, "Mommie, who are you talking to?" I smiled and said, "No, one baby, I'm just speaking out loud; do you like sitting up here?" She shook her head yes and went right back to watching the cartoons on the screen. I was thankful I could focus on the game.

Nordonia had a first and goal, but La Salle's defense held them to a field goal. It was 7-3. La Salle answered quickly, and the score was 14-3. Nordonia was on the field again, doing their no-huddle offense, and drove back to the red zone. La Salle's defense held them to a field goal again, and the score was 14-6.

I could see Nate pacing back and forth in the second quarter when La Salle had the ball. I could tell from the way he was carrying himself in the rain that he wanted to take more control of the game than he had. He wanted to leave no doubt that this was the tightest team in America. When you play unselfishly as a team, you cannot be beat. The first four downs seem to come easily between Larkin's, White's, and Watson's rushing. But La Salle was fourth-and-six on Nordonia's 23, with 8:11 left in the second quarter, when Nate sent his field goal team out to set up and then uncharacteristically called a timeout. I never really figured out who actually said this because each coach always says someone different. I do know there was chatter on the sidelines and over the headsets. I was later told that one of the coaches said, "I didn't come here to kick a fucking field goal; I came here to win." With that, the offense came back on the field, and Watson completed a pass to Johnny McNally for a first down. On the next play, our quarterback, Watson, ran it in, and La Salle took a commanding 21-6 lead.

Nordonia took the field, and you could see the determination in their quarterback. He was not going to back down. He wasn't going down without a fight, and he had the guys on his team to fight. On 3rd and 14, Murray sent a screen pass to Ward for 19 yards, but right there on the sideline, hitting him hard as he could as Ward ran out of bounds, was Pierre Hunter. The crowd reacted, "OH!" Hunter stood over Ward, and the yellow flag went flying in the air. Nate said after the game that this penalty was worth it because the rest of the night, Ward played like he didn't want to get hit. I can still, to this day, close my eyes and see that hit and hear the gasp from the crowd.

Denzel Ward was a fourth overall draft pick, a Pro Bowler, and a community-minded individual. He is a shutdown corner for the Cleveland Browns, but at that moment, he was just a high school kid dreaming of winning a state championship, and the La Salle defense was not giving him any opportunity to show what he was capable of. With the fifteen-yard penalty, Nordonia drove the field and scored. It cut La

Salle's lead to 21-13.

La Salle answered back, but the extra point was no good. The score was 27-13. Nordonia got the ball back with 33 seconds left in the half. They went for it on second-and-one. Murray tossed a sideline pass, but it was intercepted by Avery Larkin, who ran it in for a touchdown. The score at halftime was 34-13. Nate ran with his team into the locker room. They were quick to get off the field. There was no sign of overconfidence, like the game was over and we'd won. It was more like, "There is more work to be done."

I was pacing in the box. The marching bands took the field, and usually I enjoyed watching the halftime show, but I was ready for this game to get going again. Soon, warm-ups began, and Nordonia was ready to accept the kickoff to begin the second half. I wondered if Nate regretted not deferring to the second half since he won the coin toss. As I looked down, he was on the sidelines in the middle watching the field with that intense stare, which only he can give.

Nordonia picked up a fourth and two, and it looked like they might gain some momentum coming out after halftime. Jordan Thompson put a stop to third-and-ten; he sacked the quarterback for a loss of 16 yards and forced a punt. As their punter went to punt, he was blocked, and senior John Junker ran it in for a 15-yard touchdown. The crowd went crazy as La Salle took the lead, 41-13. Nordonia took the field again, only to be rushed on third-and-seven, causing a fumble and allowing Junker to recover. La Salle scored and now led 48-13.

The running clock was implemented. It was the first time it had ever happened in a state championship game. A running clock, or mercy rule, happens once a team is in the lead by more than 30 points; a running clock is implemented. Nothing could stop it now. We won the game 55-20. A Red Coat came up to the box to escort Ella and me down to the field for the state championship trophy ceremony.

I had tears in my eyes as I made it to the field. The rain was coming down lightly, and Ella was holding my hand. Eli was somewhere in the pile of boys jumping on top of each other as they hoisted the trophy in the air. My parents and Nate's parents were beaming as they walked across the field. It was as if time stood still and everything was in slow motion. I closed my eyes as I let the raindrops hit my face, and they mixed with the tears of joy. I wanted to savor this moment. No one could comprehend what this meant to me. All the sacrifices I had made as a wife, a mother, and the growth I had experienced as a person.

As the team was being led off to do their media interviews, Nate hugged me, took Ella in his arms, and kissed me on the forehead. "We did it, babe. We really did it," Nate said, smiling and drenched to the bone. I shook my head, not believing he was wearing only short sleeves. Just looking at him made me cold. Thayer gave me a big hug as he headed to the locker room and said, "You better grab Eli; he's running around here like a crazy kid." Thayer beamed that smile as he ran into the locker room to celebrate with his teammates.

Nate and I walked into the media room set up for the players and the head coach. He insisted on taking Ella (who, let me remind you, was three and a half years old) to sit on his lap during the interview. Eli stood beside him, beaming ear to ear. Nate started the interview by chit-chatting with reporters, and Ella listened to him talk, and then mimicked his motions and moved her mouth close to the microphone, not really saying anything. It was so cute that all the reporters in the room sighed together and laughed. Ella put her hands over Nate's face in embarrassment. Nate looked at me and said, "Here, maybe you should take her for this moment." I laughed along with the reporters and then sat back to watch the team.

The first question went to Jordan Thompson, and the reporter asked, "What did Coach do differently this year to get you ready for this?" Jordan answered

Nate and I with the La Salle State Championship trophy after winning the Division II state football title in 2014.

without hesitation, "Umm, I think it began at Camp Higher Ground. I kind of expected, not to be cliché or anything, that it was going to be like *Remember the Titans*. We were going to run through the woods and stuff." All the other players were laughing and shaking their heads, and Nate was just sitting there with a smirk on his face. Jordan continued, "Coach had the idea that he wanted us to be the closest, tightest-knit group in the nation. I felt like we came back, and it wasn't just on the field, it was off the field, and at school, we started hanging out, and the level of care everybody had on the team was just a lot more than in years past."

I listened closely as reporters asked a couple more questions. Nate's answers weren't long, but very pointed. The boys had humble answers when questioned about where they should be ranked. Ranking didn't matter unless they shared everyone's opinions. I looked at Nate and started to think about what this all meant. It was more than just the win, and not just that it was the first for this program. I realized he was so much more to a program than a head coach. He taught young men to take care of each other on and off the field, and he led a program humbly, even in success. Who wouldn't want him to coach their program? Would we be heading to a college program? I mean, Nate was still young, but in just five years, he had turned around two programs that were now both state champions. I knew the phone calls would come; that's how it works. You don't necessarily go looking for a job; they come looking for you. The question was, would I be willing to move again? What if this could be the beginning of the end at La Salle?

As I left the press conference and walked back across the field to the room where they had ushered all the players that weren't being interviewed, I saw the A.D. of La Salle walking towards me, and I couldn't help myself. "Good luck trying to keep him here. They are going to come for him," I half shouted and laughed out loud. He just laughed and said, "We will see!" He kept walking.

We were ushered into a building that had a small stage surrounded by the fans, the student section, and parents. Thayer and his aunt were at a table with our family, and he was getting a sweatshirt made that said state champs. Nate walked in soon after with the captains, and everyone cheered. Nate got on stage, said a little something, and shouted, "Thank God you're a Lancer!" and the crowd erupted. One by one, Nate called each player up by name and hung a medal over their neck. After the last player got his medal, we cheered and passed the trophy around and took pictures with the players. One of my favorite pictures to this day is with quarterback Nick Watson on his knees with Eli and Ella surrounding him, smiling so big, and, of course, Eli's sporting his jersey with the #28 - Jeremy Larkin. I would put some of the pictures from that day on our Christmas card.

We rode the bus home almost empty as players left with family and friends to celebrate. It was well past midnight when Nate carried the trophy into our house in Mason. His Grandpa (Pop, as our kids called him) was in the local nursing home, and Nate wanted to be sure that Pop saw it. They got a picture together. His grandpa was able to come in a wheelchair to a few games, and he may have been Nate's biggest fan. The next morning, we went to see Grandpa Plummer, and he couldn't stop beaming. It was quite a touching moment.

• • •

Christmas came, and we celebrated with family and friends. In January, Nate was busy keeping the team focused on the next year. We had Martin Luther King Day off that Monday. Nate, the kids, and I went to his parents' house for lunch. Nate's phone rang, he looked, and whispered, "I'm going to take it upstairs, it's a coach." I just nodded because this was normal. When he came down the stairs, he was bewildered. "You are not going to believe this," he said with a little surprise in his voice. "That was Lee Owens, and he wanted to know if I would be interested in the Massillon head coaching job."

I couldn't believe what I was hearing, and I think Nate was in disbelief, also. Massillon was the job any coach would want. If you know anything about high school football in Ohio, you know about Massillon. It has a storied program that is filled with some of the greatest coaches of all time. The most well-known and winningest coach in the history of Massillon was Paul Brown. He went on to coach at Ohio State, and created the Cleveland Browns and Nate's favorite team, the Cincinnati Bengals. Other famous head coaches for Massillon include Chuck Mathers, Lee Tressel, Earl Bruce, and Bob Cummings. To even think Massillon would mention Nate Moore's name took your breath away.

Nate's dad, of course, immediately said, "Well, tell us." We all stood there, waiting. Nate just began very matter-of-factly, "Well, Lee Owens used to coach for Massillon and now is the head coach of Ashland

University. It seems like Massillon fired their head coach, offered the job to someone, and that person backed out. Lee wants to suggest me for the job."

I just stood there with a lot of thoughts flooding through my head. Was I willing to just pick up and move to another town? I had things going on. I had made a commitment to Hannah that we would complete an Ironman race together. Nate and I were close to both our families and had amazing support. Eli was settled in at grade school. Ella loved going to preschool and hanging with Pop at Bob Evans once or twice a week. Would I be willing to pack up where I was comfortable just so Nate could work on rebuilding another program? Was I willing to be away from our family support system and my best friend? My parents were definitely getting older, and I was their only child.

Nate interrupted my thoughts, saying, "I don't know if I can leave my guys. I don't know if I can leave Thayer. I feel like he needs me and has a chance to make it, and I'm not sure if others will understand all the support he needs outside the classroom. And what would you do about a job next year?" I just shrugged my shoulders. I loved my job, but being in a private school doesn't contribute to the state teacher's retirement. We were still paying on student loans, so I had been thinking that I would like to get back into public education.

"You can't not go and at least listen to what they have to say and see if it is something maybe you are interested in," I said in my most supportive voice, although I knew I would be the one giving up the most. Nate shook his head as if in agreement, "I don't want this plastered all over the media. I want to do this quietly, so if it doesn't work out, I can keep operating as normal." I agreed and asked, "So when do they want you to come?" Nate looked at me and said, "Immediately, this weekend." Wow, this was going to be a whirlwind.

The anticipation of the next few days set in. Nate and I headed to Massillon for the weekend. My Uncle Phil and Aunt Julie lived in Norton, about twenty-five minutes north of Massillon, so we opted to stay with them and let them show us around. We tried to keep a low profile in town. But when you are pushing 6'5 like Nate, you tend to stick out like a sore thumb.

To Nate, this became a no-brainer. He loved a challenge, and Massillon was going to be a challenge. Expectations were going to be high, and so was the pressure. Nate made a few calls to other coaches inquiring about the job. Everyone told him *not* to take it. There were too many issues and unknown strings that came attached to a job like Massillon. He was told that if he couldn't win there, it might end his career. That kind of talk only made Nate want it more. He figured if he could go to Massillon and win a state championship, that would solidify that he was meant to be a head coach.

After a weekend of intense interviews that lasted four to five hours each day, Nate was offered the job. There would be a job for me with the school in the fall. Nate and the committee agreed that it wouldn't be announced to the media until he had a chance to tell La Salle and his team that he was leaving. That didn't happen. It got leaked to the media before Monday morning, and when Nate got to work, things changed rapidly. The principal at La Salle would not let him address the team and decided to have Nate report each morning to his office away from everyone. If Nate saw Thayer in the hallway, Thayer would walk the other way. That one hurt Nate the most because Thayer was the reason Nate hesitated leaving La Salle. He wanted to stay to give that kid a chance, and worried he was letting Thayer down. The way this was handled let everyone down. It still amazes me how it all played out. In the business world, people switch jobs and put in their two-week notice, and it isn't a big deal. But in the high school coaching world, sometimes it feels like it is treated like a betrayal, instead of a thank you for what you've done. I will never really understand this.

Nate was let out of his contract with La Salle a few weeks later and headed to Massillon to begin rebuilding the program. I stayed with the kids in Mason and finished out my school year at my job. I kept Eli and Ella with me, so they could finish the school year out where they were comfortable. Thayer would still meet with me and the kids every other week to stay on top of his school work, but never really asked about Nate.

I didn't have any feelings this time about the distance because I understood the process. Nate and I were a team. Yes, this time we spent six months apart before we were living together as a family again. But this was our life. It was our path. Almost immediately, I knew we may have taken on a bigger task than we bargained for. For Massillon, the City of Champions, expected change, and a championship NOW, not in the distant future. And Nate's plan succeeds when you buy into trusting the process, and that takes time. The question was whether the clock would run out before it took hold.

Part 3

Becoming the Light

—Chapter 12—
Welcome to Massillon

"True love is selfless. It is prepared to sacrifice."

~Sadhu Vaswani

Massillon year one was rough on the field. We went 4-6 and lost to McKinley in the final game of the season, which is a big no-no. There is no bigger rivalry in high school football than the Massillon-McKinley game. Both towns expected to win, and Nate didn't. Meanwhile, La Salle had a shot at winning a back-to-back State Championship. They played Massillon's next-door neighbor, the Perry Panthers. Massillon also seemed to have a rivalry with Perry. (*Did Massillon have a rivalry against every school?*) I had much to learn. One might say I was a little naive about how much football mattered in this town of around 20,000 people. Possibly, I didn't think everything through when I posted on social media that I would be supporting La Salle in the State Championship by wearing red and encouraging others to join me. I basically went viral in Stark County. People said I should be fired. How could I root against Stark County kids? It got so bad that even the editor of the local paper wrote an opinion piece titled "Is Becca Moore the worst coach's wife in Stark County history?" I endured a social media blast of posts and tweets. Here are a few that I kept, bad grammar and all:

119

Jake Barth @barthjake   1m
This is honestly super trashy and
unprofessional. Can't believe you
wouldn't root for a school so close to
you.

Andrea
@apipero1

I thought it was a kid saying this not the
Massillon coach's wife, wow. Sad, I live
in Massillon.

@beccamoorecw So..Mrs. Moore...lets talk
football. Let's talk about how stark county has
welcomed you and your husband to our football
community with open arms. Let's talk about how
not many people were ok with the way the
Massillon Football team was ran this year but
gave your husband the benefit of the doubt
because we all know that change takes time to
happen and no one is downing him for his losing
football season. Now let's talk about how
ignorant and bitter you sound by your immature
and disrespectful attitude toward your
neighboring football team. I don't know how
things are done in Cincinnati but here, in Stark
County, we support our community and all the
teams in it!
#maybeyoushouldgobacktowhereyoucamefrom
#coachmooregetyourwifeundercontrol

Kandice Birchfield
@Kandicelynn

@beccamoorecw I highly suggest you
watch what you say about Perry Ms.
Moore

Paige Miller @pmillaaa14   39s
You're a disgrace to the Massillon
community @beccamoorecw

Micheal Douglass
Becca is the "queen" of Massillon football?
I've seen bags of trash with better looks AND
more class! Yes I went there! She's a Barbie
wannabe that widely missed the target!
31 minutes ago · Like · Reply

Tim Cooper @Tcooper923   22s
Shout out @beccamoorecw for being the
most hated woman in Massillon.

⌐illie
@_mariomillin

Aw I'm offended by your trashy ass

Breezy ⚕
@_brycewilliams

You're fuccing dumb , shut up

Lisa Berarducci
@laberarducci

@beccamoorecw how can you cheer
on the team Perry is playing Perry is
local LaSelle is not. This is very dam
rude
11/28/15, 3:33 PM

samantha warwick @samanthawarwi...⏰ 5m
@beccamoorecw jealous much? Your
words show no class!! I hope you have to
eat your words! These are kids you are
speaking about. Go Perry!!

chip belanga @PastorChip1   4m
@beccamoorecw you should be
ashamed of yourself. This is the worst
sportsmanship I have ever seen from
someone working for high school.

Dave Lapp tagged you in a **post**.
8 hrs · ⚖

I don't know about you, but I would love for Massillon
to kick this skank to the curb, I mean several points
have been made, one- we in Stark county cheer on all
stark county teams, football belongs to stark county!
Two- cheering on your former team and school is
acceptable, trying to belittle another school is not!
#nobullnation #meanstinks as referred in Becca
Moore 'S page!!! Three- winning championships is
alot tougher when you can't recruit your players!!!!
Four- asking the TIGERS nation to wear red, is like
asking the dentist to pull out your good teeth!!! So I
guess what I'm saying is this lady has noooooo clue
about stark county football, or the Massillon/ McKinley
rivalry, I guess that explains why Massillon wasn't
coached up for THE GAME!! Don't worry folks, I doubt
she or her husband will be around much longer,
Massillon doesn't pull crap like this lady, oh and
there's an expectation of winning as well, not to
mention Massillon boosters, won't want to have to
keep cleaning up after this chic!!!!

The superintendent at the time called me in. "So what do you think, should you take the post down and apologize?" He asked calmly and coolly. I answered without hesitation, "No, I'm not giving in to what people think I should be or say. I am going to cheer for La Salle. Eli still has kids there that he thinks highly of. So no, I am just going to let it blow over." He smirked, "Pretty much what I thought you would say. Okay, good luck."

Nate, Eli, Ella, and I attended the game with two of our current players at Massillon. We sat on the La Salle side, and I cheered for Thayer and the other players that Nate had coached the year before. La Salle won, and Perry didn't even stay on the field to watch La Salle get their trophy. I was thankful that Nate always tried to model the idea that when you lose, you must respect your opponent and stay through the ceremony, even when it hurts. As we left the stadium, Perry fans booed and yelled slanderous words at us. Nate had to pick up Ella and get us to the car quickly. I learned I was really going to have to grow a stronger backbone if I was going to survive at this place.

In January, Thayer's mom, MeLisa Thompson, reached out to me. Thayer's grades had fallen, and he was on the verge of being kicked out of La Salle, and she was worried about what that would mean for his chances of getting offered college scholarships. I asked her to send me his grades and his current IEP (Individualized Education Plan) so I could see if they were providing him with what he needed to be successful. His grades weren't good at all, and he was starting to miss a lot of school. Thayer had college offers, but I knew those offers meant nothing with those grades. Everyone thinks that when you get an offer, it is yours for whenever you want to commit, but that isn't true. Other kids get offers, and if they commit before you, those offers are gone. If your grades don't match what is required, those offers mean nothing. Of course, most people don't see or know that. They just look at this kid with all the offers, thinking he is going places. I knew Thayer was in jeopardy of going nowhere. His sweet mom needed help, but just didn't know where to start or what to do. Nate had been his accountability partner and the one who kept him on top of his schoolwork. It seemed others had tried to help, but just didn't have the accountability piece. Nate and Thayer were close, and Thayer looked at Nate as a father figure, so with him being so far away, Thayer's struggle became more visible to his mom.

I calculated Thayer's grades. If he didn't get a certain grade in each class at the end of his junior year and take at least two college classes that summer, there was no way he was going to be eligible to accept a scholarship. His mom called me again in February as we went over grades and different scenarios he could consider. She sighed, "Becca, I don't know where to begin to get Thayer a tutor, or why he goes places to study and things don't get done. Could you and Nate just take him?" I paused. *What? Did she just ask us to take Thayer? I think I've been in this scene before with Ashford.* This mother was willing to sacrifice her time with her son for love so he could have a chance at a better life.

I paused because I wanted her to know I was genuine, "Whatever it takes, we will help him. He deserves a chance." I hung up the phone and called Nate into our bedroom. I patted the bed and had him come sit by me. "Listen, Thayer's in jeopardy of not getting out of Lincoln Heights, and his grades are so bad he may get kicked out of La Salle. His mom wants us to take him. She feels like it's his only hope," I said quietly while he gazed past me and to the blank off-white wall of the bedroom condo we were living in. Nate said, "What did you say to her?" I looked at him and said, "I told her yes." Nate was silent. I knew his mind was playing out different scenarios of how this could go. It was going to be a battle, but he didn't hesitate when he spoke. "Then find out what the next steps are, and what we need to do to make this happen," he said without a breath or pause for concern. He continued, "But Becca, this is going to cause issues probably with OHSAA. This is going to be a story, and it could cost us our jobs. So he will come for grades, but he won't play football. I will figure out a way to explain it to him and the college coaches."

I didn't have to be told twice. The next day, I was on the phone looking for a lawyer in Cincinnati. This was going to be a process, and according to the lawyer, the outcome was going to be up to the judge. It was highly unlikely that they would let a kid leave his mother to go live with a "white" family. We couldn't just take guardianship of Thayer. We were going to have to take custody of or adopt him, and his mom would have to be willing to relinquish all her rights. We were going to have to convince the judge that Thayer's life was in greater danger staying with his mom, and the only way for him to succeed was for us to take him. We all agreed custody was the best option because adoption would take too long, and we were already running out of time.

We also agreed that both Thayer and MeLisa Thompson would

sign a waiver form from our lawyer in Stark County. We agreed that they acknowledged that they have been provided with a full disclosure of Thayer's ineligibility to participate in football, or any other sport in which he participated during the twelve months immediately preceding his transfer to Massillon.

In March, our lawyer explained the situation to us. He wrote to us the following: "In moving forward with this matter, the safest option in terms of limiting repercussions for you and the school is for Thayer to not attempt to be deemed eligible to play football, or any sport, at Massillon. It is my assessment that representatives/coaches from La Salle will likely report Thayer's move to OHSAA, and allege that a recruiting violation has occurred, even if Thayer never attempts to be deemed eligible to play sports at Massillon. As a final note, this situation, particularly the transfer of guardianship of Thayer to you, may generate a substantial amount of interest from the press, with both positive and negative stories/comments resulting from the same. You and the school should be prepared for this, and in the event you need our assistance with the same, please let us know."

We filed on March 29 and began the paperwork to petition for custody as a non-parent for Thayer, with no guarantee in Cincinnati. There was a long questionnaire to fill out from the Hamilton County Juvenile Court. The main question to focus on was question number ten: It would be in the best interest of the child or children for the petitioner(s) to have custody for the following reasons:

1. **Academics** - Academics are his mother's primary concern. Due to a disability, it has been hard for her. Thayer currently has a 1.8 GPA, which puts his collegiate scholarships in major jeopardy. He needs at least a 2.0 and a 22 on the ACT to be eligible to accept a scholarship. Mother feels that Thayer would have the opportunity to excel and reach his full potential if Mr. and Mrs. Moore took custody. This could happen because of their backgrounds in education, and given the fact that he would be enrolled at their place of work, where they could oversee his education, and tutors would be put in place.

2. **IEP (Individualized Education Plan)** - Mother has fought for years with the school of residency (Princeton Local Schools) to have Thayer tested. After enrolling him at La Salle and meeting with Mr. Moore (who was a special education teacher), Mr.

Moore recognized there was a struggle and had the process for Thayer to be tested. Upon being tested, Thayer qualified for an IEP based on his ETR (Evaluation Team Report), which showed he struggled with comprehension, reading, and writing. By the end of the third quarter of his junior year, Thayer had a 1.8 GPA, and after several meetings, Mother felt that, with his current grade point average, his IEP academic goals were not being met. Mother felt La Salle was not supporting Thayer and put more of the blame on him for underachieving, instead of focusing on his disability, and how they can modify and accommodate the curriculum in order for Thayer to be successful, not only in high school, but in higher education. Mr. Moore is a former special education teacher, and Mrs. Moore is a special education coordinator at the school district Thayer would attend. This would allow them to regulate and enforce Thayer's education, while he's at school and after school hours. Thayer's mother called and talked to the Moores about this, visited the school where Thayer would attend, and agreed that it would be in the best interest of Thayer and his future if his education and IEP were under the Moores.

3. **Relationship with Thayer** - The relationship between Thayer and the Moore family has been long-standing, deeply rooted in mentorship, trust, and genuine care. From Thayer's freshman year, Mr. Moore recognized his potential—not only as an athlete, but as a young man capable of achieving great things. Observing that Thayer possessed the physical ability to earn collegiate scholarships but struggled academically, Mr. Moore began tutoring him, monitoring his grades, and providing consistent academic and personal support. Mr. Moore went beyond the role of a coach or mentor. He ensured Thayer had essential school and personal items—purchasing supplies such as a backpack, notebooks, deodorant, soap, and even teaching him how to shave. When Thayer's transportation was unreliable, Mr. Moore personally drove him to and from school. Every Sunday, the two met to work on school assignments, and during snow days, Mr. Moore picked Thayer up to make sure his academic progress continued. Over time, Thayer became like a son to Mr. Moore. Mrs. Moore also played an active and caring role in Thayer's life. She and their children often encouraged Thayer by celebrating

his accomplishments—taking him out for meals at Chipotle, after strong test performances, and ensuring he stayed motivated. She personally transported Thayer to an Ohio State University football camp and maintained contact with him after the family's relocation, checking on his grades, offering encouragement, and attending his games. The Moore family's involvement extended beyond academics and athletics. They joined Thayer and his aunt for Family Sunday at church, attended regional and state football championship games to support him, and even included his aunt in those events. When Mr. Moore's grandfather passed away in March 2016, Thayer attended the funeral with his aunt and spent time afterward with the Moore family, reflecting the close bond they share. Additionally, Mr. Moore's parents, Jerry and Debbie Moore—whom Thayer affectionately calls "Grandma and Grandpa"—have also played a supportive role in his life, providing transportation to football camps and clothing when needed. The Moore family has taken Thayer shopping at his favorite store, Citi Trends, and continually demonstrates unconditional love and commitment to his well-being. It is the sincere belief of Mr. and Mrs. Moore that Thayer is not just a player or student—they view him as part of their family. They remain dedicated to providing him with the stability, guidance, and opportunities necessary to help him reach his full potential and one day give back to his community.

4. **Safety** - Thayer's current living situation in Lincoln Heights presents significant safety concerns. Within the past year, he was directly confronted by an individual armed with a gun who threatened him, warning that if he continued wearing La Salle clothing, he could be shot, or that the individual might "show up at his house." This was not an isolated incident. In recent months, two additional shootings have occurred in the same area—one involving a friend of the family. These events have created an ongoing atmosphere of fear and instability that no child should have to endure. Thayer is a young man with strong aspirations—he dreams of attending college, earning his degree, and one day moving his mother out of Lincoln Heights to ensure her safety and stability as well. Granting custody would provide him the security and supportive environment necessary to pursue these

goals without the constant threat of violence.

We officially filed all the paperwork on April 6, 2016. Thayer moved to Massillon, and we set into motion a rigorous diet so he could get down to 315 pounds for the summer Ohio State Friday Night Lights Football Camp. We got him registered for summer classes at Stark State, and worked on homework and studied every night. On May 31, 2016, the Magistrate decided that Thayer Munford would be placed in the legal custody of Nathaniel Moore and Rebecca Moore based on the testimony of all parties. The gavel was hit, and we walked out as a family of five.

Nate had contacted the OHSAA and let them know that we were taking custody of Thayer. The OHSAA is the governing board for Ohio High School Athletics, and they certainly have a reputation for not being sympathetic, especially to Massillon, which I didn't really understand at that point . . . yet.

The OHSAA opened an investigation into recruiting violations, even though we did not petition for Thayer to play football. A letter arrived at Massillon Washington High School on August 11, 2016, and the next day it hit the paper in big, bold headlines, along with pictures: "OHSAA Rules Munford Can't Play For Massillon."

The truth is this. We had decided with Thayer and MeLisa that he wasn't moving to Massillon to play football, because he already had enough film with two state championships. Colleges were already interested in him. It was decided that Thayer would do the workouts and be on the practice squad, but the main goals were his weight and academic eligibility for college scholarships. What no one, who wasn't in our circle, really understood was that Thayer was not even eligible to take any of the offers he had, and quite frankly, schools were starting to back out because they didn't think there was any way possible for him to be academically eligible. Yet, Nate and I believed, and we were ready to pour everything into him, so he could at least have a shot.

The letter had four pages dedicated to their investigations and findings on Thayer Munford. They started with the Football Contact: "If a Coach leaves a school to pursue a coaching opportunity at another school, the coach should refrain from any communication with any students at his or her former school. Further, as it relates to any student who might transfer to or enroll at the school where the coach is now approved as a member of the coaching staff, said transfer or enrollment shall create a rebuttable assumption of recruiting and render the student ineligible for one year from the date of enrollment.

Coach Nate Moore accepted the head football coaching position at Washington High School in the spring of 2015. It is our position that he did not adhere to the restriction found in bylaw 4-9-4 number 8. One cannot circumvent this prohibition by having one spouse doing the communication for him/her. It is indisputable that Coach Moore's wife continues communicating on a regular basis with Thayer and his family. Social media postings evidence the fact that Mrs. Moore attended Thayer's 2015 football playoff games played on neutral sites in various parts of Ohio, sitting with their family and posing for photos following the game."

Just to be honest, that photo was my profile picture for a while. I couldn't believe I was singled out in the complaint! Why couldn't I go to Thayer's games? And it is amazing to me to read that they put in writing that no player should be able to follow a coach to a new school. I wonder if they looked at any recent coaches who might have moved from a private school to a public school in 2025, and maybe a quarterback came with that new coach? Does anyone see any lawsuits about that? Me neither.

The letter went into detail about how I had transported Thayer to OSU football summer camp and to Pittsburgh Junior Day because Thayer had no ride to either event. The letter said, "Please be advised that the La Salle coaching staff and administration have vehemently denied that those statements are true." The OHSAA office went on to say they had received reliable and probative evidence that Thayer approached the head football coach at La Salle High School and was told that he would arrange a ride for him, but Thayer never stopped by to set up those dates.

The letter continued, "It is the collective opinion of many within the La Salle School Community Coach Moore's statements seem to suggest that the individuals at La Salle High School did not care about Thayer and his future. In fact, many in the La Salle Community went out of their way to assist Thayer and his family with transportation, food, gear, guidance, and academic assistance. We can find no evidence that suggests otherwise."

The next part of the letter, about scholastic performance, had me baffled. "The claim that the educational system at La Salle was 'utterly failing to support' Thayer is not sustainable. Thayer had never been identified as a child with a disability before his enrollment at La Salle High School in 2013. The intervention team at La Salle actually referred Thayer for a special education evaluation due to his lack of progress in the general education curriculum during his freshman year. This referral is noted on pages 16 through 20 of his ETR, and he qualified for services on April 17th, 2014, towards the end of his freshman year."

At this point, I was ready to scream and just lose it. Thayer's mom had tried for years to have him tested, but because he was a sweet kid, that didn't cause problems; he was just passed on. Nate realized as he began working with Thayer that there was a disconnect, and he, being a special education teacher at La Salle, had referred him.

The letter went into more details of the IEP meetings held, and that his mom attended the meetings, and only one time, of course, when Nate was providing his services in his first IEP, was there a signed modification form. Summarizing that Thayer was assigned to study table 6:45-7:35 am from October 2015 - March of 2016, and only attended five of these days. Teachers described that his performance was impeded by a lack of preparation, inconsistent effort, and absence from school. So they rejected the assertion that Thayer's failure to meet the educational objectives was by failure of La Salle High School.

"Although we certainly understand Coach Nate Moore's desire to become a role model and friend to a student who is in difficult circumstances. Such a desire should never result in influencing the student to change schools. Coach Moore did indeed exercise considerable influence over Thayer, the most significant of which involved taking legal custody of Thayer, which clearly promoted his transfer from La Salle High School to Massillon Washington High School."

By now, my blood is totally boiling, and I could have blown the roof off our condo, where we were living, like a Tom and Jerry cartoon. First off, Nate and I were not trying to be his friend. We were trying to save his life. We didn't exercise any influence over Thayer. His mom called us and asked us to save him. What would you do if someone called and asked you to save their only child? Did they think that we influenced a judge to take custody? We had to pay two different lawyers, go to court, and have a magistrate make a decision based on the circumstances. I was literally heartbroken. Basically, OHSAA was saying that we should have just walked away as a coach from a child in need. In all my years, this went against everything I was taught and how I was raised. I was ready to go to war at this point. Especially once I read the OHSAA ruling and penalties that would be applied.

1. Thayer Munford is ineligible for the remainder of the 2016-2017 School Year.
2. Coach Nate Moore is denied the opportunity to coach in the 2016 OHSAA football tournament should Washington High School qualify.
3. Massillon Washington High School is fined $5,000 payable to the OHSAA no later than October 1, 2016 ℅ Todd Boehm, Comptroller.
4. Washington High School is placed on probation for three years through the end of the 2018-2019 school year. This means that any additional violations of the recruiting bylaw shall place the school's membership in the OHSAA in jeopardy.

I looked at Nate, "I don't care what it takes, I will not let them smear our name or what we stand for." Nate just sighed. Within his first year of being the head coach, I had not shied away from controversy. I had caused a social media storm during the state finals, and now, this was probably going to make national headlines. I didn't care. I always followed my heart and did what I believed was best for the students. I didn't care what adults said or what people thought. If I had a chance to help someone have a better life, then come for me, but you better be ready for a fight because I am not going down without a fight, ever.

We were going to need the best in the business—because this wasn't just a case. This was going to be a war. And Thayer was worth every ounce of the fight.

—Chapter 13—
A Tiger Needs a Lion

"Until the lion tells his side of the story,
the tale of the hunt will always glorify
the hunter."

~Zimbabwean Proverb

When a Tiger needs a lion, they call in a lawyer who is known as the lion. Leondias (Lee) E. Plakas of Plakas & Mannos Law Firm wasn't just known around Canton—he was feared; they called him the lion. His reputation echoed through courthouse halls, whispered by those who had watched him dismantle witnesses and sway juries with a single raised brow. And now, he was about to take our case.

The morning of our first meeting, the three of us—Nate, Thayer, and I—walked into the firm's downtown office. Everything about the building breathed quiet confidence: the heavy glass doors, the faint scent of polished wood, and the air of power. We were led into a conference room with a long mahogany table that seemed to stretch on forever. The lights were low, golden and moody, like a scene from *The Godfather*.

I glanced at Thayer, who sat straight-backed but still, hands folded in his lap. Nate looked ahead, jaw set, unreadable. Then the door opened.

Lee entered without a word.

He was followed by a younger attorney—Brandon Trent—and an assistant carrying a leather-bound file. Lee took his seat at the head of the table and, without introduction, began arranging his pens. Perfectly aligned, stacked, symmetrical. It was a small gesture, but something about it felt deliberate, like a ritual. A sign of the control this man demanded—from himself and everyone around him.

The room fell silent.

Then, finally, he looked up. His eyes were sharp, assessing, like a predator measuring the distance between himself and his prey.

"Tell me," he said, voice smooth but commanding. "Why are we here?"

A chill slid down my spine. I glanced at Brandon, who offered me a quiet, reassuring smile—like he'd seen this scene play out a hundred times before.

Nate spoke first, calm and steady. Thayer's gaze never left the table.

As Lee began to jot down notes—methodical, precise—I realized something. This was no ordinary lawyer. This was a strategy, wrapped in skin.

The battle hadn't even begun, and already, it felt like the first move had been made. He was a master chess player and knew how to use the pieces he had on the board.

Plakas knew time was of the essence. He didn't hesitate. After our conversations, he decided to take the case. He said he believed us—that our motives were genuine, that we had nothing to gain and everything to lose. And when it came to Leonidas (Lee) E. Plakas, one thing was certain: he didn't lose.

The first step in the fight came quickly. On September 8th, we appeared before the OHSAA Appeals Panel in Columbus, Ohio. This was where the decision-makers would decide if we even had a chance to tell our side.

The panel, made up of former educators from Ohio schools, was supposed to represent fairness and experience. But as I drove, by myself, the two hours from Massillon, my stomach told me otherwise. Nate had practice. Thayer wasn't required to attend. So it was just me—and the weight of what this meant. Football widow, again.

MeLisa drove up from Cincinnati, slower than usual because her back had been giving her trouble. But she wouldn't have missed it. Not for Thayer. Not for this.

When we arrived, Plakas, his assistant, and Brandon Trent were already waiting outside the OHSAA office—all business, calm, and prepared. The building itself felt sterile, bureaucratic, like it was designed to drain the emotion out of anyone who walked in. I shivered and thought, *This is uninviting; they don't really care about kids.* But immediately, I pushed that thought away.

We were led into a large room, cold and lit by fluorescent lights. Long tables were arranged in a U-shape. The center table was the committee. We were set up across from them, but both sides of the room had OHSAA staff with laptops that were typing away with the sounds of keys clattering—heads down, eyes fixed on their screens—as the lawyers talked. They barely looked up when we entered, as if we were an interruption in their afternoon routine rather than a family fighting for a child's future.

A smaller table was brought out for us. Plakas and Trent immediately began laying out folders, notes, and exhibits with quiet precision—a calming of order in the middle of chaos. MeLisa sat to the left, I took the seat beside her, then Brandon, and finally Lee at the far end, closest to the panel.

I looked across at the men behind the nameplates. Every one of them was old, white, polished—the kind of men who'd likely retired from districts with perfect lawns and tidy hallways. Not one of them, I imagined, had ever sat across from a student who had to choose between football practice and a part-time job to support their family, or who carried more burdens at fifteen than most adults did at fifty.

My chest tightened. How were they supposed to understand this story—*our* story?

MeLisa shifted beside me, gripping her cane between her knees. Her face told the truth; her voice didn't need to. Every step she'd taken to get here had cost her something, and yet, she was here—determined, tired, but unbroken.

Lee glanced at her, then at me. His eyes were calm, unreadable. Then he leaned slightly forward, clicked the pen in his hand once, and whispered just loud enough for us to hear:

"Let's begin."

The sound echoed through the room like the starting bell of a fight we hadn't yet realized was about to change everything.

Plakas wasted no time painting the picture for the panel. His voice was steady, measured—the kind that made you want to lean in and listen. He began with the agonizing decision MeLisa had made, the kind that rips a piece of a mother's soul away. How she had relinquished all her parental rights so the Moores could take custody of Thayer—not for convenience or gain, but for love.

He spoke of the courtroom that had granted it, of the magistrate who had recognized the depth of her sacrifice. Then he moved to Thayer—how he'd changed. The weight he had lost, the discipline he'd found, the light in his eyes, when he talked about football. He was finally on track—not just for eligibility, but for opportunity. A chance to earn a college scholarship, to rewrite the story of where he came from. To move his mother out of Lincoln Heights.

As Plakas spoke, the committee members shifted in their seats, shuffling papers, tapping keys. Every now and then, they'd glance up from their laptops and peer at MeLisa and me over the tops of their reading glasses—glasses that hung on their noses like ornaments, not instruments of understanding.

When he finished, the room went still for a moment before the chairman cleared his throat and called on the athletic director from La Salle—Dan Flynn—to speak.

Flynn stood, tugging nervously at the hem of his red shirt with La Salle printed boldly across the top of his left chest. His neck flushed a deep red, blotches spreading up his jaw. He stumbled through his words, trying to find a balance between duty and discomfort. I couldn't bring myself to turn around and look at him, not while my stomach twisted with a mix of anger and disbelief. I only caught fragments of what he said—something about respect for Nate and me, something about meaning well.

When he finally sat down, I heard him mutter under his breath, almost to himself, "I'm going to need a beer after this." His voice hung awkwardly in the air, a strange attempt to break the tension, though no one laughed.

Then came *the* question.

One of the committee members, an indistinguishable older man with thinning gray hair, leaned forward and peered over his glasses, eyes narrowing on Plakas. "So, Mr. Plakas," he said, "It seems as if . . . getting custody of Thayer could maybe be compared to buying a house or a boat?"

Did he just compare a child to a piece of property? I was in shock. The typing stopped. Every keyboard went silent. A woman sitting to the right of the panel lowered her head, visibly ashamed.

MeLisa's shoulders dropped. She bowed her head, gripping her cane tighter, and began gently tapping it on the floor—a soft rhythm of pain, anger, and restraint.

My blood boiled. The room blurred. Before I even realized it, my body was rising out of my seat. No one—*no one*—was going to reduce what she'd done, what we'd all fought for, to a *transaction*.

I was halfway up on my feet when I felt a hand on my leg.

Brandon Trent.

He looked at me—calm, steady, his eyes saying *not now*. I froze, caught between fury and the quiet strength in his gaze. Slowly, I sat back down. I reached for MeLisa's hand, squeezed it hard, and whispered, "We'll get through this."

Plakas stood without hesitation, collected and controlled. Not a hint of emotion crossed his face.

"Well," he began smoothly, his voice carrying through the room, "Thank goodness the courts are not in the business of children becoming transactions of sales or trades. That's why this was handled through the courts and not through commerce."

He didn't raise his voice, but somehow, his words filled the space. The man who'd asked the question blinked and leaned back, suddenly aware of the silence that had swallowed the room.

A few closing remarks followed, but they barely registered. My thoughts were a blur of disbelief and anger. When it was finally over, we walked out together—Plakas, Brandon, MeLisa, and me. The fluorescent lights of the hallway felt too bright, too harsh after what we'd just sat through.

Outside, Plakas turned to us, composed as ever. "I don't know what they're thinking," he said, "but I've already prepared an injunction to be filed in court once the ruling comes down. That's our next step."

We nodded. There wasn't much else to say. I hugged MeLisa tightly before heading back to my Jeep, her cane clicking softly on the pavement as she walked away.

On the drive home to Massillon, I couldn't stop replaying the words, "So getting custody of Thayer could be compared to buying a house or a boat?"

How could anyone compare a sacrifice like that? A mother giving up her rights so her son could have a better life, a better chance, a future. Where would I be if Mommie B hadn't given me up? I wasn't a car, a house, or a boat. Neither was Thayer. Emotions were beginning to blind me and overcome me like a Tsunami. I wasn't sure I was going to survive all this.

Were we, as a people, as a society, really that blind?

Six days later, the OHSAA released its decision. The appeal was denied. Thayer Munford was declared ineligible for the 2016 season. All sanctions against Massillon would stand.

• • •

When the news broke, Lee Plakas told the local paper that Massillon intended to take the case to Stark County Common Pleas Court.

The battle lines were drawn. Plakos filed the paperwork the next morning for an emergency injunction hearing.

Lee's assistant had called the night before with clear instructions. Thayer and Nate needed to wear suits. Becca, something simple—a pantsuit, no sparkle. Keep it professional. What? When *didn't* I dress professionally? Sparkles aren't attire for a courtroom? Hadn't they watched *Legally Blonde*? It always seemed to come back to my outfits.

We didn't sleep much that night. Every time I closed my eyes, I saw Thayer's face—the weight of waiting, the hope tucked under the surface of his calm. We knew this hearing could change everything, but no one dared say that out loud.

It was a Tuesday, September 20, 2016, and when we entered the Stark County Common Pleas Court. The late-summer heat hadn't let up, and it seemed to cling to everything, thick and heavy. By the time we pulled into the courthouse lot, the sun was already beating down on the pavement, making the air shimmer.

Lee had told us that Judge John G. Haas had drawn the case. "He's fair," he'd said. "Experienced. Seasoned." I held on to those words like a lifeline. Fairness felt like all we could ask for.

Nothing, though, prepares you for walking into a courtroom when the city is watching. The air buzzed with chatter and the click of camera shutters. Reporters were waiting in the courtroom, pads of paper and pens out. A local news crew had set up in the courtroom, and the familiar swirl of orange and black from Massillon fans mixed with the suits and ties of courthouse regulars.

And then there was Scott Graber—our self-appointed school/city critic—standing just inside the courtroom doors, camera in hand, already recording. As Nate and I held the doors open for MeLisa to enter,

INDEPENDENT PHOTOS KEVIN WHITLOCK

■ Massillon football head coach Nate Moore (left) and Thayer Munford (far right) listen along with Moore's wife, Rebecca, as she wipes a tear while listening to Munford's mother, MeLisa Thompson, speak about wanting a better life for her son and for him to get a chance to attend college during a hearing held in Stark County Common Pleas Judge John G. Haas' courtroom Tuesday morning. ONLY ONLINE: For a photo gallery, visit IndeOnline.com.

'WHIRLWIND TIME'

Moores, boy's mother stand in court to defend decision to bring Thayer Munford to Massillon

Nate, Thayer, and I sit together in court during the trial over Thayer's eligibility—a moment that would later appear on the front page of our local newspaper, capturing the weight, love, and resolve we shared.

Scott made a low, cutting remark about her weight, his voice dripping with smugness.

I felt the heat rise in me before the words even reached my brain. My mouth opened, ready to fire back, when—out of the corner of my eye—I saw our assistant superintendent, Mark Fortner, standing a few yards away. He shook his head once, slow and deliberate. A silent plea: *Don't give him what he came for.*

I swallowed my anger, turned away, and followed MeLisa inside.

The courthouse smelled faintly of old wood and paper—something about it felt heavy, sacred even. Mommie and her best friend Thelma arrived not long after, both dressed in their Sunday best, matching wigs and handbags in hand. They found their place in the second row, sitting upright, dignified, like they'd come to church. Always watching over me, helping me cross the bridges of life I struggled to navigate.

The rest of us—Nate, Thayer, MeLisa, and I—sat on the front bench. Thayer tugged at his tie, his nerves showing in the small movements of his hands. MeLisa held her cane in between her knees, her eyes focused straight ahead.

When the bailiff called, "All rise," the entire room shifted. The chatter stopped. The creak of the wooden benches was the only sound.

Judge John G. Haas entered, black robe draped over his shoulders, his silver hair catching the light. He moved with the quiet assurance of someone who'd carried the gavel for a long time—long enough to know that every decision left a mark.

The robe represented authority, yes—but also the promise of *blind justice*. Whether that promise would hold, none of us knew.

He took his seat, adjusted his readers, and looked out over the room. The air conditioning struggled against the heat; the walls themselves seemed to hum. I could feel a bead of sweat run down the back of my neck.

This was it—the moment everything came to rest. Not on the field, not in a huddle, not under Friday night lights—but here, in a courtroom that smelled of dust, truth, and consequence.

Judge Haas looked down from the bench. I could tell—he knew exactly what this case meant.

Lee stood. "Your Honor," he began, "This case centers on a single, deeply flawed interpretation of an OHSAA bylaw—one that prohibits a former coach from having contact with a student-athlete after taking another position. The ruling rendered against Thayer Munford was not only arbitrary—it was rooted in assumption, not evidence."

His voice carried without effort, even tone, no theatrics. Just conviction. The kind of calm you could feel in your chest.

Lee paused, took a single step forward, and looked down at the papers in his hand. "I'd like to direct the court's attention to an email exchange dated May 10th—fifteen days *before* the OHSAA even met with representatives from Massillon."

OHSAA attorney Steve Craig shifted in his seat. Reporters perked up. The sound of camera shutters clicking echoed through the room.

"This email," Lee continued, "was sent by Ms. Deborah Moore, Assistant Commissioner of the OHSAA, to a member of La Salle's administration. In it, Ms. Moore expresses her personal opinions regarding this very case—opinions formed before any formal review or hearing took place."

I felt Nate's knee bump against mine. We both froze, glancing at each other—eyes wide. I could almost hear him say, "What?" Without a sound leaving his mouth.

Lee began to read directly from the email:

"It is probable that he could not meet any transfer bylaw. Change of custody to the coach is just ridiculous and will not be approved. And also highly likely he will be looking at a full year of ineligibility under section 4-9-4, subparagraph 8, following his former coach."

The words hung in the air like a bomb. You could feel the air shift, a murmur rippling quietly through the back rows.

My mind started racing—faster than I could control. *Fifteen days before?* So they had already made up their minds before ever hearing our side? Before seeing the documents, the court order, and the reasons that the mother gave everything up for her son?

The realization stung. They hadn't seen Thayer as a boy in need—they'd seen him as a bylaw.

I glanced at MeLisa. Her hands were gripping her cane so tightly that her knuckles were white. She didn't move. She just stared ahead, as if trying to understand how something so personal could be reduced to an email chain.

Lee didn't waver. He let the silence linger, then continued, steady and firm. "Your Honor, this correspondence shows a prejudgment—a predetermined conclusion about my client's eligibility before the facts were ever reviewed. It undermines not just this decision, but the very integrity of the process."

Craig stood abruptly, trying to object, fumbling for words that didn't come out smoothly. "Your Honor, this—this is being taken out of context. It was simply internal communication—"

Lee nodded and went on, each word methodical. "This is not about bending rules to benefit a student-athlete. This is about ensuring the rules are applied *fairly*—without bias, without predetermined judgment, and without punishing a young man for circumstances beyond his control."

Lee stepped back, folded his hands, and waited.

I could feel the sweat prickling at the back of my neck again, the heat of the room pressing in. Nate sat rigid beside me, eyes fixed on the table in front of us, jaw tight. Thayer hadn't moved. He looked straight ahead, expression calm, almost stoic—as if he had learned long ago not to let the world see when something hurt.

But inside me, everything was spinning.

The system we thought might give us a fair hearing had just been exposed for what it was: flawed, human, and already leaning against us. And in that moment, I realized—what happened next in this courtroom wouldn't just determine a football season. It would reveal who still believed in giving a kid a chance, or that fairness had a place in the game at all.

Nate was called to the stand. He straightened his tie and rose, his frame filling the witness chair. The courtroom lights were harsh, catching the faint circles under his eyes—about the only evidence this ordeal had worn on him. His face was clean-shaven, his expression calm, but there was a heaviness behind it.

Craig approached, legal pad in hand, already pacing. "Coach Moore," he began, voice edged with challenge, "Let's talk about your contact with the student-athlete prior to his enrollment."

Before Nate could respond, Judge Haas leaned forward. "You know," the judge said evenly, "I'm wondering—did you have any thought of contacting OHSAA before Mr. Munford enrolled at Massillon Washington to explain the situation?"

Nate didn't hesitate. His voice was steady, deliberate. "The only thing I can say, Your Honor, is that the last few months have been a whirlwind of time. Everything happened really fast. Thayer was on track to be a non-qualifier. At that time, he had eleven Division I scholarship offers— and those offers were meaningless unless he qualified academically. The verdict was simple: unless he came up, there would be nothing anyone could do for him."

Craig pounced. "So you're guaranteeing that being with *you* means he'll be a qualifier?" he said, his smirk curling at the corners of his face like he'd just found a weak spot.

Nate looked back, unflinching. "I'm sure La Salle would've gotten him through graduation. They would've made sure he was eligible for football. But that's not what this was about." He leaned slightly forward, his tone still composed. "This was about Thayer's mom realizing he was going to be a non-qualifier. He wasn't going to get to play—not just college football, but he wasn't going to be able to *attend* college. He would've been back in Lincoln Heights, whether he graduated from La Salle or not."

Craig didn't blink. "So he'd graduate—maybe he just isn't meant for college. Can you guarantee that?"

That did it.

Nate's jaw tightened, and his voice sharpened just enough to slice through the courtroom's air. "Listen, there's no guarantee in life. But I can guarantee he's got a better shot with us—and you'll see how wrong you are. We will see."

The words landed with weight. A few heads turned. Craig opened his mouth again, but Judge Haas lifted a hand.

"That right there is why you are the head coach of the Massillon Tigers," the judge said, his tone rising with authority.

A faint murmur rippled through the gallery. Nate sat back slightly, his hands clasped in his lap, regaining composure.

Judge Haas shifted in his chair, eyes narrowing as he looked over his glasses. "Coach, I see you live in Massillon Jackson. Why enroll Mr. Munford at Washington High School instead of Jackson, or even a private school, such as Central Catholic? If you'd done that, it might have avoided these recruiting accusations altogether."

Before Nate could answer, Craig jumped in again, "Also, Your Honor, Jackson is a higher-performing academic institution. Why couldn't Mr. Munford receive the same educational support there?"

The room went quiet. Nate looked up at the judge—his stare calm, but heavy. I could tell he didn't want to answer, not because he didn't have one, but because the question missed the point entirely.

"The reason we enrolled Thayer at Massillon," Nate said, finally, "is because I'm in that building every day. My office is in the high school. I can monitor him during the day. If a teacher needs to talk to me, I'm right down the hall. If he's struggling, I can check in between periods. That kind of communication—that kind of accountability—you can't do that if he's somewhere else."

He paused, letting it settle.

"That's not about football," he added quietly. "That's about giving a kid the structure he needs to succeed."

You could feel the truth in it—simple, unvarnished, human.

Judge Haas didn't respond right away. He just nodded slightly, his eyes still on Nate, as if weighing every word. Craig flipped a page on his pad, but for the first time since he'd started, he didn't seem so sure of himself.

Thayer was called to the stand.

He stood, his tall frame commanding the room in a way that was both powerful and painful to watch. There was pride in his posture, but also the weight of everything that had led him here. When he took his seat, he looked straight ahead, eyes fixed on Craig as if bracing for contact on the field.

Plakas approached the podium first and began gently, guiding Thayer into talking about his relationship with Coach Moore.

Thayer's face softened. "He was my only support," he said simply. "He actually cared about my grades. He actually cared about me as a person. It was just hard for me to go to school. I was just mad he left to go to Massillon."

His words hung in the air—unpolished, unpracticed, and completely real.

Craig rose from his seat to begin his questioning, but before he could speak, Judge Haas leaned forward, adjusting his glasses. "Help me understand," he said. "It looks like La Salle set up a study table for you. Why didn't you go?"

Thayer let out a faint laugh—half smile, half sigh—the kind of reaction that said more than words ever could. The judge and attorneys might have seen a missed study table; Thayer saw something else entirely.

"Transportation played a big role," he said. "Yes, La Salle may have set something up with one of the offensive line coaches, but I never felt like he wanted to do it. He'd come some of the time, but not all the time. They were just trying to get me to school so I could play and practice."

He paused, glancing briefly at the floor. "Coach Moore wasn't like that."

I closed my eyes. I wasn't sure if people were really hearing him—or if they were only listening for what fit their arguments. What Thayer was describing wasn't rebellion or laziness—it was survival. The kind of daily grind where gas money, clean clothes, and someone believing in you were not small details, but lifelines.

For Thayer, Nate had been that lifeline. That sense of someone showing up—every day, without judgment—had become the difference between drifting and direction. Riding with Nate, being picked up, being checked on—it had never been a burden. It was structured. It was family.

When Thayer was dismissed, he stood and walked back to the front row where we sat. His expression didn't change, but I could feel the exhaustion in his steps. Then it was MeLisa's turn.

She rose quietly, smoothing her pants before making her way to the stand. Her voice was soft but steady, the kind that carried truth even when it trembled.

"Yes," she began, "My son received assistance while he was at La Salle. Between the time Coach Moore left and when I decided to give them custody, there was help." She looked toward the judge. "There just wasn't *enough* of what he needed."

She folded her hands in her lap, searching for the right words. "Thayer needs someone with him—someone who takes the time. He learns, but it takes him longer. He needs that kind of attention, that kind of patience."

Her eyes glistened, not from weakness, but from the weight of knowing she'd had to make an impossible choice out of love.

The courtroom was silent. Even the OHSAA lawyer didn't move to interrupt.

For the first time that day, it felt like everyone in that room—reporters, fans, even the judge—saw Thayer not as a rule violation or a headline, but as a boy just trying to climb his way out of circumstances most of them could never imagine.

Then I was called to the stands.

Nate gave me the look—that same quiet look he's given me a hundred times when everything inside me wants to react. Stay calm. Focus. I could almost hear him say it without a word.

I shifted my eyes toward the gallery. Mark sat in the third row, leaning forward, his stare fixed on me as if willing me to hold it together. Just beyond him, Mommie's eyes met mine—tender, fierce, and full of that silent promise mothers have: If I could take your place, I would.

Lee motioned me to the stand. I took a deep breath and rose. My palms were damp against the wood rail as I swore in, then settled in the witness chair. Lee started gently, his voice calm and steady, giving me room to tell the story in my own words.

He asked what Thayer meant to our family. I felt my throat tighten before I even began. "He's family," I said softly. "Not by blood maybe, but by every other measure that counts." I told them how our nephew Ashford and Thayer bonded almost instantly—two boys who saw something in each other that the world too often overlooks. How Eli and Ella became like his little brother and sister, trailing behind him at the dinner table, teasing, laughing, believing in him. Ella especially. She adored him.

Judge Haas leaned forward, elbows on the bench, eyes narrowing behind his glasses. "When you first met him," he said, "didn't you look at his size and think—this guy can go somewhere?"

I smiled faintly, shaking my head. "No, Your Honor. I didn't care about his size. I cared about his grades—about giving him a chance. Size doesn't factor into that."

A few people in the courtroom scribbled notes, but I kept my eyes on the judge. I wanted him to understand this wasn't about football. It had never been.

I explained how, after Nate took the job in Massillon, Eli, Ella, and I would drive down every Sunday to meet Thayer at Chipotle. We'd go over his assignments, plan out his week, and talk about what needed to be done to stay on track. When he came to live with us, we mapped out his next year and a half, signed him up for two summer classes at Stark State College, and he was proud when he earned a "B" and a "C."

But as I spoke, my eyes flicked toward Craig. He was watching me with that same thin, polished smirk he'd given Nate. I could see it—the judgment, the doubt, the quiet contempt of someone who had never once had to choose a better path for their child, like Mommie B had done for me, Rachel had done for Ashford, and now, MeLisa was trying to do for Thayer. These were huge life decisions, and the OHSAA was boiling it down to trying to win a football game.

Not the fact of a mother surrendering her own heart, not for the sake of a game, but for the sake of their child's safety and future. More faith than this lawyer or most of the people in this courtroom would ever be asked to find. The most selfless form of love there is.

What I wanted to say was, "You have no idea what this does to a family." They want to focus on grades? They have no idea what it took for him to earn those grades. He was up at dawn for workouts. He was on a diet he hated. He was living away from his mother for the first time. He had recently learned that his birth dad had died. He never even got a chance to say goodbye. He was fighting years of habits and hurt just to sit still long enough to study. Some nights, we were still at the kitchen table at midnight, books open, the whole house asleep except us.

While my body is sitting on the stand, testifying, my mind takes me back to that summer's vacation.

Nate, Eli, Ella, and I went to Hilton Head for just a few days when the team wasn't practicing. Thayer went home to visit his mom. They didn't have the internet, but he told me not to worry, that he could finish his classwork at the library. It was the second-to-last week of his course, and he sounded confident.

Friday morning, Nate and I were walking the beach, the sun coming up over the water, and my phone rang.

It was Thayer calling from Cincinnati. Panic in his voice. "Becca, I got a test in science due tonight at midnight, and I forgot my notes and my book in Massillon."

I stopped walking. The air just left my chest. That one test—that one assignment—could determine his eligibility, his scholarships, his future.

Nate looked at me and didn't say a word. He didn't have to.

"We'll pack up the kids," I told Thayer. "Be ready. We're coming."

We threw everything in the truck—sand still clinging to the towels, Nate's coffee on the dash—and started driving. Hours of highway. There was no traffic, by some miracle. Through the day into the evening, through Cincinnati, and straight to his mom's house.

We grabbed Thayer, got back to Massillon, got him logged in, and he hit submit at 11:59 p.m.

I remember all of us sitting there in that small kitchen bar, faces lit by the glow of the laptop screen, just staring at that confirmation page. It felt like we had just won the biggest game of our lives.

I laughed through my exhaustion. "Someday," I told him, "You owe us at least one day's vacation."

Thayer grinned—that big, wide smile that could light up an entire room—and said, "I got you."

Even now, sitting in that courtroom, I could still hear him saying it. And for a moment, I didn't care who was watching or writing or judging. That's what this was about—*that kid, that chance, that moment.*

Next came the questions that were trying to make me look like I didn't understand grades and GPAs. People must look at me and think, "This girl is not smart." I really don't know what gives them that opinion, but I feel like I experience that a lot.

Craig was going through and explaining how La Salle had calculated Thayer's grades and how, if he could just get two B's and two C's, he would have a 2.0 GPA. He would need four B's for a 2.12. GPA, and he would need three A's and one B for a 2.3 GPA. I scoffed and almost laughed out loud on the stands. I looked at him and began, "You do realize he had a 1.5 his freshman year, and 2.1 his sophomore year, when Nate and I were tutoring him, and a 1.1 before he transferred his junior year. He wasn't on track to be eligible for college." The lawyer kept interrupting me, "But, he was eligible to play." I interrupted him, "For high school, but this isn't about high school. This is about succeeding beyond high school." I was beginning to lose my cool, and I glanced over at Mark Fortner, who was shaking his head and making a cut motion. I didn't care that Craig was arguing for high school; this was about life after high school. How were they not seeing that? This lawyer was not smart.

Judge Haas leaned in and asked me, "Why enroll him at Massillon?" I explained, "I'm the special education coordinator for the Massillon City Schools. He has an IEP. Coach Moore, Nate Moore, my husband, works at the high school. I'm in every building. If Thayer starts to struggle, his mom entrusted us to make sure he absolutely makes it to college. She gave her only son to us . . . I want to be where I can walk in and make sure it's being done."

Their math just didn't work. A 2.3 GPA meant he'd need at least a 19 on the ACT to qualify. That might sound simple to someone who's never sat at a kitchen table night after night with a kid fighting to believe he's smart enough to pass. But for Thayer, that 19 might as well have been Mount Everest.

And even if he finished at a 2.0, there was no miracle waiting. Colleges could technically offer an academic redshirt at that level, but the truth was—they rarely did. They wanted clean transcripts, strong scores, and predictable success stories. Thayer wasn't that. He was the messy, complicated kind of story that required faith, time, and a family who refused to quit on him.

Junior college wasn't an option either. The NCAA had locked in ten core courses that had to be completed before the start of his senior year. Seven of them had to be in English, math, or science. Thayer had already stumbled through too many of those with D's and F's, dragging the chain of his past behind him. That's why we'd pushed so hard—summer courses, college prep, tutoring every night, rewriting study habits that had never been built in the first place.

But none of that seemed to matter to the OHSAA. To them, it was simple. A rule was a rule. A line had been crossed. Custody had changed hands, and in their eyes, that meant manipulation—an adult move to win a high school game.

They didn't see what we saw. They didn't see a mother sitting in the front row of a courtroom praying that someone would believe her when she said, "I just wanted my son to have a chance."

For them, this was about eligibility. For us, it was about saving a life.

When the court adjourned for the day, Judge Haas requested the full transcripts from the OHSAA's panel hearing and ordered Deborah Moore to appear the following morning for questioning. His tone was neutral, but his eyes gave away that something had struck a chord.

We stood, quietly gathering our things. No one said a word as we walked out—Nate, Thayer, MeLisa, and me—hand in hand, the weight of everything pressing down, the courthouse hallway stretching long and silent.

Because sometimes silence speaks louder than any defense ever could.

We didn't talk in the car. The air felt thick, every one of us lost in our own prayers, our own fears. The only sound was the hum of the tires against the road and Thayer's soft, steady breathing from the back seat.

Tomorrow, everything could change.

And as we turned onto Lincoln Way, I found myself whispering under my breath, "Lord, just let them see what we see."

• • •

Day two in court began with the same tension that had hung in the air the day before. The hallways of the Stark County Courthouse were crowded and restless—reporters whispering, attorneys pacing, the hum of anticipation like static you could almost feel.

Before the session started, Lee and Trent pulled us aside. Their expressions were tight, professional, but I could tell they were uneasy.

"The judge has requested a meeting in his chambers," Lee said quietly. "He's reviewed all the public records both sides submitted."

We followed them into a smaller conference room, papers in hand, our nerves steadying with each step. We told our story—backed with documentation, transcripts, GPA calculations, and the NCAA rules we had painstakingly studied and lived by for months. We came with facts.

The OHSAA, on the other hand, came with bylaws, internal emails, and something called "Yappi."

I blinked when I heard that word. "What's Yappi?" I whispered.

Lee sighed, shaking his head. "It's an online message board. People post anonymously about high school sports."

It took me a second to process that. They were submitting a *message board*—a thread of strangers' opinions, assumptions, and gossip—as evidence of truth.

It felt absurd. Unbelievable. And yet, somehow, this was part of the process.

I remember thinking, *How could this possibly be justice?*

When the lawyers returned from the judge's chambers, I caught sight of Deborah Moore standing beside the OHSAA's attorney, Craig. She leaned in close, whispering, her arms folded tightly across her chest. Her body language said it all—she didn't want to be called to the stand. She didn't want to face questions about any emails.

A few minutes later, Trent motioned for us to follow him. "The Judge wants to see you," he said softly.

We were led into Judge Haas's chambers—a stately room lined with shelves of leather-bound law books and heavy wood furniture that seemed to absorb every sound. A long polished table stretched across the center, and the judge sat at the head, hands folded neatly on a stack of papers.

He glanced around at us, his expression was calm but decisive. "Well," he began, "I see no reason to carry this on any further. I believe we've reached a reasonable agreement that should make both parties satisfied."

I didn't move. My hands tightened in my lap as Lee began to outline the agreement.

Thayer would be declared eligible to play.

That part made my heart swell with relief—at least for a moment.

But then came the rest. We would be required to email Thayer's grades weekly to the OHSAA, so they could monitor his academic progress. Nate, not Massillon City schools, but Nate, was fined five thousand dollars for what they called "impermissible contact" with a former player before custody was finalized. And, as if that weren't enough, Nate was ordered to sit out the first two playoff games if Massillon qualified.

It didn't feel like a victory to me.

Yes, Thayer could finally play—but we were still being punished for doing what was right. For choosing to step in where others had stepped away. We had custody of Thayer. How was that recruiting? Show me another coach in the state of Ohio who went through what we did and was fined for it? Recruiting isn't the same as legal custody.

I swallowed my frustration and looked at Nate. His jaw was set, but he gave a small nod. We both knew what mattered most. This wasn't about fairness anymore—it was about Thayer. About giving him back the hope that had been dangling by a thread.

Handshakes were exchanged. Papers were signed. We walked out into the daylight, where Mommie and Thelma were waiting for us.

Mommie wrapped her arms around me and whispered, "Remember, it's about the finish line, not the race."

I nodded, though it still felt hollow. I knew she was right, but that didn't make the sting any less sharp.

The next morning, the headlines were everywhere.

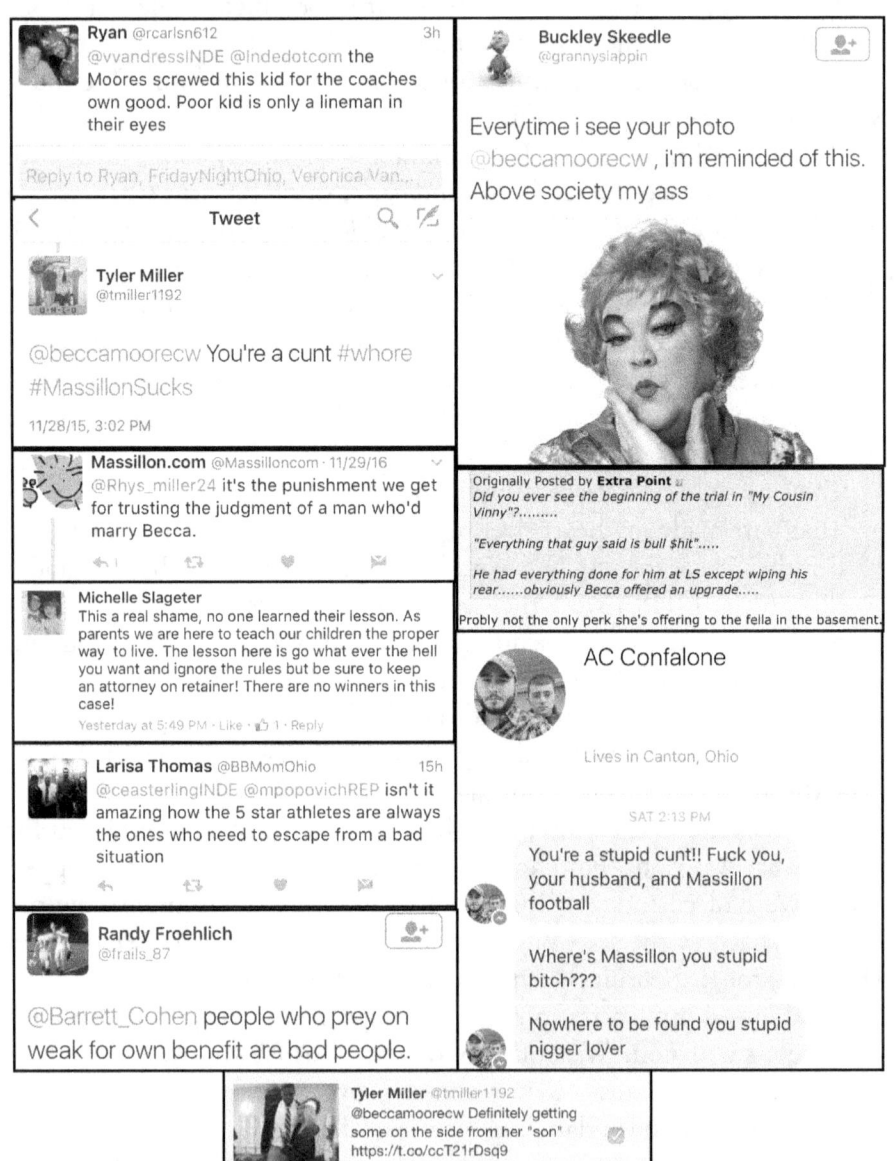

"'A' for Effort–Academics Always the Priority in Massillon Player Case"
"Munford Declared Eligible to Play Football for Massillon"
"Independent Readers React to Munford Being Cleared to Play"

And beneath that last one came the comments—anonymous voices, faceless opinions. People who didn't know our story didn't know the sacrifices, the nights of tutoring, the emotional toll. Just words on a screen, each one a reminder that the court of public opinion never really adjourns.

• • •

Despite everything, our routine didn't change. We still showed up, did the work, and stayed silent while the "keyboard warriors" kept typing. The comments came in waves—accusations, mockery, opinions from people who didn't know a single fact. We didn't respond. We didn't need to.

The courtroom battle was behind us, but the real challenge was just beginning.

Now, it was time to *actually* take care of Thayer—every single day, every single hour—and make good on the promise we'd made. Getting him ready for college wasn't just about football or eligibility anymore. It was about making sure he had the tools to build a life beyond the game.

I quickly realized how heavy that responsibility really was. Looking back caused me to feel a wave of respect and sorrow wash over me.

I had struggled with my own issues—my doubts, my exhaustion, my moments when I wasn't sure if I could pull this life off. But Mommie and Daddy had carried it for me way longer. I began to understand now how hard it must have been for them to watch me stumble, to wonder if their love would be enough to push me through. How many times had they stayed awake, hoping the next day would bring a breakthrough? How many sacrifices had they made, unseen and unthanked, to keep me moving forward? In this moment, it was humbling and terrifying all at once.

I promised myself, silently but fiercely, that I wouldn't let Thayer or my parents down.

—Chapter 14—
Life on the Line
in Tigertown

"When your back is against the wall, you will find it is a good place to push off."

~Jeffrey Fry

On October 30, 2016, Thayer Munford helped lead the Tigers to something unforgettable. That Saturday under the home lights, he helped give Coach Moore his first win as the Tigers head coach against our timeless rival—Canton McKinley. The stands shook with noise, the air electric with decades of history. I watched as Nate lifted the trophy high over his head, Thayer grinning ear to ear beside him, and Daddy standing close, pride written all over his face. For a moment, all the noise from the outside world disappeared. It was just joy. Pure and earned.

The Tigers went on to make the playoffs, but the shadow of OHSAA still lingered. Due to the sanctions, Nate wasn't allowed to coach or be on the sidelines. They forced him to sit in the press box between two OHSAA representatives, like a prisoner of his own success. It was one of the hardest things I'd ever watched him endure.

The game was chaos—penalty flags thrown like confetti, questionable calls one after another. I glanced over at Nate, fists clenched, jaw tight. When the game ended in a loss, he stood, turned to the two men beside him, and said in that calm, but dangerous tone I knew too well, "You should be ashamed of yourselves. That was poor officiating, and you took your agenda out on those kids. Now, I'm going to the locker room to talk to my team. If you want to fine me again, so be it." He walked out, down the stairs, across the field, and straight into the locker room. The season ended with that loss, but things didn't slow down.

The next mission was keeping Thayer ready—his weight, his grades, his drive. The college recruiters were circling again, some curious, others cautious. We started visiting schools: Tennessee, Ohio State, Kentucky, and Iowa State. Each trip was another reminder of how far he'd come—and how far we still had to go.

Then one morning, Nate called. "Hey, can you come over to the office? There's a coach here who wants to talk to you about Thayer—and his academics."

I walked in to find Penn State's head coach, James Franklin, sitting across from Nate's desk, his assistant beside him. Franklin stood, extended his hand, and smiled warmly. "Pleased to meet you, Becca."

The academic advisor got straight to the point. "Coach Moore tells us Thayer's on track to be eligible," he said, flipping through his notes, "but I'm not seeing it. And I've been doing this a long time."

I smiled. I love it when people doubt me. "Oh," I said, locking eyes with him, "You're going to regret saying that." He raised an eyebrow.

"Thayer finished his junior year with a 3.1. When he graduates, he'll have at least a 2.5 cumulative and the ACT score to match NCAA requirements."

The assistant laughed lightly, shaking his head. "You sound determined, but I just don't think it's a risk we should take, Coach Franklin."

I leaned forward, still smiling. "Your loss."

Coach Franklin chuckled. "You know," he said, "I'm betting on you. But I have to trust my guy. It's risky."

We exchanged polite goodbyes, but as soon as they walked out, I knew—he'd remember that conversation.

Christmas came, but the uncertainty hadn't lifted. No one knew where Thayer would end up. No one knew if any school would take the risk. Christmas is supposed to be about joy, family, and celebration—but that year, it was also about whispers and jokes.

Someone thought it'd be funny to Photoshop our faces onto *The Blind Side* movie poster and pass it around like a holiday card.

So I decided to play along. Our Christmas card that year featured our own version—bold and unapologetic. I wanted them to know we heard it all and saw it all, and we were still standing.

After the holidays, recruiting heated back up. We kept Thayer playing basketball to stay in shape—and to keep his weight in the range that college coaches wanted. Then, Ohio State called and was back in the picture.

Coach Urban Meyer wanted to see Thayer. An offensive lineman from Colorado had just decommitted, which opened a single scholarship spot—and Meyer wanted to fill it fast.

It was mid-January, a couple of weeks before signing day, when Meyer came to one of Thayer's basketball games. Nate and I sat with him in the bleachers. He didn't talk much—just watched, eyes sharp and focused, following Thayer's every movement. He studied him like a hawk, the way great coaches do when they see something they want to believe in.

After the game, Meyer asked to meet with Thayer in Nate's office. The three of us sat down, and Meyer leaned forward, hands folded, eyes steady.

"Well, Thayer," he said, "I'm impressed. I'd like to invite you for an official visit during the last weekend of the month."

Thayer blinked, frozen for a moment. Then he grinned, his voice catching. "Are you serious?"

Meyer smiled. "Yes, I am."

After they left, I broke down. All the fights, the late nights, the paperwork, the criticism—it all came rushing out. We were one step closer.

We started making plans immediately. Nate, Eli, Ella, Thayer, and I headed to Columbus that last weekend in January. We already knew: if the offer came, we'd say yes on the spot.

Because this wasn't just about football anymore, it was about faith—in him, in us, in the idea that sometimes, when you fight long enough and hard enough, the world has no choice but to see what you saw all along. But would our belief in him spill out to others and be enough?

We were so excited and knew this was going to be a huge weekend. This wasn't just another recruiting trip—it felt like the culmination of years of prayers, sacrifices, and second chances. Just when it seemed like things were gonna settle down, Nate got the call that his uncle had passed away. The funeral was scheduled at the same time on Saturday, AND they wanted him to serve as a pallbearer.

For a moment, it felt like the timing couldn't have been worse. But we knew how important both were—family and this opportunity. So we came up with a plan. Nate would go to Columbus with us on Friday night, then early Saturday morning he'd take Ella and drive to Cincinnati for the funeral. Eli and I would stay in Columbus with Thayer and keep the visit on track. Nate would make it back in time for the Saturday evening dinner with Coach Meyer's family and the other recruits. "Divide and conquer," we said. We had no choice.

This wasn't some "fun" college trip. This weekend could change Thayer's life.

When we arrived in Columbus Friday evening, the nerves and excitement were palpable. We checked into the hotel and were quickly whisked away with the other recruits and their families for dinner and a social event. The energy in the room was electric—young men full of dreams, parents trying to keep their emotions in check, coaches and recruiters scanning for something beyond talent.

Saturday morning came early. Nate and Ella dressed in their Sunday best and quietly left for the funeral. I could see the conflict in Nate's eyes—his heart was torn between honoring family and standing beside Thayer at such a pivotal moment. But that's who he was—loyal to both duty and love.

Eli and I were taken to the academic wing on campus while Thayer was escorted to begin his academic testing. Coach Meyer wanted to make sure Thayer would be able to handle the rigor of college classes. This isn't something that most college recruits have to do at an official visit. As Thayer worked through the tests, Eli and I sat in Coach Meyer's office, telling the story—how Thayer had come to live with us, what he'd overcome, and what we hoped for him.

When the testing wrapped up, we met with the academic advisors and the offensive line coach. They explained that Thayer could succeed academically, but he would need ongoing support and an updated Evaluation Team Report from his high school that outlined his learning accommodations. I assured them it wouldn't be a problem.

Soon after, we were chauffeured to meet up with the other recruits at the mall for lunch. Eli was playing arcade games when one of Coach Meyer's right-hand men, Ed Terwilliger, walked up to me.

"Becca," he said gently, "Coach Meyer needs to see you back in his office right away. He'd like you to meet with athletic director Gene Smith."

My stomach tightened, but I smiled and said, "Of course." Eli and I climbed into the car and rode back to campus.

When we arrived, Gene Smith was already waiting for us in Coach Meyer's office. Eli wandered around, studying the framed photos and trophies lining the shelves—snapshots of football glory, the kind built on grit and belief. Gene turned his chair toward me and said, "Tell me your story. How did all this come to be?"

So I told him. It made sense to me that he wanted to hear from us. Up to that point, Thayer was just a headline that had rocked newspapers through Ohio. I had to put a human face on the story. I told him about Thayer, about what led him to us, about the long nights and the promises we'd made to never give up on him. I spoke softly, but with the kind of truth that comes from the heart. Gene listened carefully, asking a few clarifying questions before turning to Coach Meyer.

"Coach," he said, "I hear and see nothing but sincerity. You have my full support in whatever you decide."

He shook my hand and left the room.

By the time Eli and I got back to the hotel, Nate and Ella had just returned. Nate looked exhausted—his suit wrinkled, his spirit heavy—but we both knew there wasn't time to rest. We had one more mountain to climb that night.

We got ready and headed to a private dinner at one of the best steakhouses in Columbus. The Meyer family was gathered in a private room, with round tables set for the recruits and their families. The atmosphere was warm, but serious. This was a family affair, not just a football event.

Dinner was served, conversation flowed, and just before dessert, Coach Meyer stood and spoke. "Thank you all for coming tonight," he began. "Before we finish, I have one question for each of you. Who has had the most impact on your life, and what does that mean to you?"

The room grew quiet. One by one, players stood and gave heartfelt answers—parents, grandparents, siblings. Thayer stood and just looked down for a moment. He straightened his shoulders.

"I have to be honest," he said quietly. "It's these two people sitting here." He pointed to Nate and me. "They took me in, held me accountable, and made me believe I could get here. I wouldn't be here without them. They sacrificed for me, never complained, and loved me like I was their own. I don't think I can ever repay them or say thank you enough. What they've shown me is what real love and sacrifice look like—for a kid who probably would've ended up on the streets."

The room went still. When I looked over toward Coach Meyer's table, I saw his wife and daughters wiping tears from their eyes. Nate leaned over and whispered, "There's no way they're not giving him an offer in the morning."

The next morning, we were called back to Coach Meyer's office. The air felt thick with anticipation. Coach looked at Thayer and said, "Thayer, I'd like to offer you a scholarship to play for the Ohio State Buckeyes. But it comes with a few conditions."

Before he could finish, tears were already streaming down my face. Nate and Thayer were grinning ear to ear, Eli was fist-pumping, and little Ella sat in my lap, unaware of how life-changing this moment was.

Coach continued, "You'll need to follow our football nutrition plan— 3,000 calories a day. Becca, you can send your weekly menus to our nutritionist. And I'd like you to come to Columbus weekly for tutoring. The tutor will report directly to our academic team. I understand Becca already has a retired teacher in mind."

Thayer nodded without hesitation. "Yes, sir," he said. "I'll do it." He committed on the spot.

Eli, Thayer, and Ella hand in hand, soaking in Ohio State Media Day his freshman year—a hard-earned moment etched forever in our hearts, built on sacrifice, perseverance, and everything it took to finally stand here.

As we walked out of the building, I couldn't stop the tears. Every sleepless night, every criticism, every moment of doubt—it all led to this.

Munford officially signed his National Letter of Intent with Ohio State on February 1, 2017, completing a long recruitment process to his "dream school". He posted on Twitter later that day, along with a letter posted by Ohio State football.

SELECT

Dear Buckeye Nation,

I am choosing The Ohio State University over other schools that have offered me scholarships for several reasons. The first is the outstanding level of academic support. The tutors, the coaches, the learning specialists — they all genuinely care about your academic success. I take getting a degree from The Ohio State University very seriously.

The second reason is that I love this place. It is a big school with a small feel that makes me feel right back at home. With over 200 majors to choose from, my goal is to graduate with a Bachelor of Science in Education, Sport Industry. With a huge alumni base, future internships, job possibilities and the networking system, there is no limit to the things I can accomplish.

Thirdly, I feel confident that I will be successful athletically at The Ohio State University because it is the school closest to mirroring the support staff I currently have as a high school senior. I looked around one day and realized I wanted so much more than my current situation. I didn't want to be stuck not having a job and just staying home. It is through all my life adversity that I have learned to become stronger and use the positive support available to be successful on and off the field.

SELECT

I hope that I can inspire the younger generation in Lincoln Heights to see that putting in the work in the classroom, finding just one person to support you (a teacher, intervention specialist, coach, etc.) and staying away from all the nonsense will allow you to achieve a college degree from a place like The Ohio State University.

I want to be the first person in my family to go to college and get a degree. This is my number one goal. Football will take care of itself. If I just do what I am supposed to do and stay healthy and focused, Plan B is to go to the NFL Draft.

I could not have achieved any of this without the support and guidance from Coach Moore and Becca. Without them and Coach Stud, this day would not have been possible.

Sincerely,

From January through June, we kept our promise. Every Sunday, I drove Thayer down to Columbus with Eli and Ella so he could work with my former mentor, retired teacher Fayth Lawson. He spent up to three hours with her each week, ending every session with an assessment sent to Ohio State academics. While he studied, the kids and I would fill the time at a nearby park, a movie, or the mall.

Each week, I emailed Thayer's meal plan to the team nutritionist—

breakfast, pre-workout, lunch, snack, dinner, and evening snack. He struggled with that part, and we'd sometimes find candy wrappers tucked away in his room, small signs of resistance. And honestly? I couldn't blame him.

In June, we dropped him off at his dorm and ate at the football facilities one last time as a family and said our goodbyes. Thayer, in his college career, was named Second Team All-Big Ten 2019, 2x First Team All-Big Ten 2020, 2021, First Team All-American, 2021.

However, the proudest moments were that he was named to the Dean's List in 2020 and that he walked across the stage to screams from family and friends with a degree in Human Development and Family Science from The Ohio State University. He stayed that fall for the extra year players were allotted due to COVID and was drafted by the Las Vegas Raiders in the 7th round, 238th overall pick in the spring of the 2022 NFL draft. Only .016 percent make it from high school to playing college to the NFL draft.

From a kid who the OHSAA thought of as just a transaction to an NFL player. I'm still astounded.

Nate, MeLisa, Thayer, Ella, Eli, and I pause for a family moment on OSU Media Day—joy and excitement overflowing—unaware that time would later soften the edges of this picture and change what the moment would come to mean.

—Chapter 15—
Finding Hope
Takes Patience

"Every new beginning comes from some
other beginning's end."

~Seneca

After everything we had gone through with Thayer, I was looking forward to life settling down. But sometimes God has a way of rearranging the story you think you're living.

Earlier in the week, Nate called and asked me to come to practice. One of the players had been living with his grandmother, and after a heated argument in the home, things escalated. The grandmother's son had called the police, and they were on their way to take the player to juvenile detention while things got sorted out. Nate didn't want the whole team distracted by the situation, so he asked if I could sit with the boy until the officers arrived.

So I drove down to the high school, and there he was—leaning against the brick wall by the double doors. Thin, a little smaller than I expected, with an expression that gave nothing away. I walked up, trying to sound gentle.

"Hi, I'm Coach Moore's wife, Becca. I'm just going to hang out here with you for a bit."

He didn't say a word. Just gave a slight nod, eyes fixed ahead.

I tried again, keeping my voice steady. "So, your name's Terrence, right? What position do you play?"

Nothing. Just silence, and that blank stare.

I gave him a small smile anyway, hoping to break through. "That's okay. I get it. This is a lot. But you're not alone. We'll help you through this. I promise, we'll figure it out."

Before I could say more, the police car pulled up. In a matter of seconds, they had him in the back seat and were gone—swift, quiet, leaving me standing there wondering what was going on.

I hadn't really given much thought to Terrence after that first meeting, and Nate didn't mention him again. Life moved forward, and with a new football season going on, I just assumed whatever happened with him was handled by someone else.

On a fall Friday afternoon, I was preoccupied. We had a playoff game later that evening, and my mind was already juggling the details of game day. I happened to be at juvenile court with another student, waiting in the lobby, running through mental checklists, when a lawyer approached me.

"Are you Becca Moore?" he asked.

I smiled politely. "Yes, that's me."

"Could you follow me to the magistrate's chambers?"

I froze for a second. My brow furrowed, but I stood anyway. Silent, confused, my heart pounded a little harder. What in the world could this be about? I was just at the courthouse to drive a student there for a simple traffic ticket.

As I followed the lawyer down the hall, every step of my glittering silver stilettos echoed a little too loudly, like a drumbeat announcing something I couldn't yet see. I tried to keep calm, but inside, my thoughts spun: *Why me? Did something go wrong? Am I in trouble?*

We walked into a small room where the magistrate and a guardian ad litem were waiting. Their faces were serious but not unkind. I sat down, hands folded tightly in my lap, bracing myself.

The magistrate began, "I've heard the story of you taking in a boy before and helping him out."

I nodded slowly, cautious but honest. "Yes, we did."

He leaned forward, lowering his voice as if this were a private plea. "Well, we're kind of in a predicament here, and I thought maybe you might be the person to help us out. You see, Terrence's grandmother doesn't feel he can be safe with her anymore. His mom doesn't want him. The only option left is to make him a ward of the state—foster care until he's eighteen. But I heard you were in the building, and I knew your story with the other boy, so I thought . . . maybe you might be open to considering one more."

For a moment, the room went quiet. My breath caught, and I felt the weight of his words pressing down on me. I already knew, deep inside, what my answer would be. It wasn't really a choice—not for me. If I said no, Terrence would vanish into a system that often swallowed kids whole. At fifteen, his chances of finding stability, of making something out of his life, were already so fragile.

But then my other thoughts came rushing in: *What about Nate? What about the kids? We've just gone through so much already. Do I really have the strength for another one?*

I drew in a slow breath, steadying myself. I knew I couldn't live with the guilt of turning away. Not when God had placed the question right in front of me.

So I smiled softly, pushing past my doubts. "Of course. It would be our pleasure to help Terrence. What do I need to do?"

Relief washed over the faces in front of me. The guardian ad litem leaned back in their chair, shoulders unclenching. "We'll type up the papers and court-place him in your home. That's all for now."

I nodded, but inside my chest was a swirl of emotions—resolve, fear, compassion, and a hint of dread. I had just agreed to something that would change all of our lives.

So without even calling my husband, I signed the court papers with a shaky hand, the reality of what I had just agreed to settling heavier than the ink drying on the page. My stilettos carried me down the hallway almost on autopilot until I passed the room where his mother and grandmother were sitting. I paused at the doorway, not daring to go in but unable to look away.

How could they sit there so calmly, backs straight, faces distant, while their child—their grandson—was about to be handed over to strangers? My chest tightened with a mix of sorrow and anger. To me, it felt like abandonment, a severing of bonds that should have been unbreakable. But then, a memory flickered. I had once sat in a courtroom myself, faced with impossible choices, knowing that sometimes sacrifices had to be made to save a life. Still, this didn't feel like a sacrifice. This felt like an inconvenience—like giving up because it was too hard.

I turned away before bitterness could take root. Terrence needed someone who would see him, not someone who resented his past.

When I reached the holding cell, the air seemed colder, heavier. My pulse quickened as I stood waiting, listening to the muffled voices and the metallic jingling from the other side of the door. Then, they brought him out.

The sight knocked the breath out of me. Shackles around his ankles, chains clanking with each step. His wrists were bound in cuffs like he was dangerous, like he was beyond redemption. My stomach twisted, and before I could stop myself, a small gasp escaped. *What had this boy done to deserve such treatment?*

And then another thought shot through me, sharp and uninvited: *What if Eli and Ella are in danger? What if bringing him home puts all of us at risk?*

The officers removed the restraints, the sound of metal scraping against metal echoing in the room. Terrence rubbed his wrists briefly, then let his arms hang limply at his sides. His eyes lifted to meet mine, guarded, but not defiant—just empty, like no one had ever expected him to hope for anything better.

I forced a steady smile. This boy didn't need to see my doubts; he needed to see something solid.

"You remember me, right? Coach Moore's wife, Becca?" My voice was softer than I expected, almost pleading for connection. "Well, it seems like you're coming home with us for the time being."

For a moment, nothing. Just the weight of silence between us. Then, finally, he gave a small nod, eyes dropping back to the floor, and whispered so quietly I almost missed it, "Okay."

That single word carried no fight, no relief—just resignation. As if he had learned long ago that his voice didn't change outcomes. Standing in that stark hallway with Terrence beside me, I knew this was different. This was going to take different skills than Thayer needed. Did I have those skills?

I didn't call Nate on the way home. I knew better—he was already locked in, preparing for the game. A phone call from me in the middle of that would only throw him off. I just sent a quick text: On my way with Terrence. I figured he'd piece together the rest soon enough.

I can't even recall the exact moment I told Nate everything. The details blur, probably because the night was already full—Terrence, the playoff game, the quiet weight of what had just happened. What I do remember is after we won, we stopped at Wendy's drive-thru with Terrence, Eli, and Ella in the car, all of us hungry, and riding that little high of victory.

When we pulled up to the speaker, I turned to Terrence and said, "Order whatever you like."

He looked at me, wide-eyed, almost disbelieving. "You mean . . . I can order more than a 4 for 4? Like I can order two, maybe three, 4 for 4s?" The words hit me harder than I expected. I tilted my head, confused at first, then it sank in. "If you're hungry, order whatever you want. As long as you eat it, I don't care." He ended up ordering four 4 for 4s. I don't know whose eyes were wider. Terrence's because he was getting to order and eat all this food, or Eli and Ella at the shock of seeing someone ordering and then eating all that food.

That night, my bill hit well over fifty dollars, and I didn't regret a single cent. What struck me wasn't the food—it was the realization. This boy had probably lived with limits pressed down on him so hard that even something as small as ordering fast food felt like crossing a forbidden line. Hunger, both the physical kind and the deeper kind, was written all over him. I made a mental note right then: Food was going to be an issue, and if I wasn't careful, it could become a battle none of us was ready for.

When we got home, I led Terrence to the room that used to be Ella's. It still looked like a little girl's room, soft and unfinished, but Ella hadn't been sleeping there for months anyway. She'd long since taken to wandering into our bed at night, curling up against one of us until morning.

Terrence had nothing—just the clothes on his back. Tomorrow I was supposed to meet his grandmother, who promised to pack him a suitcase. The thought of a boy needing his life reduced to one suitcase, handed off like a formality, broke me in a way I couldn't quite name.

Later that night, Nate and I lay in bed, the house quiet except for the light breathing of Eli in the next room and the occasional creak of the floorboards settling. He was mostly silent, the weight of it all sitting between us like a third person in the room. I finally rolled over, pressing the words out of my chest before they could choke me.

"You have to give this a year. No judgment. If we don't do this, everything we've built—everything we've stood for—crumbles."

Nate sighed, staring up at the ceiling. His voice was low, tired. "I know. Doesn't mean I have to like it."

And that was the end of it. The line was drawn. Terrence was ours, and whether we were ready or not, we had to figure out what that meant.

This wasn't Thayer. Thayer had a mother who loved him, even if she couldn't always show it the way he needed. Terrence's story was different. His story was threaded with loss and rejection, with trauma that stretched deeper than I could see—and probably deeper than he could put into words.

Still, as I lay there in the dark, I made a promise to myself. I would give him everything I could—guidance, structure, love, the chance to believe he mattered. I couldn't fix the whole past, but I could help write a different future.

I had one year. And in my heart, I believed that would be enough.

●●●

Terrence didn't interact with us much at the beginning. He had a routine that rarely changed: get up, eat breakfast, make peanut butter and jelly sandwiches, get on the bus, go to school, football practice, then come home, and disappear into his room with the door shut. The interaction was minimal, and Nate didn't like it. When Terrence came to the dinner table, he would eat as much as he could without saying a word. Nate took the silence as ungratefulness, but I saw it differently. To me, it felt like Terrence was afraid—afraid that if he got too comfortable or too connected, something would happen and the support he had found with us would vanish. Then what would he have left?

Around that time, we were working through some things with Thayer and Ohio State Football. It was winter break, and the team was preparing to play in the Rose Bowl. Thayer was going to be sidelined with an injury, but he still wanted Nate and me to come so he would feel supported. So we booked flights to Los Angeles, leaving Terrence, Eli, and Ella at home with my aging parents.

The day before the game, my phone rang in LA. Eli's voice came through, high-pitched and panicked, screaming and crying that we needed to come home immediately. My heart dropped. "What happened?" I asked urgently, glancing at Nate, who was already pacing and clenching his fists.

Nate cut in before Eli could answer. "I don't care what happens—if he puts his hands on my son, he is done."

"Calm down, both of you," I said, trying to keep my voice steady.

"Eli, tell me exactly what happened."

Eli swallowed hard on the other end. "We were arguing over something, and he came at me, so I threw my bowl of cereal at him. Then he lost it and hit me in the back of the head. Please come home. I'm scared."

Nate exploded in the hotel room, his voice echoing off the walls. I told him I would look for a flight, but first I needed to talk to my parents. Daddy got on the phone and explained that he didn't quite understand what had happened, but he thought it was settled. They told Terrence he had to stay upstairs until Nate and I got home.

"Put Terrence on the phone," Nate growled.

When Terrence reluctantly answered, Nate's voice was firm and sharp. "Listen here—if you touch Eli again, you're finished. It's over. No one is coming to save you."

Terrence tried to explain himself, his words halting, but Nate cut him off. "I don't want to hear it. You are a guest in this house. You will do everything Grandma and Grandpa Garber tell you to do, or you will not like the consequences. And I promise you—there will be consequences."

When we arrived home, there was no easing back into normal life. The air in the house was heavy, like everyone had been holding their breath until we walked through the door. Nate called for a family meeting at the table, and there was no mistaking the seriousness in his voice.

Our old historical house had a way of making moments feel bigger than they were. The dining table—solid oak with tall, castle-like chairs—set the stage. Nate sat at the head, as if presiding over a courtroom. To his left sat Thayer, Eli, and me. To his right, Terrence and little Ella. The room felt divided before anyone spoke.

Nate's voice was low, but sharp when he began. "I am not happy about what happened. Honestly, I think we should just turn you back over to the courts and see what happens, because this kind of behavior is unacceptable."

The words hit hard, and for a moment, no one moved. Then Thayer leaned forward, his voice steady and protective. "Eli is my brother. Ella is my sister. We are family. You can't act like that. We want to help—but not at the cost of one of us getting hurt. I understand your pain and confusion, but if anyone can help you, it's here. You won't get another opportunity like this."

Before the weight of Thayer's words could settle, sweet Ella chimed in, her little voice clear and certain. "I didn't like the fighting, but I think you should get another chance." Her innocence cut through the tension like sunlight breaking into a storm.

I took a deep breath and glanced at Nate. His jaw was clenched tight, eyes hard. He was done—more than done. He wanted no part of this mess anymore. Still, I pressed on. "Okay, look. You can't touch Eli or Ella, because it's wrong. If you want to stay here, you're going to have to see a counselor or therapist and follow strict rules. Otherwise, you'll become a ward of the state. And Terrence, the statistics for making it out of that are pretty low. But understand this—if Eli says he wants you gone, you're gone."

Every pair of eyes turned to Eli. Terrence just stared blankly, no expression at all. Eli shifted in his chair, his voice shaky but brave. "I don't like what you did. And I did throw milk on you. I know you're in a tough spot, and I want to forgive you and move on. So I'm okay with you staying because Mom says everyone deserves a second chance—so as long as it never happens again."

The silence that followed stretched forever. Finally, Nate pushed back his chair and stood, his voice final. "Well, that is that. Let's never have this conversation again—because it won't end like this next time."

The chairs creaked as everyone rose, but the weight of the moment didn't lift. We had drawn the line. What happened next would depend on whether Terrence could stay inside it, whether he wanted help, change, and to get over his bridge that seemed to be falling apart. Would he take the guidance? Or would he fall through? The choice was now his to make.

So this became the beginning of our relationship with Terrence and the beginning of the end of a relationship. When COVID hit, we were in the middle of building a house in Massillon that would have an in-law suite for my parents to move into. COVID slowed everything down, and Ohio State sent its players home. Suddenly, we found ourselves all under the same roof for the first time, and it wasn't easy.

Thayer wanted to go live with his girlfriend and her family a couple of towns over, and I was completely against it. For one, no one knew what was really happening with this virus. Two, we were still responsible for Thayer—his health, his training, his weight, and making sure he stayed eligible for Ohio State. When you've got four kids at home trying to manage online school, and two adults working from home, even a big house can feel suffocating.

But there were moments of light, too. Thayer pushed Eli and Terrence hard in workouts, dragging them along to the basement or the yard, turning chaos into competition. Eli complained about it, but secretly loved the challenge. And Terrence—he thrived. He grew stronger, more disciplined, and slowly began to find his voice. Thayer's relentless drive became Terrence's fuel, and by the time his senior season came around, Terrence was voted a captain of the football team. For a boy who once shut himself behind a bedroom door and spoke to no one, that was no small thing.

By August, we had finally moved into the house we'd been building. It was supposed to be a fresh start—room for everyone, a place where family could fit and grow. But with fresh walls came new pressures. Thayer's mom needed a place, so she took up space in the unfinished side of the basement. My parents moved into their side in late October. The house was full, but the fullness didn't always feel like togetherness. Sometimes it just felt crowded.

Still, even as Terrence grew on and off the field, the cracks at home widened. What had started as a fragile hope of building trust was slowly bending under the weight of too many personalities, too much history, and not enough space, and Thayer wanted space. As the fall season played out, Thayer returned for another season at Ohio State after graduating. Life felt like it was shifting in ways we couldn't control.

One late night, Nate's phone buzzed. It was Thayer. I watched through the window as Nate stepped out to the little stone porch and sank into a chair, his shoulders heavy. Thayer's voice came through, steady but final. "Listen, I appreciate what you did for me, and I'll be grateful, but I'm going to move on. I've got a girlfriend and her family, and I can afford my own things now because of NIL [Name Image Likeness] deals in college. I just don't consider you family anymore."

I could see Nate bow his head, his hand rubbing his eyes. He sighed the way you do when you've lost something you can't get back. The truth was, Nate had always loved Thayer like his own son, and hearing those words was like being cut open. When he finally came inside, his face looked hollow. "Well, Thayer doesn't consider us family anymore. I told him his mom will have to move out as soon as possible, because we were doing him a favor by having her here."

I cried as I told him I was sorry. Sorry because deep down, I knew I had pushed too hard—pushed Thayer to stay focused on football, pushed

Thayer, Nate, Terrence, Eli, Ella, Pepper (our loyal German shepherd), and I gather for what would become our final Christmas photo together in 2021—a moment now held with deep love, gratitude, and ache.

away the outside things I thought could wait. I thought I was protecting his dream of the NFL. Instead, he felt we were too controlling or that we wanted something from him in the end. We had never taken a dime from him or his mom. We just welcomed them into our home.

A few weeks later, after living with us for about a year and a half, Thayer's mom moved out. At that point, the communication between all of us came to an end.

Terrence saw all of it. He watched Ella scratch Thayer's face out of every picture she had of him, watched her cry into her pillow night after night. He watched Eli try calling, texting, trying anything to pull Thayer back in—but nothing could change his mind. The silence of those weeks felt like a death in the family. The hardest part was that Thayer was still very much alive, just out of reach. Grieving someone who hasn't died is a strange kind of ache.

In that hollow space, new bonds began to grow. Terrence and Ella leaned on each other. He became her protector, her steady place when her big brother's absence hurt too much. He and Eli grew closer too, brothers forged in loss. More and more, Terrence would look at us and say the words we weren't used to hearing: that he was thankful, that he appreciated us, that he loved us.

When he graduated from high school early in January, he gave Thayer the credit, saying he wouldn't have pushed himself if Thayer hadn't shown him how. That discipline earned him a full-ride football scholarship to the University of Pittsburgh.

While in high school, Terrence thrived being part of the DECA (Distributive Education Clubs of America) Business program, earning top honors. In his Junior Year, he was the district champion in Business Services and a state qualifier. In his Senior Year, he was the state champion in the Stock Market Game Competition and International Qualifier (Placed 6th out of 1,200 competitors in the Midwest region). Terrence graduated early in 2021 and did not compete in the Business Services event. He could have qualified for internationals in that event, according to his teacher.

Terrence would go on to graduate from the University of Pittsburgh, be named in the 2022, 2023, and 2024 All-ACC Academic Football Team, and in 2023, be named to the National Football Foundation's prestigious Hampshire Honor Society, start his master's degree, and eventually transfer to the University of Connecticut to finish out his final year of football eligibility.

Meanwhile, Thayer's path led him to the NFL. From a distance, connections were still there. Eli and Thayer got back in touch eventually. Eli even flew out to Vegas to see Thayer one summer before his senior year, and Thayer gifted him a jersey. Thayer told Eli that he wanted to see Ella, too, but she couldn't bring herself to face him. Her heart wasn't ready, and the hurt hadn't healed.

Life is always on the line in Tigertown. I really believe you can change your life and your outcome if you are willing to. When I look back on everything, I remind myself that we did what we said we would do. We guided Thayer to graduate from high school, to stay eligible, to take a football scholarship, and to graduate from college—not just any college, but The Ohio State University. Because of Thayer, we gained Terrence. Nate gave Terrence that year, and it made a difference. Terrence completed our family.

I will never forget the day Terrence looked at me, completely out of the blue, and said, "You know I got to make a phone call every day for the nine days while I was in the juvenile detention center. I called my birth mom every day." He paused, and I stayed quiet, just waiting. His eyes shifted away as he continued, "She never answered. Then they told me someone was there to get me when I went to court, and I figured it was probably her. Turns out it was you. You didn't ask questions, you just said, 'Let's go.' So thank you for always showing up."

Those words sank deep into me. I thought of the picture that hung in my room when I was a child—the angel guiding children across a broken, decrepit bridge, keeping them from falling into the treacherous river below. I am no angel, but maybe, sometimes, I could be the one who helps steady someone's steps. Maybe that was enough when things were on the line, because it had gotten Terrence and Thayer across.

My life has been a constant collision of where I've come from. I've known what it feels like to be left behind, and I've known what it feels like to be chosen. Maybe that's why I fight so hard for others—because I understand the edge between despair and grace. When lives are on the line, I remember both sides of my story. The pain taught me sympathy. The love taught me strength. And somewhere between the two, I found purpose.

—Chapter 16—
Beyond the Lights

"You make a living by what you get. You make a life by what you give."

~Winston Churchill

My Grandma Combs never turned down an opportunity to help someone in need. She lived with a kind of unwavering generosity that was stitched into the fabric of who she was. One time, after carefully selecting and buying my grandpa a brand-new suit, she gave it away the very next day to a traveling missionary who spoke at their church and mentioned that he didn't own one. My grandpa didn't grumble or ask questions. He simply smiled and shrugged. He knew it was her calling—her unique, sacred way of giving.

After they retired to Oak Ridge, Tennessee, my parents took me down there every summer to spend two weeks with them. This was a different world. No FaceTime, no internet, no cell phones. A long-distance phone call from Tennessee to Ohio was a rare luxury, especially when your grandmother gave away every spare dime without hesitation. But oh, how those two weeks were worth more than any conversation over the phone. They were magic.

The mornings started early with Grandma in the garden. We'd walk barefoot into the dew-soaked grass, pulling weeds, watering roots, and gently talking to the tomato plants and bean stalks like old friends. "Grow strong," she'd whisper. "You'll feed many around my table." She saw food not just as nourishment, but as an offering—an act of love. It wasn't unusual for her to invite a stranger from church to Sunday lunch without a second thought. Her table always found room for one more.

Mid-mornings were reserved for time with Grandpa. We'd walk hand-in-hand to a weathered printing building beside Mt. Pisgah Baptist Church. Inside, long wooden tables stretched endlessly, each one covered with stacks of delicate paper. We'd start at one end and work our way down, picking up page after page of scripture, carefully collating them in the stifling heat—no air conditioning, no fans, just the sound of pages rustling and the occasional creak of floorboards. Grandpa would smile and remind me to lick my finger to grip the next page, a quiet little ritual. We were assembling New Testament Bibles, destined for faraway villages in Africa. At the end of each session, he'd take me to a large map and point out the pins marking where the Bibles were headed. "Each pin," he'd say, "is a place where someone's going to hear about Jesus because of the work we're doing." I remember the pride swelling in my chest—I felt like I was part of something eternal.

Evenings were just as sacred. After supper, Grandma and I would head to the creek bed with our cane poles. She taught me how to bait a hook with care and even how to speak to the worms. "Now listen here, little worm," she'd say softly, "You're going to help bring us a fish, and we thank you for it." I'd throw my head back laughing every time, but to Grandma, even worms deserved gratitude. She believed everything that gave something—whether it was food, joy, or shelter—should be acknowledged.

By the creek sat a tree with a trunk shaped like a chair, naturally carved over time into the perfect resting spot. Grandma would settle in with her stories—tales from her childhood, or secondhand adventures from missionaries who had passed through their home. I remember thinking I might want to be a missionary one day, to go out and help people. But I couldn't imagine ever leaving Tennessee. As a child, it's easy to believe that the things you love will never change, that summer will always come, and that people will always be there.

But time, of course, moves on. Seasons shift, and childhood gives way to adulthood.

What I didn't realize back then was that those summers were quietly preparing me for something far greater than myself. They were laying the groundwork for the life I would eventually live—especially the role

I would come to play in helping kids, guiding them, and offering them the same kind of steady, selfless support I once received beside a garden bed or at a printing press in Oak Ridge, Tennessee.

Selfless support had been etched into the back of my mind since those long, sunlit summers in Tennessee. It was in the soil, the stories, the slow, deliberate way my grandparents gave—no matter the cost, no matter the judgment, no matter the outcome. Helping others was never about convenience. It was about conviction.

When the phone rang just before football practice, and I saw Nate's name flash across the screen, I answered, expecting anything and everything. We were just over twenty-four hours away from the regional championship against our longtime-playoff nemesis—Akron Hoban. Everything about that week had been high-stakes, high-pressure. And this was not the moment for surprise phone calls.

I picked up quickly, heart already beating faster. I didn't even get a word out before Nate launched in—his voice tight, sharp, strained.

"Listen, I don't have time to go into details, but the US Marshals just came in and arrested TK, and I'm not sure what's going to happen next. I just thought—you should hear it from me."

For a second, I couldn't breathe.

TK? Our starting running back, TK?

TK was a kid who loved his family with everything in him. A kid who said "Yes ma'am" and "No sir" without thinking. He prayed before practice and thanked God after every touchdown. He worked twice as hard without ever asking for credit.

How could he be mixed up with the police? Not the police. The US Marshals?

I felt the heat rise in my chest—grief, rage, confusion all colliding. I inhaled, long and slow, steadying myself the way my grandmother might have done before walking into a room where she knew someone needed her.

"You should've called me sooner," I said firmly, then hung up and did the only thing I knew how to do in a moment like that.

I got to work.

Had I heard Nate right?

The US Marshals came to a high school and arrested TK? That can't be right, but Nate is not known to embellish anything. He is direct and calculated.

I stood there, phone still in hand, heart pounding. This couldn't be happening to a kid like TK. It felt extreme. Overreaching. Like someone had intentionally lit a match and tossed it into the middle of our team, the eve of the regional championship against a team Nate and his team hadn't been able to beat. I'm not one for conspiracy theories—but this? This felt personal. And it felt targeted.

I went into full crisis mode.

Call after call. Lead after lead. I tapped every contact I had, trying to locate TK. Nothing. He wasn't booked at the juvenile detention center, which didn't make sense—he was only seventeen. So where was he?

Hours passed in this frantic fog until, finally, around 6 p.m., a connection at the detention center called back. "He's here," they said. My stomach dropped.

And then came the detail that nearly took my breath away: the US Marshals had "mistakenly" processed him as an adult. They had taken him to an adult jail. A 17-year-old. A high school student. A kid.

I found out that it wasn't until the moment of fingerprinting that an honest guard—thank God for that man—looked up and said, "What the fuck are you doing here with this kid? We can't put him in here." Only then was TK rerouted to the juvenile facility. What would have happened if they had put him in there? Lawsuits for years, but the damage to his mental health and quality of life would have already been done.

I was numb.

When Nate finally walked through the door later that night, back from practice and the team's Thursday sideline meal, I didn't wait. I pounced, like a storm ready to break. My voice came out sharp, quick, "What in the world went down today?"

He paused, like he still couldn't make sense of it himself. "It's all so strange," he said slowly. "This morning I started getting phone calls from weird numbers—guys saying they were detectives or officers, telling me they had a warrant for TK's arrest, and they'd be taking him at the beginning of the game tomorrow night."

I stared at him, wide-eyed. My breath shallow. "You're telling me this now?"

He nodded, almost in disbelief himself. "Then I get a call from one of our former players' dads. He says US Marshals are being sent in—guns blazing."

I physically gasped. "To a high school? Filled with kids?" My hand flew to my chest. I couldn't help it. This wasn't just overkill. This was an attack. On TK. On us. On Massillon.

Nate's voice dropped. "What's worse is that they released his name on the radio. It hit the press before we could stop it—even though he's underage. It's a complete nightmare."

I scoffed. "You think?"

He went on. "I pulled the SRO (School Resource Officer) into it, told him everything. He started working backchannels, trying to confirm what was going on. And yeah, the US Marshals were coming."

He paused again, staring out the window. I watched the weight of the day settle on his shoulders like an anchor. "Between the principal, the superintendent, the SRO, and me, we worked out a plan. We brought TK to the back of the building. Quiet. Discreet. This would keep the kids safe. Keep it contained."

My heart shattered as Nate spoke the next words. "They cuffed him right there. At the back door of the school. TK looked at me and said, 'I love you, Coach Moore,' and walked to the car, hands behind his back. No fight. No fear. Just faith."

I could hear the sound of heartbreak. I could feel the sting of injustice burn through my chest. I should have gone to law school. I hate injustice, and this reeked of it.

"I had to get myself together," Nate said, his voice almost a whisper. "I still had to run practice. I still had to tell the team. And then I thought— I'd better call Becca."

I almost screamed. "I could've used a full day, Nate. Not just a few hours."

He looked at me, exhausted. "What did you find out?"

I took a breath, steadying myself. "This supposedly happened over the summer, but it's now they came for him? The day before regionals? He's in front of a judge tomorrow at 8:30 am. I lined up a lawyer with some help. His parents are getting to see him tonight. I'm going to court in the morning. I need to see how this plays out, because something's off. Something's not adding up." This felt like someone was trying to sabotage the game, and they were willing to take a kid down to win. "They are saying something about juvenile felony assault or battery charges, and that a man no longer has a quality of life because supposedly TK hit him and knocked him off his bike, and the man hit his head," I explained.

Nate nodded slowly, taking in all the information I just spewed out.

"Yeah, you should probably drive my truck. Everyone knows the color of your Jeep. Just in case. This all feels . . . off. Like someone's got a vendetta."

He sighed. That sigh meant the conversation was over—for now.

I laid there later, in the still darkness of our bedroom, eyes wide open, staring at the ceiling like it might suddenly give me answers. I replayed everything—every detail, every second. I mapped out a hundred ways tomorrow could go, cause what could TK have possibly done that could cause something like this to happen?

But nothing could've prepared me for what actually happened the next morning.

When my alarm went off at 4:30 a.m., the room was still cloaked in silence. Nate lay beside me, breathing steady, his chest rising and falling in the rhythm of uneasy sleep. The house was dark, heavy with the weight of the day ahead. I rolled out of bed quietly and laced up for my game-day ritual: a run at the Jackson YMCA. It's where I cleared my head, found my fight, and steadied my nerves—but this morning, it felt more like a battle cry than a routine.

When I got back, the quiet lingered. No words—just long, knowing glances exchanged in the stillness of our bedroom. A nod from him. A nod from me. We both understood the stakes. This wasn't just about football anymore. It never really was.

We had two obstacles in front of us: the initial court hearing and the half-day school attendance cutoff. If TK didn't physically walk through the school doors by then, he wouldn't be allowed to play in the game that night. School rules. Ironclad. No exceptions. The window was tight—razor-thin.

Nate leaned against the doorframe of our bedroom, his figure backlit and slouched, trying to look composed but clearly feeling the weight. He cleared his throat and said quietly, "Listen, at the end of the day, it is what it is. You're at the mercy of the court. All you can do is be there—and support TK and his family."

I nearly smirked.

Underestimated—again. Most people do. And honestly, I don't mind. But when I see injustice? When I see a kid caught in the middle of something bigger than himself, that flips a switch in me. And if this wasn't a case worth fighting tooth and nail for, then I didn't know what was.

He stepped across the room, kissed me softly, and walked out just as fast. No fanfare. Just quiet solidarity.

I turned to my closet and spoke out loud to no one but the truth. "Okay, no flashy shoes today," I muttered, scanning the rows. My black sequined stilettos caught the light, tempting me. I laughed out loud. "Ahh, you'd cause a scene." My eyes settled on a pair of plain black leather stilettos. Classic. Strong. The kind Grandma Garber, my Daddy's mom, would have approved of—though she always said a single pair of church shoes could last a woman a lifetime. That wasn't my style—I had over a hundred pairs. But today called for something simple, sharp, and unshakable.

Next came the dress. I chose a plain black, lace-sleeved number that brushed my knees—conservative enough for court, but with just enough backbone to remind people who I was.

I lined my eyes in black, a steady hand painting quiet fury, and finished with red lipstick. Not for glam. For war. Red meant I was ready to fight.

I looked at myself in the mirror. No fear. Just resolve.

"Whatever it takes, Becca . . . you get him out."

With that, I grabbed my bag, walked out into the cool morning air, and climbed into Nate's black Dodge Ram. I started the engine, turned left out of the driveway, and headed toward Akron—more than thirty minutes early.

Because when a kid's future is hanging in the balance, being early is the bare minimum.

About twenty minutes from the detention center, traffic on the highway came to a dead stop. I hadn't moved in thirty minutes. Panic was setting in fast—not only could I be late, I might miss the hearing entirely. My hands gripped the steering wheel tighter. I didn't know what to do, so I called Nate. He answered on the first ring.

"I'm trying to get off the highway, but it's bumper to bumper," I said frantically. "There has to be a major accident—I'm going to be late or miss the hearing altogether."

Without hesitation, Nate said, "Whatever it takes—drive through yards, ditches, whatever. Just get there."

That was enough for me. I laid on my horn, yanked the wheel to the right, and started driving half on the grassy median and half in the ditch. I didn't dare look at any other drivers—I knew the looks I'd get would only make it worse. I just kept going.

I gunned it past a truck on the shoulder of a two-lane road, swerving around mailboxes and bouncing through front yards, all while silently praying no one had security cameras—or that I wouldn't get arrested. Someone's definitely going to report a black truck, I thought, and for a moment, I laughed. Good call, Nate. There are probably more black trucks in Ohio than blue Jeeps. That gave me hope.

I pulled into the parking lot of the juvenile detention center ten minutes past the scheduled hearing. My heart was pounding as I rushed through the metal detectors, gave my name, and boarded the elevator up to the courtroom.

When I entered the room, it was packed. Every seat behind TK was filled. He sat with his family and his lawyer to the left of the judge, right in my line of sight as I walked in. Everyone on his side looked like they were headed to Sunday service, the women's hats bold and towering. No one turned. No one even flinched. I quietly slipped into a seat on the left side, second row from the back.

The judge sat high above the courtroom, cloaked in her black robe, gazing down on us all. TK's lawyer was finishing up; the only sound in the room was the soft rustling of papers. The judge spoke, her voice calm and deliberate:

"Thank you, counselor. Now let's hear from the prosecution."

I nearly scoffed out loud. I had to choke it back and clear my throat.

This was the prosecution?

She looked like she had just rolled out of bed. Her hair was matted, her wrinkled black skirt landed awkwardly mid-calf, and her white shirt—also wrinkled—was barely tucked in. She had thrown on a black blazer, like a kid dressing up as a lawyer for Halloween. I knew I shouldn't be judging her appearance—but how could anyone take her seriously when it looked like she didn't?

That thought would come back to bite me.

The prosecutor stood slowly, her expression cold, her voice sharp and laced with something close to hatred. Every word oozed with malice and contempt. I sat there, flabbergasted.

"Your Honor, this is a young man who poses a clear flight risk and is a danger to society," she began. "He left another man clinging to life. That man now requires full-time care in a facility. His family is devastated and unable to care for him due to the trauma caused by the defendant's actions. We ask that he be held in custody until a trial date is set. There's no reason to consider the fact that he's a student—or that he's a football player trying to play in some big game tonight."

I gasped, quickly covering my mouth. Did she just say that? Did the prosecution seriously reference a football game as part of her argument to keep a teenager behind bars? What does that have to do with anything?

For a split second, I wondered if this was some twisted reality show. Was I being punked? This had to be a Lifetime movie. Will anyone believe me when I tell them she referenced a football game in court? My mind was spiraling—Is this really about a game? Is someone so desperate to keep TK off the field that they'd orchestrate this? Is he being framed?

I had to do something.

Then the judge's voice cut through the chaos in my head.

"Is there anyone from the victim's family who would like to speak?"

Without hesitation, I stood.

"Your Honor, my name is Becca Moore. I serve as the Parent Involvement Coordinator and Special Education Coordinator for Massillon City Schools. I know TK. I've worked with him. He is a respectful, dedicated, and honorable student. He deserves the presumption of innocence until proven guilty—just as the court system promises. To keep him locked up pending trial could jeopardize a bright future, and for what? Based on accusations that haven't yet been proved? He is more than a football player—he's a young man with dreams and integrity. And frankly, Your Honor, in my opinion . . . TK is the victim here."

I sat down, heart pounding.

The prosecutor's eyes burned through me like daggers. She was seething. I met her stare, stone-faced. *You can't break me,* I thought. I've already been broken. I rebuilt myself. Stronger. Smarter. So if it's a fight you want—game on.

The judge's voice broke the tension.

"Thank you, Mrs. Moore. I couldn't agree more. Innocent until proven guilty is the foundation of this courtroom. I see no prior offenses. We'll set a preliminary hearing for next week. Good luck at your game tonight. You are free to go—for now."

With a firm strike of the gavel, the court shifted. People stood. Papers shuffled. The prosecutor passed by me slowly and glared. I smiled—calm, deliberate, defiant.

TK and his family rushed to me.

"We don't have much time," I whispered urgently. "We need to get you to school on time—and I think we may be followed. Everyone leave separately. Different directions."

TK, ever gentle and grateful, pulled me into a hug. "Thank you, Ms. Becca. I'm ready."

We hugged all those who had come to support him and scattered to our cars like a rehearsed plan. TK ducked into the back of my truck. Just as I predicted, when his dad turned left out of the parking lot, a police car followed. His mother pulled out, and another police car followed her. They had to follow the speed limits. No one followed me.

I turned right.

I picked up my phone and dialed the Assistant Superintendent Mark Fortner—just as we'd discussed.

He picked up on the first ring.

"You ready?" he asked, voice steady and full of belief.

I smiled, eyes on the backroads ahead.

"You know I am," I said. "Let's roll."

The Assistant Superintendent guided me through the back roads, giving calm, steady directions—how many miles until the next turn, what to watch for—so I could focus entirely on getting us there fast, but safely.

Mission accomplished.

We pulled into the school parking lot with seven minutes to spare—just before the cutoff to be considered present for a half day and eligible to play that night. When we walked into the hallway, there they were—the high school principal, the superintendent, and Nate—standing shoulder to shoulder, waiting for TK.

As soon as TK saw them, he walked up and gave each one a hug. He looked each of them in the eyes and told them how much he appreciated their support. It was one of those surreal moments you never forget—where time feels like it pauses and you realize you're standing in something bigger than just the present. I don't think any of us could fully comprehend what we'd just witnessed or what it meant. Not yet.

I turned to the principal.

"Hey—TK's in the same clothes as yesterday, and he hasn't had a shower. Is there any way he can use the locker room before heading to class?"

There was no hesitation. Within seconds, TK was whisked away.

As he disappeared around the corner, I pulled out my phone and began texting his dad: Bring him clean clothes to school.

I paused, looked down the hallway just in time to catch a glimpse of TK disappearing with the principal.

When I looked back, Nate was watching me. He mouthed, "Thank you."

I smiled, nodded, and turned to leave.

There was still a full day ahead. Meetings. Students. Work to be done.

But Friday night lights were waiting.

It felt like poetic justice when the Massillon Tigers clinched their third consecutive regional title—and ended Hoban's reign as a four-time state champion, dashing their dreams of five in a row. TK ran with fire that night, finishing with a game-high 87 yards on 17 carries. He carried more than the ball—he carried everything that had tried to stop him. Always pointing up to the sky after each run, to give someone else the glory.

We went on to win the following week's game and advanced to the state championship. There, under the weight of so many dreams, we fell to Cincinnati La Salle, 34–17. (Yes, Nate's former team. I can't make this stuff up.) The season ended with a 14–1 record. On paper, it was a remarkable run. A nearly perfect season.

Later, David Lee Morgan—a teacher at Massillon and the running backs coach—would write a book about that year, *15 for 15*. The pages would mention that TK had been uncertain for the regional title game.

But that was all it said.

No one really knew.

No one knew that while the season had ended . . . the real battle had only just begun.

•••

TK was going to need a good lawyer—because they were coming for him. Hard.

We knew we had to find someone outside the Akron area, someone without ties to the local system. I made a few calls to lawyer friends in Stark County, and one name kept coming up again and again.

If you want the best shot at the best outcome, you need Max Hiltner.

So I made the call.

We arranged to meet at a quiet coffee shop—just TK, his dad, Hiltner, and me. I didn't know what it was going to cost, but I already knew I'd do whatever it took. This felt too orchestrated, too off. I wasn't going to let TK's life be ruined by what felt more and more like a setup.

We arrived first and took seats off to the side. TK and his dad sat quietly while I scanned the door, nerves buzzing. Then I saw him.

He moved with quiet confidence, not arrogance—just presence. His sharp blue suit was tailored perfectly to his lean frame. His dirty blonde hair was neat and styled with precision, and his icy blue eyes locked in on us the moment he stepped through the door. He approached with a warm smile and a firm handshake.

"That's a nice watch," TK said with a grin, noticing it right away. His smile could light up any room—even this one, where we were carrying so much weight.

Max laughed. "Yeah, sometimes you've got to reward yourself when you work hard." Then he looked at TK and added, "Call me Max, by the way."

Right then, I knew. He's the one.

Max had a way of making everything feel instantly more manageable. He listened intently as TK described everything—what had happened, what hadn't, and how things escalated. Max didn't interrupt. He didn't rush. He just listened.

Then he leaned back, fingers resting lightly against his chin.

"Very interesting," he said. "I think I can help. And I'd be willing to take on your case—but I won't lie to you. I'm not cheap."

TK's dad nodded solemnly. "We understand."

I looked Max in the eye. "I'll be in touch in the next few days."

Back in the Jeep, I called Nate.

"This is definitely the guy," I said. "If we want a fair shot, it has to be him. There's no one else—my gut is screaming it. But it's going to cost us."

Nate exhaled deeply. "Don't tell me. Just do what you think is right."

That was all I needed.

Max was our guy.

And I'd find a way to get him paid—even if it meant walking into the bank and taking out a loan.

That's how much I believed in this kid.

That's how much I knew.

This was an injustice.

We went back to court a few weeks later. I don't remember what the weather was like or what I wore—I only remember the weight. The weight of watching a kid fight for his future while the system looked for ways to clip his wings. The prosecution wanted house arrest. An ankle monitor. A seventeen-year-old boy boxed in by four walls and fear. They argued he should only be allowed to stay in Massillon—even though he'd been spending weekends with his grandmother in Akron. It was all control. Nothing about this felt like justice.

Thank God for Max.

Max stood in that courtroom and didn't flinch. He argued for TK to be allowed at our house too—for tutoring, for structure, and for that flicker of a dream that TK still held onto: college football. The judge approved it. A small win. But we knew there was more coming.

Weeks later, Max called us in. The look in his eyes when he opened that conference room door told me everything I didn't want to hear. He cleared his throat, as if it were physically painful to say what came next.

"I'm going to be honest with you. I've never seen or experienced anything like this—and I've tried a lot of cases."

Then he laid it out: the prosecution wanted to try TK as an adult once he turned 18. A felony charge. For what?

He showed us the eye witness statement. My blood ran cold.

It described a young Black man. Muscular. Longer hair in twirls. White ribbed tank. White Nike shorts, swoosh on the right leg. White Nike tube socks. Nike slides.

To. The. Tee.

Max hit play on a video—TK walking off an elevator after visiting his grandma—wearing exactly that outfit. Like someone had watched it, then rewound the tape and wrote the script. I asked Max, "Is it normal for a witness to describe someone in that level of detail?"

He chuckled—then turned serious in a blink.

"No. I don't think I've ever seen a police report like this."

My thoughts started racing. *Was the report filled out by a cop? Was it connected to Hoban? Or Saint V's? The rivalry. Politics. The power. Was it all this deep? Could someone be so bitter about a game . . . that they'd burn a kid for it?*

TK's mom asked softly, "What can we do?"

Max's voice shifted—gentle but grave.

"I'll keep negotiating with the prosecution. But I think we may have to go to trial. That's more expensive. It's your call."

I leaned in.

"I want the charges dropped. This is ridiculous. It feels personal. Targeted."

Max didn't argue. He just nodded. Slowly. Like he had already been thinking the same.

Outside, TK looked at me and smiled.

"Keep the faith, Ms. Becca. It's going to work out." He comforted me. While wearing a damn ankle monitor.

After football ended, I couldn't bear to see TK locked down, both in body and spirit. I got permission for him to play on my wheelchair basketball team. That's where he met Alayna. My girl. My firecracker on wheels.

Alayna was born with spina bifida and never once let that define her. She used it like armor— her own kind of magic. She was the kind of kid who made you believe again. She and TK clicked instantly. No complaining. No excuses. Just respect. Just joy. She called me the "crazy lady in stilettos." I called her one of my best defenders. We had done Girls on the Run together, track, and now hoops. And her light pulled TK right into our

Alayna and TK pose together after a wheelchair basketball win, their smiles overflowing with joy, love, and the unbreakable spirit that always lit up the court.

orbit.

Watching them out there on the court—two souls who'd been handed so many reasons to fold—but who just kept showing up . . . smiling . . . fighting—I swear, the joy was almost holy.

The court ordered that each Friday, TK would have to check in with a probation officer and get drug tested. I would drive there each week. I'd sit in the Jeep, in a parking lot that made my stomach turn—surrounded by pain, addiction, hardened eyes. Still, he never once complained. Not about the drive. Not about the ankle monitor. Not about having his world shrunk to a triangle: school, our house, and wheelchair basketball. Always smiling. Always looking out for me.

"You good, Ms. Becca?"

Every time. Like I was the one in trouble.

Then, in March, Max called.

"Becca, this might be the most bizarre case I've ever had."

He didn't even try to sugarcoat it. He'd hired a private investigator. The "witness" who ID'd TK had vanished. According to the officer who took the statement—whose bodycam just so happened to be off when he talked to this mystery witness—the man had changed his name, moved to Georgia, and joined some religious group.

I literally choked on the phone.

"Oh, wait—there's more," Max said.

There always is.

The investigator couldn't find any trace of the witness. No name change. No new identity. No person. The "victim" whom TK supposedly attacked? A known alcoholic. Detoxing in the hospital, he flailed and fell out of bed, cracking his head. The hospital had ordered a brain scan. A detail the prosecution conveniently left out.

TK hadn't pushed him off a bike. He hadn't given him a brain injury. He had confronted a man who had pulled a knife on his grandmother. And for that, they wanted to bury him.

If it hadn't been for Max—if we hadn't had a lawyer who believed in us, who dug, who hired a private investigator—TK would be sitting in adult prison. I know it. I felt it in my bones.

I cried. Not just for TK, but for every other kid like him without a Max.

"What's next?" I asked quietly. "With this evidence, I'm going to force the case into Stark County. Where it belongs, since TK resides there.

Then, we push for dismissal."

"Done," I said. "Whatever you need—I'll get it."

TK's life was held hostage from November to July. From the day before Regionals until the doors of Stark County Courtroom slammed shut behind him, and slammed the doors shut on his recruiting while we waited. Despite pissing off the Summit County prosecution, the case was moved to Stark County.

Max walked in with everything that day: the investigator's report, a letter from Alayna and her mom, a letter of recommendation from Nate, and everything and anything that could anchor the truth in a system

---

Your Honor:

We are writing to urge leniency in the sentencing for Terrance Keyes.

We have only known Terrance since October of 2019; no amount of words can really describe the impact he has had on our family. I would like to give you a perspective that shows that he has more to give than the actions that he is in front of you for.

My perspective is a mother of a 13-year-old young lady that has spina bifida. Alayna has played wheelchair basketball for Massillon Tigers for 4 years now. Each year a couple able-bodied high school students join the team to assist the players with disabilities. The 2019-2020 season started off just like the rest of the previous years. After the first couple weeks it was clear that this year was going to be different and the difference this year was Terrance being a part of the team. I am sure you are thinking, why is it different? Terrance was present at every practice and was at every game, even the early Saturday morning double headers! I want you to understand that there was a difference between Terrance and the other able-bodied players. His presence was not just coming to practice then leaving. He was there for the other players by taking time to high five and talk to each of them. If he noticed one of the players getting upset, he would go to them and give them some encouragement. He had a special connection with my daughter, and she looked forward to seeing him. Terrance would take the ball out and pass to my daughter then he would stay beside her the whole way down the court encouraging her. They also liked to play tricks on each other and the funniest one that Alayna still talks about was when she scared Terrance with a fake mouse at practice. Talk about screaming like a girl and running away! It was the funniest thing, but you have no idea the joy and laughter that Terrance brought to my daughter this year.

Terrance was also willing to lend a hand with loading and unloading the wheelchairs for the away games.

In the short time that we have known him, Terrance has been a leader, reliable, trustworthy, kind and a deceit young man.

I believe that Terrance will make a great impact on the community with the proper guidance and support. We look forward to seeing his smiling face supporting the students this next upcoming season at the games.

I appreciate you taking the time to read this letter and I hope that you will give him the opportunity for a second chance and that will not impact his future growth. Terrance does have plans to go to junior college in Texas this coming fall. Then he plans on transferring to a division 1 school and hopes to come back give back to the Massillon community.

Alayna would like to take a moment and let you know that she felt he was very supportive and didn't treat her differently. He knew that I had issues with one of my hands and he would adjust handling the ball to accommodate me.

Sincerely,

Monica Mendenhall and Alayna Mendenhall

Monica Mendenhall   Alayna Mendenhall

---

built on shadows.

We watched them disappear into the closed courtroom. TK, his mom, his dad, and Max. The door clicked closed. And all we could do was sit outside.

Wait.

Pray.

And hope that justice, for once, wouldn't be a ghost.

Max led TK and his family out of the courtroom. His expression gave nothing away at first, like he wanted to hold the moment in his hands before releasing it.

We followed—me and Nate, just a few steps behind, bracing.

And then, outside those courthouse doors, Max turned around, his face breaking into the kind of smile that only comes when the impossible just became real.

"Well, we're done," he said. "TK is free to go. No record. Nothing. The judge said in all her years sitting on the bench, she had never received a report from a probation officer or letters of praise like she had for TK." He paused, smiling even bigger. "I'm going to be honest—this is a first for me, too."

I didn't say a word. I just broke. Tears hit my cheeks before I could stop them. I wrapped my arms around TK's grandma, who had prayed and fought with more strength than I'd ever seen in a woman her age. And I started making the call to the secret angel who was the benefactor that brought Max into this story. To the person who believed with us from the start. Who helped save a life in silence.

Justice wasn't a ghost after all.

It was flesh and blood. It had a voice. And this time, it spoke on TK's behalf.

He was free.

Free to go to college.

Free to play football.

Free to be exactly who he was meant to be.

Two years later, he would earn his associate's degree in Business. And that kid with the ankle monitor and a quiet strength that could move mountains—he never once wavered in who he was.

When I look back on those long months, when TK's life was held hostage by fear and false accusations, I realize something that still stays with me:

I learned more from TK than I ever could've taught him.

He never let bitterness in. Never once acted like a victim. Not through the court hearings, not through the ankle monitor, not through the endless Fridays in that Akron parking lot where broken men passed us by like shadows.

Instead, he gave back.

He showed up for the kids on the wheelchair basketball team, especially Alayna. He helped her shine brighter. He made her laugh harder. He lifted her up without even knowing he was doing it.

TK didn't see his circumstances as punishment. He saw them as a path. And that path was lined with the kind of grace you don't teach. The kind you just carry.

People say when you're a hammer, everything starts to look like a nail. I think that's true.

But I also think when you see yourself as a victim, you begin to see victims everywhere—even in places where only ghosts exist.

TK and Alayna never saw themselves as victims.

They were light-bringers. Fighters. Quiet warriors in a loud, broken world.

And I will spend the rest of my life honoring what they taught me.

You don't get to choose what life throws at you. But you do get to choose what you carry, and how.

And TK?

He carried it with faith, like my grandparents.

With love.

With a smile.

And with a strength that never wavered, and I'll never forget.

—Chapter 17—
The Ending Is Only the Beginning

"The end of one journey is simply the start of another. You have to let go of the past to open the door to the future."

~Unknown

For every story that ends in triumph, there are others I carry like stones in my chest—secret griefs that never quite go away. For every headline or handshake, there have been heartbreaks, funerals, and phone calls I'll never forget.

William was one of my first students who taught me how heartbreak comes. He was chasing a dog in the summer heat, ran into the road, and never made it back. He was buried in his Spider-Man costume. It took me days to breathe again after that funeral.

There was Alyssa. I told her if she stayed off probation and graduated, I'd be there—a hundred dollars in hand. I kept my promise and showed up to graduation with a card stuffed with a hundred-dollar bill. Three years later, she was found in her apartment, beside her little boy, gone from a drug overdose. When they asked if anyone wanted to speak at her funeral, I couldn't find words. I just wept, silently asking myself what more I could've done.

Jamir—God, I worked with him for months. We were on the edge of something beautiful. He missed eligibility for a full ride by 0.01. I cried for four hours the day we found out. I felt like I had failed him. There was Kyree, who barely had a quarter of school with us. We kept

I was there to celebrate Alyssa's high school graduation, and my heart shattered when the call came that she was gone—a loss that, like others, still haunts me and lives quietly inside my heart.

in touch all year, and he made it to graduation. He was supposed to leave for college, but three days before he was set to leave, he was gunned down before his second chance could even begin. I found myself again at a funeral, questioning what I could have done differently.

Lauren is one of the most beautiful girls I've ever seen—her mom is an addict, her grandma did the best she could. I spent more nights than I can count driving back and forth to Akron, dragging her mother out of some place I had no business being. One time, I crawled under a garage door on a floor filled with used needles and God knows what else. The next day, I was almost written up for bringing Lauren and her friend, high and drugged out, onto school property. I didn't even know. I was just trying to give that girl a shot at graduation. She called wanting to go to school, and I took her. She never graduated.

Then there was Alex, who had a baby at age eleven. I went to the hospital with Nate after she had the baby. She and her family decided to keep the little girl. We walked in, and she was sitting there watching cartoons while the baby slept in a bedside crib. I remember Nate looked at me and said, "I can't do this again. That was so tough to see." I spent hours and days helping her through depression while she navigated being a new mom. I tutored her and kept her on track. I hauled her out of bed and to school, and she finally got back on track. Then, in her sophomore year, her stepdad died. Her mom spoke little English and was scared they would be deported, so they fled during the night to a different state. I worked trying to get them into a school in the state where they landed, but the school wouldn't allow them to enroll. We cried on the phone together because we both knew there was nothing either of us could do.

Those are just a few I carry, but there are so many others that I worry that I failed. It plays in my mind over and over again. Worse, were the times I had to walk away from someone, accepting that the person I was trying to help couldn't be helped because they didn't really want to help themselves.

All these kids—the faces, the names—blur my vision as a spotlight catches my eye. My mind clears as I sit in front of a crowd of over 300 people waiting to hear me speak. Nate—my husband, my constant— finishes up his introduction at the Pro Football Hall of Fame Luncheon. While others were sitting there eating their lunch, I was reflecting on how I got to this moment.

I didn't know if I could follow Nate. I swallowed the lump in my throat and looked out at the crowd, each face a stranger, yet somehow familiar because they were here to hear about hope. About perseverance. About what it means to keep showing up—even when your heart is broken and the world is against you. Even when the wins feel small and the losses feel enormous.

Because the truth is, I've had failures. I've been called out over and over again. I've had disappointments. I've felt like giving up more times than I can count. But I didn't. And if you're reading this, it's probably because you haven't either.

And that's where you and my story begin, in the moment we didn't give up.

Time stands still as I walk to the podium.

It's as if my entire life just played out in slow motion, the sound of old film whirring through a reel—flip, flip, flip—projecting flashes of memories across my mind. I stand here, heels planted, heart steady but full, and I can feel the weight of every moment that led me here. Before I begin the speech, I pause—not out of fear, but reverence. Reverence for the girl I once was, for the miles I ran, and for the life that could have broken me . . . but didn't.

In the reel of my memory, I see a small ranch house in Oak Ridge, Tennessee. Adults gathered in a quiet circle—some on chairs, some on beds, some on upside-down buckets—sitting in a discomfort that went far deeper than the furniture. There's tension, and grief, and the silent mourning of something slipping away. A little girl peeks through the doorway in a red plaid Christmas dress, innocent and unaware that this is the day everything changes. That her whole future—the very shape of who she will become—is being decided in whispers and worried glances.

Then the image shifts. A man behind a heavy oak desk. A final decision made. The same little girl, this time in pigtails, lacy socks, and patent leather shoes, walks hand in hand with new parents. Behind them stands her birth mother, broken and crying, making the impossible choice to let her go. The pain on her face is something that would haunt me for years, even when I didn't understand it yet.

The screen goes black. Not sad. Not peaceful. Just silent. Just dark. There are no dresses now, no shoes, only echoes of voices: "Hold on. You'll make it. Keep going." And somewhere inside that darkness, I see a mirror. A hospital gown. A bruised face. Swollen eyes. And then a scream.

But just like that—the flash of a stage. A college campus. Laughter, celebration, a chance to shine. I step forward, eager to use my story for good, only to feel a hand jerk me back. "You need to learn your place," a voice hisses. "Your story is too much. No one will believe you. Sit down." And just like that, I'm silenced. Again. The dress, the heels, the hope—all pushed aside.

Silence.

And then a new scene. A man. Steady, unwavering, eyes filled with certainty and promise. He takes my hand and says the words that would change everything: "I will love you for the rest of my life, in sickness and in health, for better or worse." A kiss. Applause. A life beginning again. An angel?

That kiss. I felt it recently, and it pulled me right back here—to now.

I take a deep breath, step forward, and pull the mic down.

I look out over the crowd, and I feel the weight of Nate's introduction still hanging in the air. But this moment, this microphone, this voice— it's mine now.

And I begin:

"What a privilege and honor to stand before esteemed guests, fans of the game of football. Thank you to the Pro Football Hall of Fame Luncheon Club for allowing me to come and speak. Thank you to Massillon City, Massillon City Schools, and our superintendent, Paul

Salvino, and the Massillon Booster Club, who I continue to drive crazy at times just being, well . . . me. Thank you to my love and undoubtedly the most important person in my life, and in this room, Coach Nathaniel Moore.

'Persistence is the key to my life. You fall down, you get back up, and you go again' - Lew Hollander (oldest Ironman Finisher).

I have been judged on the kind of person I am by the way I dress my whole life. I didn't wear pants till seventh grade, just dresses, and heels, or patent-leather shoes, and trust me, kids had a lot to say about that. It became either you love me or you hate me.

When I met Nate, he was an assistant to the offensive-line coach at Chaminade Julienne in Dayton, Ohio. I had spent the year before coming back to Dayton traveling and teaching English in Thailand. I had promised my best friend I would come home for a year. Nate and I were both teachers at City Day Community School, a charter school. He taught PE, and I taught first grade. You could almost say it was love at first sight, if you believe in that. I've experienced it, so I do. I dropped my class off at PE and felt the butterflies in my stomach. I ran down the stairs and quickly called my best friend and said I think I met someone important. Nate and I started to hang out, and I'd show up with cookies before his football game on Fridays. (He complains he doesn't get those cookies anymore.) I remember watching him run across the field and thinking there was something special about him. Two months into dating, he told me his aspirations of becoming a head coach, and he wondered if I could handle that. I thought, *It's a job. It would be fine. I mean, how hard can it be? You win some, you lose some, whatever. It's just a game.* See, I went to a private school that didn't have high school football, so I didn't live and breathe football. So I didn't really grasp the concept, or really how much the game would change from 2005 until now, or how important a strong partnership would be.

When Nate and I were at City Day, we started a basketball team. Neither one of us really knew much about basketball. But coaching that team to the one win of the season really sparked something in me. Seeing their faces, when we won that one game, after loss, after loss, had sparked something in them, and it inspired me to look for ways to help students find that spark.

As Nate worked his way through his coaching career, I began working my way through mine. With a degree in journalism and early childhood education, I realized that if Nate was going to be moving, I would need to be able to market myself. So I returned to school and got a masters in School Counseling from the University of Dayton, and a masters in Administration from the University of Cincinnati. Those two masters would be key for me when we made the decision for Nate to take the head coaching job at Massillon.

Why do you ask? Well, after immediately confirming he was taking the job, and I would be taking a job in the fall of 2015, the social media attacks began.

- She's just getting a job because of her husband. She isn't even qualified. They just made up one.
- Who would hire her? She is such a diva!
- Winning is great and all, but I've heard rumors that the team GPA is the lowest that it's been since Becca Moore came to town.

Then I made the mistake (to some people) of posting that I would be cheering for La Salle in the state championship game in the fall of 2015 against Perry. The tweets and memes intensified. Letters telling me that I know nothing about the "backyard battle", traditionally the first game of the season (which has actually never happened since the fall of 2015, we have met in the playoffs.)

- #notwelcomecoachmoore
- Shout out to Becca Moore for being the most hated woman in Massillon.
- shocked by Becca Moore's lack of class
- Question for Becca Moore, educator, 1st or cheerleader

Then, to put the nail in the coffin, the local newspaper wrote an opinion article titled "Is Becca Moore the worst coach's wife in Stark County history?" As you can imagine, neither Nate nor the superintendent at the time was happy. When the superintendent called me into his office and said, 'What do you think you should do?' I remember thinking, *I am not going to apologize for what I said. I'm just going to have to show who I really am.* I remember looking at him and saying, 'We'll have to just work harder to prove everyone wrong who thinks they know me. I have to have an identity outside of Nate and football. I have to go back to what I'm good at, helping kids find that spark, that motivation.'

I went home and screenshot every awful thing that was posted about me. I read it to our son Eli, and continued to, every time someone posted something negative or made a meme. I wanted Eli and Ella, as she began to get older, to learn that what people type or put out on social media is their opinions. It does not mean that is who you are, and it does not define you. Because of this, I have seen resilience in my own children that I never expected to see.

It was after this that things began to change for me. I was able to work with the athletic department and start Wheelchair Basketball. It was here that I would meet some of the most amazing student-athletes. For reference, to play wheelchair basketball, you could have two able-bodied athletes, and then you had a list of qualifications; you didn't have to be wheelchair bound. Fun fact: as I was working with our school's physical therapist to get a list of students to talk to who would be eligible to play on the team, I met 4th-grader Alayna Mendenhall. I went to the door, and she was going out for the bus. I was wearing my signature stiletto heels and dress. I told her wheelchair basketball was going to be fun, and she would be an excellent athlete. I later found out she went home and told her mom that some crazy lady in heels was trying to get her to play basketball. I would from then on be known as the crazy lady in heels. Alayna is a senior this year, and I have been her coach for wheelchair basketball and seated track her whole athletic career. She is a true example of what it means to be a Tiger. Through sickness, surgeries, and setbacks, she has walked the warpath that Coach Moore has described as tenacious and disciplined at all costs. Alayna constantly reminds me why I want to work with kids and why I continue to look for programs to incorporate in school that will give every student a chance to find that spark.

It was through wheelchair basketball that I was reminded how important being a student athlete is to all. No matter their ability. Savannah (one of my wheelchair athletes and seated track athletes) said in an interview, 'When I get to put on our uniform and go out there, I feel like a Tiger. I am really representing Massillon.' Her saying has stuck with me way past her graduation. Each year after the football season, Coach Moore and I would meet and ask two players to be on the team. We have had players such as Seth Blankenship, Jayden Woods, Austin Brawley, Andrew Edwards, Zach Catrone, Terrance Keys, Jr., Zion Pfeifer, and our son Eli Moore. We won zero games our first year. Each year, we would win one more. Then, in the 21/22 season, I had the privilege of coaching with former football player and now teacher/coach

Benito Salzar. Together, we were able to coach the team, beat a five-year undefeated Wooster team, and become the state runner-ups in the Wheelchair Interscholastic Sports. My favorite things about coaching wheelchair basketball were seeing our athletes improve and inspiring our teachers and administrators when we would have a scrimmage with them. Our kids were tough. One of my favorite memories was running into Seth Blankship, and him saying one of his most rewarding experiences in high school was being on the wheelchair basketball team. And of course, my competitive nature had to let Coach Moore know.

From wheelchair basketball to my love for all things track and field, we were blessed to be able to get chairs for our seated athletes to compete in throwing and rolling on the track. We have been able to take seated athletes every year since 2019, with the exception of the COVID season that was canceled. This will be my girl Alayna's senior year. If you want to see a sight, come to senior night in the spring, and you will find me in heels, crying on the track. I have been her only coach since she started in 4th grade, playing wheelchair basketball, and then transitioning to track as a 7th grader. In all those years, I have never heard her once complain or tell me the workout was too hard. Along with coaching the rollers, I had the privilege of teaming up with Greg Corsale, and we won the 2021 OHSAA Junior High State Championship Boys Division with names such as Tyler Hackenbrack, Braylon Toles, Mike Wright Jr., Jaylen Slaughter, Mylen Lenix, and Jamir Gamble (And believe me, I reminded them that they won a state championship with me first, and I have a ring to prove it). Winning the boys state championship indoor in 2023 was kind of icing on the cake. Just call me by my nickname, given by former-kicker Vinny Keller, #TheRealCoachMoore

We added Girls Flag Football, and we will be the first team in Stark County to have a girls team, and I get the privilege of being the coach. I take pride in this because we continue to grow and allow students to have opportunities to be student-athletes. To learn how to walk the warpath and learn how to deal with what life throws you.

Working with the community in Massillon and partnering with so many great people, we (And I don't say I, because it takes multiple people to be able to accomplish things) have been able to feed families weekly, and send home snacks with eighty kids with our Feeds Kids First Program. We have been able to bless families at Thanksgiving and Christmas with turkeys, meals, and presents. There is so much good in

Massillon; so much that this community prides itself on.

That brings me to the saying that people who aren't from Massillon smirk about: Massillon Against the World. Until I moved here, I didn't really understand it. I always looked at myself as Becca Against the World, and I've been okay with that. But being part of Massillon gave me a new understanding of how people don't want to accept or respect other people's legacy and traditions. They would rather hate or dismiss success by calling out things such as saying paper champs, or you only won one.

After the state championship win, a couple of weeks later, life began to get back to normal. My sister texted me, "Call me when you get a minute; you are not going to believe this." My sister Rachel is one of our biggest supporters. I think she has been to every Massillon-McKinley game since Nate has been coaching here. She comes to playoff games and brings the rest of the family. She owns a little beauty shop in New Lebanon, Ohio, population around 4,000. She is a nail tech at her shop. So I called her, and she told me one of her regular clients came in to get her nails done. She went on to tell me her client asked her what she is doing this upcoming weekend.

My sister said, "Becca, I told her I am headed up to Massillon because my nephew is graduating." The client responded, "Oh, that demon city." Rachel says, "Becca, I was looking at her and was like 'What do you mean?'" Her client began to explain, "We played Massillon in the playoffs, and they just ran the score up on us." By now, I am laughing, and I am thinking this cannot be happening. Rachel continued, "So the client says, 'The coach's wife does some show, like she's a talk show host, called *Tiger Talk*. She thinks she is funny and only laughs at herself. She also walks on the sideline wearing some orange snowsuit, like "Look at me."' Rachel interrupts her, 'You know that's my sister, right? The head coach is my brother-in-law.' The client looked at her, "She isn't your sister." Rachel just laughed and pulled up a picture of us together. It turned out the client was the mother-in-law of one of the coaches from Cincinnati Anderson, whom we beat 55-7 in the State Semifinals.

I laughed as I hung up the phone. So it continues, and so it will always be. As Denzel Washington said, 'It's not about what you have or even what you've accomplished. It's about what you've done with those accomplishments. It's about who you've lifted up, who you've made better.' People have this preconceived notion, these ideas about

Massillon. They think they know, but they don't know. It was here before Nate and I arrived. It will continue once we are gone. It will always be Massillon/Becca Against the World." I stepped back from the podium. I got through it. I heard a sound. It was the applause. I had done it. I had started the process of telling strangers my life.

The applause faded, but something stayed with me—something I couldn't shake. Not just the humbling words, or the inbox full of encouragement, or the people who came forward with quiet apologies. It was the look on Nate's face as I got in the truck—the same man who had walked beside me through fire and silence, through courtrooms and hospital rooms, through victories and defeats that no one else saw. That look said, "You did it. You stood tall. And they saw you for who you really are."

Since that day, our girls flag football team went 11-3, beating McKinley and Akron Hoban twice, which I am not afraid to remind Nate of, jokingly, of course. I was honored as the Cleveland Browns Coach of the Week, and got to watch as our girls stand up with other girls as the OHSAA announced at a press conference held at the Pro Football Hall of Fame that Girls Flag Football would now be a sanctioned sport in Ohio. What a journey—from being the girl who felt like no one believed in her, to now coaching the very girls I once was—helping them write their stories in sweat and sideline grit, one down at a time.

And through it all, I haven't changed the outfits, the make-up, and especially the shoes.

I glance down now at my sparkling silver stilettos, matched with a black pencil skirt and just enough glitter to remind the world: This girl is not going anywhere quietly. The heels are louder now, but so is the strength behind them. That little girl they once counted out—she didn't just survive. She rebuilt.

Would life have been easier without the adversity? Maybe. But easier isn't always better. Easier wouldn't have built the fire in my bones or the steel in my spine. It wouldn't have made me a fighter, a truth-teller, or an advocate. It wouldn't have given me this voice.

So no—I wouldn't trade a thing. Here's the truth:

Where you come from shapes you, but it doesn't chain you.

Flashbacks may visit, but they don't get to decide your future. You do.

I've walked through valleys I never wanted to enter—abuse, loss, trauma, a courtroom, a funeral aisle, and a dean's office where I was told

I didn't "look the part." But through it all, God or I never let go.

Even when I didn't recognize an angel's hand, it was there—steady, strong, unmoved.

"Keep going," was whispered in my ear, even when I could barely lift my head.

I remember the angel on the bridge. Children crossing a rickety, broken bridge with jagged, missing boards and dangerous waters below. But there—quiet, glowing, fierce in presence—is an angel.

Guiding. Watching. Protecting.

That image has never left me.

Because for every shattered memory, every cracked board underfoot, there was a divine presence holding me steady, or a person, friend, family member. When I should have fallen, I didn't. When the trauma should have taken me out, it didn't. When shame should have silenced me, it didn't.

Romans 8:28 says:

"And we know that in all things God works for the good of those who love Him, who have been called according to His purpose."

That means all things—the abuse, the injustice, the accidents, the heartbreaks, the nearly invisible wins, and the moments no one else saw.

He wastes nothing.

Not even this.

So go ahead—step forward. In your best dress, your loudest heels, or your quietest strength.

Prove them wrong. Not out of bitterness, but out of joy. Out of healing. Because scars aren't a weakness, they are proof that you won.

Prove them wrong. Out of holy purpose. Out of knowing that you were guided across a broken bridge, not just to survive—but to shine a light to lead others safely across.

So in your time of need—when the night is thick and the pain is too loud to pray—if we can just trust, even a little, there are angels. Maybe not with wings, maybe not with halos, but real ones. They show up. And they will guide us—stumbling, sobbing, shaking—across whatever broken bridge we're standing on, looking across to the other side. No matter how deep the water looks below, no matter how splintered the boards are beneath our feet, we will find our way. We're not alone. Not now. Not ever.

—Epilogue—

"You have to be brave with your life, so that others can be brave with theirs."
~Katherine Center

Since writing the last chapter, I was able to read most of this manuscript to Mommie, as she lay in her hospital bed. She took her last breath at home on August 1, 2025. The house was quiet, filled with the soft sound of gospel music and the gentle hum of heaven opening its doors. Family surrounded her. Love surrounded her. The hospice nurse stood at her side as I sobbed, unable to hold back the flood of years, memories, life lessons, and gratitude.

The nurse wiped her tears and whispered, "She was deeply loved. You don't see that much anymore at the end of life."

And she was right.

Mommie was loved deeply and completely—not just because of who she was, but because of how she loved others.

I have no regrets, except that I hadn't finished this memoir before she left. But maybe that was the point. Maybe she knew I needed to walk through this last chapter with her before I could write the ending. I finished it two months later, and every word felt like a conversation with her.

Mommie was an avid reader—books were her love language. Our home was filled with them, scattered across coffee tables, tucked into corners, piled high in the garage and basement. Stories lived in every room. She was the first to read my first book *Massillon Against the World,* and the first to hear me read what I wrote for what became *this* book.

She used to smile and say, "One day, Rebecca, you'll write your story—when the timing is right." And as always, she was right.

When we celebrated her life, it was exactly that—a *celebration*. Pictures and videos told the story of a woman who had poured herself into everyone she met. Letters were read aloud—from former students, families she had cared for, and friends whose lives she touched. Pastor Lawson's son, Chuck, played the hymns she loved on the piano, his hands moving with the kind of reverence that fills a room with peace.

Daddy spoke, calling her the love of his life—his greatest blessing. He said she had accomplished so much that one day couldn't contain it all, but above everything else, she loved Jesus and wanted others to know His grace and His love.

One night, before she came home from the hospital, Mommie reached for my hand. Her voice was soft, but her words carried eternal weight. "Please, Rebecca," she whispered, "sing for me one more time."

I laid beside her on that narrow hospital bed, her hand stroking my hair as tears fell like rain down my face. "I don't know if I can," I said through a shaky voice. "But I will for you."

She smiled and kissed my forehead. "You can," she said, "Jesus will help you through."

And He did.

At the funeral, Nate picked up his guitar. I took a deep breath and began to sing "Face to Face." The first few notes trembled, but then peace filled the room—the kind of peace that only comes when heaven is close. As I reached the lyrics, "when we all see Jesus, no more sickness, no more sadness, no more pain," I closed my eyes and placed my hand on Nate's shoulder. He leaned in as I finished the song—I have no regrets.

Her life—and her death—reminded me that we are only here for a little while. The time we are given is not meant to be wasted, but poured out—in love, in gratitude, and for us to be humble in service to others.

So, I plan to keep living. To coach girls flag football in the spring and help the sport grow into something that builds confidence and community. To return to the trails with Hannah and run farther, longer, harder—100-mile races, maybe even more—because strength is built in motion, and the mind can only grow if you keep challenging it. To help all those along the way who may be paralyzed in fear as they start to cross their bridge.

And above all, I'll keep building bridges in case someone needs reassurance. Because Mommie taught me that love is the bridge—the one that carries us from pain to peace, from one heart to another, and from Earth to heaven.

I already experienced a moment my Mommie would have been so proud of. It was the night when Thayer came to senior night for Eli. Together, lined across the field, were Daddy, Thayer, Nate, Eli, Ella, Terrence, and me. We walked Eli, as a family, across the field, as Eli beamed ear-to-ear and dressed in his orange Massillon uniform. The same all-orange uniform that Thayer had worn on his senior night. I knew Mommie was smiling because we live for others, not ourselves.

I will keep walking in my stilettos, wearing my sparkles, and doing my best to live as a servant to others. Until one day, I too see Jesus—face to face.

On Eli's senior night with the Massillon Tigers, our family came together in love and pride—Daddy (Grandpa Garber), Thayer, Nate, Eli, me, Terrence, and Ella—and I know my Mommie was smiling down on us all.

Standing with my parents on Massillon's field at the ring ceremony after Nate won his second state championship, and Massillon won its first in the playoff era.

—Special Thanks—

Hannah Ross (my best friend): We've been running side by side since the seventh grade, through every finish line, heartbreak, and start line life has thrown at us. From the very beginning, you've been more than a friend—you've been family, a sister in both spirit and sweat.

We've shared miles most people couldn't imagine—across roads, trails, oceans, and finish lines. We've crossed time zones and finished tapes, trained before sunrise, and laughed long after sunset. Together, we've conquered two Ironmans, countless marathon races, and the quiet moments in between—the ones that test not just our bodies, but our faith, our patience, and our hearts.

What I treasure most isn't the medals or the miles, but the way we've always shown up for each other—even when the race wasn't on a course, but in life itself. You've seen me at my strongest and at my breaking point, and through it all, you've never stopped believing that I could keep going.

As we take on new challenges—the longer races, the harder climbs, the tougher days—I know we'll keep pushing each other, not just to be faster or stronger, but to be more alive. Because every finish line we've ever crossed together has reminded me of one simple truth: some people run to escape the world, but we run because we've found our place in it.

Thank you for every step, every laugh, every finish line, and every word of encouragement. Thank you for being the kind of friend who doesn't just run beside me, but believes in me enough to help me build bridges where roads once ended.

Here's to the next race—and to every new start line we'll face together until we cross our final finish line.

To my sister Rachel: Girl, we have been through it. We've walked through storms that could have easily broken us, yet somehow, side by side, we always found a way to keep moving—sometimes swimming, sometimes barely treading water—until we could finally pull ourselves up onto that bridge together. Through it all, you've trusted me with your life, with helping to raise Ashford and Mamie, and with pieces of your heart that I will always hold sacred.

What we've endured, what we've overcome, has only made our bond stronger. I love how close we've become, how deeply we understand each other—the kind of closeness that doesn't need many words, just a glance that says, "I've got you."

I cherish knowing that when I'm out there running my ultras, you're waiting for me on the other side—cheering, believing, ready with that smile that says I can do anything. And oh, how I adore our wild DIY projects—the ones that drive our better halves absolutely crazy until they see what we've created and can't help but be amazed. Those moments, big and small, are the threads that have woven our story together.

You are my sister—not just by title, but by heart. One of my very best friends. I know we won't always see eye to eye, but I also know this: no matter what life throws our way, we'll always be one call away from each other because that's what we do. We show up. We have each other's backs—always.

Thank you for walking this journey with me—for the laughter, the tears, the late nights, and the unwavering love. I wouldn't have made it this far without you, and I wouldn't want to go any farther without you by my side.

To my baby sister Melissa: You, my dear, are the heartbeat of our family—the spark that keeps the laughter alive and the light that reminds us to cherish every fleeting moment. You have this beautiful gift of knowing when time matters most, of capturing the memories that might otherwise slip away. You remind us—with every photo, every laugh, every "come on, let's take one more"—that life is precious, and love is worth preserving while we have the chance. For that, I thank you with all my heart.

Even though we may not be as close as either of us would like, please know that I am always cheering you on—even in the moments when you drive me a little crazy. Beneath it all, I see your heart: generous, full of love, always reaching out to make others feel seen and cared for. That spirit shines so brightly to everyone lucky enough to be around you.

Keep that light burning. Keep loving as fearlessly and unconditionally as you do. And never stop being unapologetically you—because you, just as you are, make this family whole.

Mommie B: To the one who gave me life. "Greater love hath no man than this, that a man lay down his life for his friends."—John 15:13 (KJV)

Every time I read this verse, I think of you. Because to me, it isn't just scripture—it's the reflection of your love, your courage, and the profound sacrifice you made so that I could have the life I live today.

I can only imagine how hard that choice must have been—to give me up, to let me go, trusting that it was what I needed to thrive. That kind of love takes a strength beyond words. It is the truest form of selflessness, the kind that not everyone in this world gets to witness or understand. But I do. And I carry it with me every single day.

Without your sacrifice, I wouldn't be the woman I am today. The lessons I've learned, the people I've loved, the life I've been blessed to live—all of it exists because of your courage. You gave me the chance not just to survive, but to shine. And even when that must have been difficult for you to watch from afar, you never stopped letting me be me.

Thank you for your love, your faith, your quiet strength, and your willingness to give me the gift of a full and beautiful life. I hope this story—our story—serves as a light for someone else who needs to be reminded that even the hardest choices, when made in love, can create something extraordinary.

Scott: To my gadabout friend (as my Daddy would say), who somehow became both my editor and partner-in-chaos. When we first sat down to talk about what this book *might* look like, neither of us knew it would turn into years of laughter, tears, detours, and a state championship pact. Which led to you winning your first award as an author that didn't cover *Twin Peaks* or *Moonlighting*. Ha!

The "book" was supposed to come first—but our friendship clearly had other plans. You inspired me to dig deeper, rewrite fearlessly, and find my voice again. You took what was once "just a project" and helped turn it into a memoir—something raw, real, and completely unexpected.

Your patience, humor, and perfectly-timed one-liners made the process (almost) painless. You taught me that laughter really can rewrite a bad day—and sometimes, that's all we need to keep going.

Thank you for being the "Section 14 guy," my *Tiger Talk* co-host, and the friend who reminded me that joy always sneaks in, even when life feels heavy. I hope this book makes you proud—not just as a publisher, but as someone who helped me believe in my story again. To the sweet old lady at Tremont Coffee: We weren't really fighting; we were able to work it out and publish the book.

TK: There's so much I want to say, and I'm not sure words can ever do it justice. Your senior year wasn't just a chapter of your life—it was a testimony. At seventeen, you faced a system that tried to break your spirit, yet you stood firm with grace, faith, and unshakable loyalty to your family. You never complained, never lost your smile—and in that quiet strength, you showed all of us what true resilience looks like.

You inspired me more than you'll ever know. Watching you handle life's weight with such light in your eyes reminded me of what faith, courage, and love really mean. I'll never forget that Thanksgiving Day—two families gathered as one, laughter filling the air, hearts full of gratitude. That moment will stay with me for as long as I live. Thank you for trusting me to tell your story. You often say, "I love you," and I want you to know, I love you too. Keep shining that light of yours. The world needs it, and you were made to illuminate even the darkest places.

Pastor Lawson & Fayth: To the two people who showed me more patience and grace than anyone ever has—Pastor Lawson and Fayth— thank you.

Pastor Lawson, you walked beside me through my darkest valleys and celebrated with me on the mountaintops. You counseled me through years of pain and healing, never once wavering, no matter how far you had to drive or how heavy my heart was. You reminded me what steadfast faith looks like in action. I'll always smile thinking about our shared belief that Tennessee is heaven on earth—and how you tried to convert me into a Dr. Pepper fan. You can keep that one, but the laughter we shared over it will always stay with me.

Fayth, my educational mentor, my guiding light. I don't know if any words can truly capture what you've meant to my life as an educator. When I was just starting my teaching career, you came into my classroom—not to judge, but to lift, to teach, to show me what it means to reach kids whose worlds felt broken. You taught me how to build trust before lessons, how to teach reading in a way that touched both mind and heart. Years later, when I was in Massillon and struggling to find my footing, you were still there—just a phone call away. Watching you tutor Thayer on those quiet Sundays reminded me that true educators never stop teaching, never stop believing, never stop remembering their why.

I miss you both deeply. But every time I start to question my purpose, I hear your voices, steady and sure, reminding me who I am and why I keep going. Your patience, love, and faith in me live on in everything I do.

Grandma and Grandpa Combs: Thank you for summers spent in church and by the creek beds. Teaching me that life is a balance, and we only have one life that will soon be past, and only what's done for Christ will last.

To My Combs Family: I truly believe it would be nearly impossible to find another family like ours in this day and age. Through the good times, the heartbreaks, the tough losses, and the quiet, saddest of days— we have always shown up for one another. No matter the miles between us, love has always bridged the distance, pulling us together exactly when we've needed it most.

The roots of our family tree run deep—built on the foundations laid by Georgia, Gordon, Ashford, Charles, Edward, Harold Paul, Eddie, and Susie. Though I never had the privilege of meeting Susie, I see her spirit shining through her children—some of the finest souls this world will ever know. Each of you has inspired me to live with gratitude, to serve others, and to understand that giving of oneself is one of life's greatest rewards.

Our yearly summer weekend at Buckhorn State Park in rural Kentucky remains one of the sweetest traditions of my life—forever etched in my heart as the best kind of summer magic. To now bring my own children there, to watch them feel that same love, laughter, and belonging that shaped my own childhood—that is a gift beyond measure.

I may not carry the Combs name, but the truth is, it flows through my veins all the same. The love, the loyalty, the laughter—it's who I am. And for that, I am endlessly grateful to be part of this family.

Grandma and Grandpa Garber: Thank you for choosing me, expecting me, and instilling in me the love of family that runs deeper than just blood.

To My Garber Family: When I was adopted, I came into this family as the youngest grandchild—and from the very beginning, I was wrapped in love. There was no hesitation, no question, only open arms and warm hearts. I was Ruth and Bruce's daughter, and that was that. You all embraced me so completely that I never once felt like anything but family.

Some of my fondest memories are those summers on the farm— long, golden days spent exploring the fields, and quiet evenings gathered together without screens or distractions. Just laughter, stories passed from one generation to the next, worn photo albums on the table, and that familiar ride on the tractor over the hill to bring in the cows as the sun went down. Those moments were simple, but they built the foundation of who I am.

Thanksgiving and Christmas with Grandma and Grandpa Garber, visits from Uncle Arlin and his family, Uncle Howard, and Aunt Linda with Brian and Tammy—whom I was blessed to spend the most time with—filled my childhood with love, laughter, and belonging. It was never about what we had, but who we had.

Through every season of my life—graduations, marriage, children, and even loss—you have stood beside me. You've shown me, by your actions, what unwavering loyalty, faith, and family truly look like. You have taught me that real love isn't just spoken; it's lived, every single day.

There will never be enough words to express how deeply grateful I am for each of you. Your love and support have been my steady ground, my reminder that family is not only who you're born to—it's who chooses to love you, wholly and forever.

And to Daddy's girls (you know who you are)—you are the shining example of sisterhood, strength, and grace that every woman should be blessed to witness. Your bond is a light that continues to guide and inspire. From the depths of my heart—thank you for being my home, my history, and one of my greatest blessings.

Geo and Laura Villegas: Wow, my loves. You are two of the kindest, most genuine souls I've ever met. Thank you for capturing not just my cover, but the heart and vision behind it. Somehow, from just my words, you knew exactly where to go and how to bring it all to life—from the perfect back cover shot to the author photo. I didn't even know I could love this much.

You took something I've always felt so uncomfortable doing—taking pictures—and turned it into pure art. You made it feel effortless, natural, and full of joy. Your love, faith, and light shine through everything you do—in your church, your community, and in your work.

I only wish we lived closer, because I'd choose to do life and create with you any day. Knowing you're forever part of this journey warms my heart every time I see that cover. I can't wait for more adventures together—this is just the beginning.

Minster Community: To the ones who believed in a young family—I can never thank you enough. Your kindness and support, from the moment Nate accepted his position, to the years that followed, and even after we moved on, have meant more than words can say. I will always cherish the joy of small-town football and the incredible sense of camaraderie that defined the village.

I'll never forget the evenings when the kids stayed out until the streetlights came on, or the friendships and memories that continue to warm my heart. Thank you for embracing us, believing in us, and reminding me what true community feels like. The village of Minster will always be my very own Pleasantville.

La Salle Community: Thank you for the two years that taught us resilience under the pressure of a role that came with tremendous visibility and media attention. To those who supported us, offered understanding, and even to those who voiced their concerns—you all played a part in shaping our journey. Through it all, we grew stronger as a family and were reminded that faith and doing what is right may not always align with popular opinion, but they always stand the test of time.

I am incredibly proud of that 2014 state championship team and all that was accomplished. Your belief in Nate not only fueled his success but also opened doors and opportunities beyond anything we could have imagined.

Massillon Community: To a community that became home. You've taught me more than I could ever put into words. I'll be honest—it didn't happen overnight. You didn't embrace me right away, and I understand why. You were cautious, skeptical, watching to see if I would truly understand what this place stands for. And truthfully, I didn't make it easy. But over time, you showed me—through your quiet strength, your pride, and your unwavering spirit—what legacy really means.

You taught me that tradition isn't just something we talk about; it's something we live. You showed me that building a winning culture goes far beyond the scoreboard—it's about character, heart, and the way we lift each other up when life gets hard. I've taken that lesson deeply to heart. I've tried to carry it beyond the field, to pour that same spirit into the lives of the young men and women who walk through the halls of our schools, learning what it means to be part of something bigger than themselves.

My love for this community stretches far beyond the Friday night lights. The cheers fade, the seasons change, but what remains is the sense of belonging, of purpose, of family. Long after I'm gone, I hope the wins on the field are seen as only a small reflection of the deeper victory—the imprint we've left on the hearts of those who've grown up here, loved here, and called this place home.

Thank you for allowing us to raise our children here, to grow roots, and to experience what true community really is. This town—its people, its spirit, its heart—has changed me in ways I'll carry for the rest of my life.

To my doubters: who tried to suppress my light, you taught me to rethink, recoup, because there is always a way, just sometimes not the way you planned.

David Bushman: Thank you for always checking in with Scott about the progress of my book and asking when it would finally be finished. Each time he mentioned it, I was reminded that someone genuinely cared about this story and believed it was worth completing. Your time, interest, and thoughtful edits mean more than words can express—thank you for investing in both the book and in me.

Jen Ryan: Thank you for taking the time to read my book before it went to press and for offering your honest thoughts on every single chapter.

Your willingness to pour into this project means more to me than you know. Because of you, you made me believe the heart of the story is clear, the message is strong, and readers will feel the connection I prayed they would. I'm so grateful for your care, your insight, and your belief in these pages.

Mary Miller (St. Marys School District): To an incredible leader and inspiration. You opened a door that led me into some of the best and most meaningful educational years of my life. Serving as your school guidance counselor and watching you lead with such strength, grace, and authenticity—especially as a woman in a predominantly male-run district—was truly inspiring.

You gave me the freedom to be myself, to think creatively, and to try things far outside the box—all in the name of connecting with kids and building bridges that mattered. Those opportunities didn't just make me a better educator; they shaped me into the leader I am today. And I'm not sure you even realized the impact you were having at the time.

When you called me about Alyssa's passing, it touched me deeply. You knew how much she meant to me and understood that I would want to be there to honor her. That simple act of compassion reminded me again of the kind of leader—and person—you are.

From the bottom of my heart, thank you for believing in me, for leading by example, and for showing me what true strength in leadership looks like.

With heartfelt gratitude, your former guidance counselor.

Stephanie Wijesinghe: Although your name doesn't appear in the pages of this book, your presence has been written into my life in countless ways. From our days at Kennesaw State University to now, your friendship has meant the world to me. Somehow, you always seem to know when to reach out—whether it's a simple text, a word of encouragement, or a Bible verse that finds me exactly when I need it most.

I love you deeply. Thank you for being a constant in my life, especially in the moments when I've needed strength, faith, and a reminder that I'm never truly alone.

Thelma Avore: To my Mommie's best friend and confidant—your love and support through the years have been truly priceless. Thank you for always believing in me, cheering me on, and standing beside me through every season, especially in my latest time of loss. I hope this book fills your heart with pride and reminds you of how wonderful it was to be part of Mommie's life.

To all the athletes I coached: I hope you truly know what an honor it was to coach you. You each inspired me in ways that can't be fully captured in words, only felt deep in the heart. I'll carry with me the memories of every tough practice, every team-building moment, and every spaghetti dinner that brought us closer together. Thank you for letting me be a part of your journey. You changed me for the better, and I will remember you always.

Thayer: You have been one of life's greatest teachers. You taught me to stand up and fight for those who deserve a chance and a voice, and to trust that truth always finds its way through. From you, I learned that love and forgiveness aren't weaknesses—they're the hardest, bravest choices we make. You showed me that loss and redemption walk hand in hand, both shaping who we become.

Thank you for always being there for Eli—you mean the world to him. You've opened doors for so many others, often without even realizing the ripple effect of your courage and trust. Your impact runs deeper than words could ever capture, and I hope you know how much your presence has mattered.

Terrence: To the boy who completed our family. You came into our lives carrying the weight of uncertainty—cautious, guarded, unsure if love could truly last. But with time, patience, and faith, you began to let the walls down. You allowed healing to take root, and in doing so, you showed the world—and all of us—that when someone is given a chance and chooses to believe in it, they can change the entire course of their life.

Watching you grow has been one of the greatest joys of my life. You didn't just join our family—you embraced it with open arms and an open heart. The day you wanted to share our last name was a moment I will never forget. It wasn't just a name; it was a declaration of belonging, of love, of the home we built together.

You've become a shining example for Eli and Ella—showing them what perseverance, courage, and kindness truly look like. Your journey of resilience and strength is nothing short of remarkable. The love and gratitude you show never go unnoticed; every time you say "thank you," every time you express how much you appreciate me, I feel it deeply. You remind me that love—real, patient, healing love—changes everything.

Our long talks, those late-night conversations about life, purpose, and faith—they mean more to me than you'll ever know. This small chapter about you could never fully capture the man you've become. You are living proof that grace transforms, that second chances matter, and that hearts can find their way home.

I am endlessly proud of you—not just for what you've overcome, but for who you are: a man of strength, integrity, compassion, and heart. To call you our son is one of the greatest honors of my life. And to be your mom—that is one of my life's greatest blessings.

Eli: To the boy who made me a Mommie. Watching you grow into the young man and leader you've become has filled my heart with indescribable joy and pride. From those early days on the sidelines—eyes wide with wonder—to the moment you ran onto the field waving the American flag, every step of your journey has moved me beyond words.

I love the bond you share with your Grandpa Garber and the quiet beauty of your Friday breakfasts together. Someday, you'll understand just how much those moments mean—and how deeply they shape a life.

You wear your heart on your sleeve, yet your strength runs so deep that even your teammates see and respect it. You've taught me more than I could ever put into words—about love, resilience, and what it truly means to believe in someone.

In a world that has not always been kind, you have stood tall, stayed true, and shone even brighter. I am endlessly grateful to be your mom, and I cannot wait to see all that your future holds.

Ella: To my favorite daughter—well, my only daughter. When we found out you were a girl, my heart overflowed with excitement—and a little fear. It's not easy growing up in a world that so often tries to tell girls who they should be, how they should act, or what they should look like. I've watched you find your own way through all of that, and I couldn't be prouder.

From your very first days of school, I would say to you—and you'd repeat—I am smart. I am beautiful. I am kind. I am strong. And most of all, I will be kind. Those words have always been more than just a mantra; they are who you are.

I've tried to teach you that you can't control what others think, say, or post, but you can control how you respond, how you treat others, and how you carry yourself. And you, my girl, have done it all with grace, confidence, and integrity.

I love the way you live—boldly, joyfully, and fully. You dive into friendships, sports, and each new day with a light that inspires everyone around you. Keep growing in that light, becoming the woman I already see inside you—strong, compassionate, and true. I am beyond proud to be your Mama, as you call me. You are precious beyond compare, and I thank God every day for the gift of you.

Daddy: To the man who saved my life —You taught me that real love exists—the kind that sees you, believes in you, and never asks you to be anything other than who you are. You chose me when you didn't have to, and you loved me when you didn't need to. Through your quiet strength, you showed me grace, forgiveness, and how to live a life rooted in gratitude, no matter where the road leads.

Thank you for letting me be me—wild, free, and unrelenting. I know there must have been moments when you bowed your head, wondering how to guide a spirit that refused to be tamed. But your example spoke louder than words ever could. It reached me. It changed me.

You have been my steady, silent support—the constant heartbeat of love that has carried me through every storm. I hope you know that everything I am, and everything I strive to be, is touched by your influence. And I hope, more than anything, that I've made you proud.

Mommie: To the woman who was perfectly content to be the light in the shadows. You never sought the spotlight or tried to claim any part of my life; you were simply grateful to be a part of it. Like Daddy, you chose me to be your daughter, and that gift places me forever in your debt.

Your grace, your quiet love, and your unshakable confidence inspired me to live a life of servanthood—giving without ever expecting anything in return. Your impeccable style—the matching heels, the carefully chosen jewelry—has found its way into my own closet, a beautiful reminder of you.

Your love of books, scattered across the house like whispered stories waiting to be discovered, is a legacy I promise to carry on. You once told me that reading takes you on adventures, inspiring you in ways you never could have imagined—and that truth continues to guide me.

But above all, you taught me to love Jesus and to trust Him even when my heart is reluctant. I miss you every single day, and that ache is a testament to the depth of your love and the beauty of your soul.

Nate: To the boy who changed my life.

I never went searching for love—but somehow, love found me the day you did. It came softly, with laughter and butterflies that danced endlessly in my stomach. I never believed in love at first sight . . . until you looked at me, and the world quietly shifted into place.

Your patience through the years deserves a medal—no, an entire monument. You once told me I was like an onion, full of layers to peel back, one at a time. Well, my love, you've reached the very center. Every layer, every piece of me, belongs entirely to you.

What we have lived together, most people would need several lifetimes to experience. You are my rock—my steady, unwavering truth. My angel in chaos. My light in every dark place I've ever wandered. I hope you've felt me beside you, too, guiding you home in the quiet moments.

The world may never truly know who Nate Moore is—the depth of your spirit, the kindness of your heart, the way your soul keeps growing brighter with every passing year. But I do. I see it every day.

Thank you for loving me—even when it wasn't easy. Thank you for letting me be wholly myself, for believing in me, for urging me to finish this memoir when I doubted I could.

If I've made you proud, then every word, every tear, every moment of this journey was worth it. Because in the end, our love, against all odds, has always won.

Forever and always,

Becca

If you have a nice comment about the book, please email me at mylifeinsstilettosinfo@gmail.com. Connect on Facebook: Author Becca Moore, or Instagram: beccamoore75

Book Club
Discussion Topics
Part 1: Crossing the Bridge

Discuss the following points:

- Face your bridge. Stop pretending it isn't there. The fear, the loss, the pain—name it, stand before it, and take the first step.
- Refuse to be a victim of your past. Your story may have started in brokenness, but it doesn't have to end there.
- Tell your truth anyway. Even when people doubt it. Especially when they doubt it. Speak to what you know is true.
- Build while you walk. The bridge beneath you may not exist yet or need replaced—but every act of courage, forgiveness, and love lays another plank.
- Trust the crossing. The waters below will always roar, but they can't touch you when you keep your eyes on what's ahead.
- Leave light behind. When you make it across, don't forget to turn back and shine your light for the next person who is still in the dark.

So this is your goal, my message, my hope: Keep crossing the bridges.

Don't let the waters of your past convince you that you're unworthy of crossing. Don't listen when people say your story sounds too impossible—because that's exactly what makes it miraculous. You survived what should have destroyed you.

The bridge doesn't have to be perfect. It just has to hold long enough for someone to make it to the other side.

Part 2: Accepting the Angel

- Let people in. The walls that once protected you might now be keeping healing out.
- Recognize your angels. They don't always look the way you expect—sometimes they come as friends, teachers, coaches, or even strangers who care enough to see you.
- Stop apologizing for needing help. You don't owe anyone perfection. You're human, and healing sometimes takes community.
- Receive without guilt. Accepting kindness doesn't make you a burden—it makes you brave enough to trust again.
- Look for divine timing. Sometimes the right person at the right moment *is* the answer to the prayer you thought went unheard.
- Allow yourself to be carried. There are days when your strength will falter. Let someone else steady you without shame.
- Say thank you—and mean it. Gratitude opens the door for more light to enter your life.
- Become teachable again. Angels often come to show us a better way—humility is the bridge between being helped and being healed.
- Winning is not your endgame. Take the lessons you've learned from winning and set your sights on new goals that will take you out of your comfort zone.

So this is your goal, my message, my hope: Trust the process.

For a long time, I didn't trust angels—not the ones with wings, or the ones walking around in the flesh. When you've been left, when you've been told you're unworthy, help starts to feel like pity, and love starts to feel like a setup for pain. I told myself I didn't need anyone. That I could carry my story, my scars, and my silence all by myself. There were times I prayed for strength, and instead, someone showed up. There were times I prayed for answers, and instead, I got a friend who simply sat beside me. And slowly, I realized—maybe accepting help wasn't weakness. Maybe it was faith in motion. The picture of the angel on the bridge shows it clearly: the children aren't walking alone. The angel's presence doesn't erase danger—it just gives them the courage to keep moving. That's what real help does. It steadies your steps until you remember how to walk again.

Part 3 : Becoming the Light

- Live as proof. Your survival is your testimony. Let people see what faith, grit, and grace can build out of what was broken.
- Shine, don't shout. The brightest light doesn't need to demand attention — it simply glows, quietly guiding others forward.
- Share your story. The very thing you thought disqualified you might be what saves someone else. Speak it with courage and honesty.
- Hold the light steady. You can't walk the bridge for them, but you can make sure they know where to step.
- Be patient with the ones still crossing. Everyone moves at their own pace. Offer presence, not pressure.
- Pass it on. The help you once received was never meant to stop with you. Be the angel now — build, lift, guide, love.
- Keep your heart open. Even as you lead others, stay humble enough to keep learning. Light grows brightest when shared, not guarded.

So this is your goal, my message, my hope: Remember your crossing.

Never forget what it felt like to stand on the edge of your own bridge—it keeps your compassion alive. When you look back, and for the first time, you see someone else standing where you once stood: afraid, uncertain, carrying the weight of their story just like you did.

That's when you understand — your healing isn't the end of the story. It's the beginning of someone else's.

Becoming the light isn't about perfection or pretending the pain never happened. It's about using your scars as lanterns—proof that darkness can be survived, and that hope can be rebuilt plank by plank.

The angel in the picture doesn't just protect the children—she illuminates the way. Her presence gives them permission to take the next step. That's what you become when you decide to shine: a steady presence in someone else's storm.

Because in the end, that's what this journey is about–Crossing the bridge, accepting the angels, and becoming the light that helps others find their way across.

—Appendix—

Nate Moore's Speech

I knew I had to include this moment in the book because of the way Nate spoke—so full of truth, tenderness, and conviction. When people ask me, "Who is Nate Moore?" this is what I want them to see: a husband who loves his wife without hesitation or ego, a man who stood in front of a community and showed the world exactly what that love looks like. When I received the One Tiger Heritage Award, he didn't just introduce me—he honored me. And I will never forget it.

The words Nate spoke that day, when I received the One Tiger Heritage Award, will forever be inscribed on my heart. Nate has a way of moving an audience—taking them on a journey through laughter and tears—and leaving them inspired to believe and longing for a love like ours. How could this girl have been so blessed to be broken and end up sitting and hearing a speech like this?

Nate, dressed in his orange suit jacket, black pants, and an Obie tie, slowly walked across the stage to the microphone. As per usual, he had to adjust the mic to his 6'4 ½ stature over the wooden podium. He reached in and pulled his note cards out of his breast pocket, which was over his heart. That gesture there got me, and I knew this was something he held sacred that he was going to share.

He began in his solemn, yet commanding voice, "It really is an honor to be here today. It really is an honor for your wife to get this award, and to be honest, we were both kind of taken aback. It's such a tremendous honor, but there have been some giants on this stage. It is really hard to see ourselves in that category. But this lady has been here for four years and has done some incredible things in those years. We have been married for fourteen years, and never in fourteen years did I think this is where life was going to take us. We were just two teachers who met at a charter school in Dayton, Ohio. I was teaching elementary physical education, and she was hired somewhere in the middle of my first year there as a first-grade teacher. I kind of kept to myself in the gym most of the time. But she came in, and I couldn't help but keep myself from venturing out and walking down that first-grade hallway. I kinda wanted to see what Becca was doing. Did she need any help? So I found myself trying to help her very often. Coaching at Chaminade Julienne High School in Dayton, she started coming to games. The kicker was when, in one Friday game, she brought me a plate of cookies. They were made up of footballs and helmets decorated in our school colors, blue and green. I could tell she worked hard on them, and we weren't dating officially. This looked pretty good. A lady who spends time on stuff like that is a good sign. It's the last batch of cookies she's ever made." Everyone in the audience burst out with laughter, while I sat on stage laughing and shaking my head.

He continued, "You know our life has taken us on all kinds of turns. She's an unbelievable partner to have. The previous speakers have a common theme: she is fearless. If you are going down a dark alley, she may not look like it, but she is the one you want with you. She is a fighter. She is not scared of anything, not scared of any situation. A lot of people tense up and really start to back down in life situations, and she never flinches, ever." Nate had to pause and compose himself for a moment, and I felt the warm tears forming in my eyes.

With a breath, he continued, "You know the stuff she has already done in Massillon is unbelievable, and she has done it from day one. And often, being the head football coach of Massillon, it's a big, big job, and I can't do it all by myself. Everything I have asked her to do, she jumps right in. A kid may need a bag of groceries, or clothes, or needs tutoring, and she finds a way to get it done, and doesn't ask me questions. When I asked her to do ACT prep for ninety players, her answer was yes. She set up a classroom, taught it, and did it selflessly, like she does everything else. You know my falls are pretty busy, and you think in the winter, I would be a little less busy, but it's not. She is in wheelchair basketball, and I am helping her load and unload chairs. You think, maybe in the spring we will have a break. No, she is doing two sections of Girls on the Run. It just never stops, and neither one of us would change it for the world. She does great things for the school, for the city, and for the football program.

"Personally, we have had several big changes in our lives. And not a lot of people would do things like that. We had been married five years, and her sister was in a bad place, and her nephew needed a place, and we took in Ashford for three years, and were happy to do that. Then, you look over the last couple of years, and the very public scrutiny we went through with Thayer, who is now a part of our family. People were saying we were doing it for this reason or this reason, but the fact is that it's just who she is. The fact is, Thayer's mom called her up and said, 'I don't think Thayer is going to make it out of La Salle, and I don't think he is going to make it out of Lincoln Heights, Will you guys take him?' And it was yes without hesitation. It was just yes, fully aware it was going to cause issues, and people are going to have a problem with this, and nobody is going to understand. There is going to be finger-pointing, and people are going to think that we are dirty, that there are other motives. She doesn't care about anything or any of that. She cares about one thing. She cares about doing what she believes is right. And Thayer is doing unbelievably well now. He is doing great at Ohio State, and he is a member of our family, and what she has done for him is unbelievable."

He pauses, "Then you fast forward a little bit again, and then all of a sudden you get another guy in need, a member of our team, and he is here today. He was in a bad spot. We had the ability to help him, and that was really it. We had a bedroom, and she went to get him, no questions, that was it. A lot of things really don't add up. You got this beautiful girl, you see her, and you think she has had everything in the world. What possible motivation does she have to do all these things that she's doing? Is she doing it for optics? She wants everyone to think she is better than everyone else. And you guys know we are all friends around here, but there have been some really terrible things said about her on social media, and around. At the same time, I kinda get it. On the surface, it seems unbelievable. So I am going to try to make it make some sense for you."

At this point, I held my breath. Hannah, sensing, reached over and gently placed my hand in hers. I had no idea what he was going to say or do. But you could hear the urgency, conviction, and passion in his words as he took a breath to continue.

"I think this is important, and this may be a little uncomfortable, but I think it is important to understand why she does those things. She helps people who need help, and she is fearless about it, fearless." You could hear the agony in his voice and the struggle for the words to come. He said, "I don't know if I can do this." Mommie B said out loud in the audience, "Yes, you can."

Nate gazed out into the crowd, "I'm going to tell you a story about a little girl. Who grew up in a home with domestic violence, with alcohol abuse, and the worst kind of violence against women you can imagine. And she watched these things happen to her mother, and she couldn't do anything about it. And these things also happened to her, and she couldn't do anything about it. She couldn't save herself, and she couldn't save her mom. But she could try to save everybody else. There are a lot of people who would have been crushed by those things. Crushed. But she made a promise that if she got out of that situation, she would use that to help people. And that is what she has done. That is her motivation. That is why."

Continuing and looking out over the crowd, Nate said, "Usually, I get to stand here and talk to you as the head coach of Massillon." Nate then proceeded to take off his orange jacket and hand it to the president of the One Tiger Heritage Club sitting on the stage. Then he took off his tie and handed it to him. Then turned back to the mic, "But today I stand here before you as Becca Moore's husband, and I'm damn proud of it."

As Nate walked across the stage to clapping and cameras flashing, the host said, "Becca, I couldn't speak after that. I hope you can."

I can't tell you what I said, or how I made it through. I just knew I had been true to myself and made the best decision for me fourteen years ago, and today would go down in my life as the moment I knew.

Then there is the truth that always finds a way. Here's the truth: at the end, when we take our final breath, everything else falls away. What remains is the legacy we leave behind. Did we help others cross the bridge to safety, or did we leave gaps that caused them to stumble and fall into the swirling river below?

ABOUT THE AUTHOR

Becca Moore lives boldly in Massillon, Ohio, where passion, purpose, and perseverance shape every part of her life. She serves Massillon City Schools as a special education coordinator and parent involvement coordinator, advocating daily for students and families while building meaningful community connections.

A lifelong coach and mentor, Becca has proudly led Girls on the Run, Girls Flag Football, Wheelchair Basketball—guiding her team to a state runner-up finish—and Junior High Track, where she captured both indoor and outdoor state championships and earned Junior High Coach of the Year honors. Her coaching philosophy is simple but powerful: believe big, work hard, and show up for others.

In 2024, Becca coauthored the award-winning book *Massillon Against the World*, preserving the unforgettable oral history of the Massillon Tigers' undefeated season and first-ever on-field state championship, led by her husband, Coach Nate Moore. Storytelling has always been part of her calling, supported by degrees in Journalism, Early Childhood Education, and a master's in School Counseling and Administration.

When she's not working or coaching, Becca is chasing her next challenge—training for marathons, Ironman competitions, or ultra races alongside her best friend, Hannah. Above all, she treasures time with her husband Nate, their sons Terrence and Eli, daughter Ella, and their loyal German Shepherds, Echo and Kilo.

Driven by heart, fueled by grit, and committed to living her best life, Becca Moore believes the journey matters just as much as the finish line.

MORE TO READ

BY BECCA MOORE

BEST NON-FICTION BOOK

AT THE 2024 BOOK FEST AWARDS

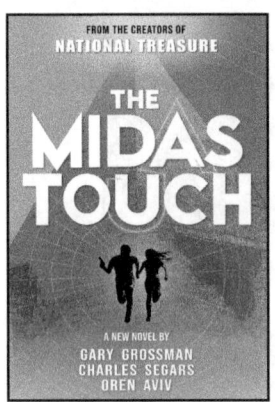

www.ingramcontent.com/pod-product-compliance
Lightning Source LLC
Chambersburg PA
CBHW061732120626
46550CB00005B/1774